LOSING
MY RELIGION

Craig W. Thomas

Juma

First published in 2002 by
Juma
Trafalgar Works
44 Wellington Street
Sheffield S1 4HD
Tel. 0114 272 0915
Fax. 0114 278 6550
Email: MLacey5816@aol.com

ISBN 1 872204 95 3

Printed by Juma.

cover design: IDFP (www.idfp.co.uk)

Preface

Craig Thomas has been cursed since birth, and the evidence is before you. Cursed with talent, in everything, but where to channel it? Sportsman, Musician, Historian, Cod Shamen to all of those who are in receipt of his friendship (and we are a select bunch, let me tell you). Right now we are seeing something that has been a long time coming, the first of many declamatory, inflammatory and downright compulsive treatises on anything that captures his obsessive, but butterfly mind. In an epoch choc-a-Hitler with so called "style" writers who are all too eager to proclaim that Shit is the New Piss, Craig's déshabillé honesty is like a fresh glass of lime and soda on a July 1976 afternoon. Caught in possession of the most contrary of natures, he always does what his instincts tell him are the Right Thing. Whether that is singing Stevie's "Loves In Need Of Love Today" a capella in a cardboard packing factory to a bemused clutch of Mrs Cutouts, declining the hand of the most eligible girl in the school because she lived one stop too far on the bus route, or passing over job offers in order to concentrate on his writing, he doesn't care to take the obvious route and remains cliché free. Getting this story out to a wider public, is hondootedly, The Right Thing. Look, growing up in our village, you had to confront the existence of Mabel Junior. My family lore says that, after TWO WEEKS at school, aged 5, I rang my friend Billy Keeble and said we should attack her ....."with spears and guns". I'm glad my plot was foiled, because when I became tight with Craig in our teens, I developed a fascination for this lovely, but severe woman. What led to the Olympian smoking, the malapropisms, the friendly and wise advice, the immaculate and quotidien cherry pie, and the ability to send my friend Craig into a tortured fever? I wondered what powers led him into the mire I would find him in most summer holiday mornings, all Stygian gloom and stale bacon fat, as we prepared for a day of leisure prior to Mabel's return from work. We were too young to know that Craig's exposition of all things Mabel is a monument to the sheer wisdom you need to accumulate by living your OWN life before you are able to forgive the sins of your forebears.   It's a Gallagher and Lyle essay all right. (Heart on Your Sleeve, stupid). No eyes on the prize, no cultivation of image. Just the way he thought, it always was and will always be. It's beyond football. To me, its football as classic escapism. He needed to lose his religion to find peace with himself. You've got Sly Stone to thank for the most serious recommendation to READ this thing. If you don't like it, you really have a "Permanent Crease in Your Right and Wrong."

Steve Perren

Before we start.....

I'm feeling a little philosophical about this. I mean, why am I even doing this? For a start, no-one actually reads the author's thanks apart of course from those who might be expecting to get a look in. Then there's the thought that perhaps only about forty seven people may actually buy this book. I do not feel good about putting on airs here with a 'thank you' page for forty seven people. Finally, there's the fact that to write Losing My Religion and then get it published was, apart from a number of other things, an exercise in understanding the importance of friendship. So. Philosophical is the key note of the afternoon.

Somehow, along the country back roads (crammed with pretentious arses in huge faux-rural assault vehicles) of life, I got it into my head that if I was to embark upon something of a writing a book type project, I would have to gather around me as much expertise and encouragement as I could.

And I was lucky. Without the example of Nick Manns, a somewhat rising starlet of the teenage fiction world, and Brian Glasser, author of In A Silent Way, the major Joe Zawinul biography, I would never have taken The Voice seriously. Both could write a long treatise on the theme of 'encouraging the wet, whining would-be author' knowing as they both do what to say and when to say it. It was like breast milk to an infant. Then there was Josh Alexander, an American bloke, with a classic New World 'go for it' attitude, who though he needs to put on a little weight is a walking, talking advert for a continuation of the Hands Across The Water approach to the good ol' US of A. You may never have met Dave Radford, which is your loss entirely, but look out for his upcoming book on Seventies football, 'The Radfordgate Tapes'. He proof-read for me and was always, always there with the right words too.

Then there was Steve Perren. You probably don't know Steve either but every home should have one. Tall, fantastic eyes, full head of hair, the lot. Most importantly he send me an email from work one day saying he was laughing so much at chapter six he was on the verge of getting the sack. You're a schmo trying to get a first book published, boy, you need this sort of thing really, really badly. The honour of writing the preface seems to have gone right to his head - I am not remotely the Renaissance Superstar he's trying to make me out to be, as anyone who has seen me trying to negotiate any given set of seven days from close quarters will be glad to tell you - but still. Like I say: friends. If you don't have any: get some. Work on it. Go into therapy if necessary. Do whatever it takes. Then set them to work for you. It's amazing what they'll do for you.

Another if. If you're anything like me, you're probably thinking: 'he's going to mention his wife and kids in a minute (boring), or if he's not, he must be gay.' Let's put it like this. I do have a wife. She comes into the book at some point, so that should be enough for her. But do you think my life would be worth living if I didn't mention her on this very page and say 'darling you were wonderful?' Bear with me. Darling you were wonderful. And kids, we got kids. How many do you want? There are three in the Thomas household and they too will make my life a misery if I don't report to you the fact that they are: Nastassja (Dostoyevsky and Kinski by way of Simple Minds, you want honesty for your money? Look at it, I admit to Simple Minds); Lyall (Mays, Pat Metheny's [who?] keyboard player with a face like a nerd) and latterly Jordan (The Comeback, Prefab Sprout's brilliant album from 1990). And to give them their due, they put up with my moods and hermit seclusion as I wrote evenings into frantic Derbyshire nights throughout the opening months of 2001. What am I saying: I loved writing this book.

A big thanks next to Martin Lacey at Juma for saying 'yes I'll publish this' where others said 'I like it but...' O ye of little faith.

A large nod too to Bob Wort for permission to reproduce parts of his stupendous watershed article for the Crooked Spireite on a stinking dog's jacksie of an afternoon at Ninian Park about ten years ago. And one to another Martin for his support: I hope this tops you up, Mart in a different way.

Finally, there are bottle of Scotch sized bouquets of thanks to give: to the young lad Ben Worthy whose friendship and talent inspired me, to Savannah Stevenson, whose talent frightened me (into action), to Hayley Snowden, whose determination to make the best of herself and do always good things inspired me to find the hard working me, to Stephen and Bill for laying out a clear road to walk down (this should be a vat of Lagavulin, in truth) and to the Australian touring side of 2001 who pulverised England yet again and who were constantly there to tell me, 'whatever you do, do not on any account stop before you have won the game.'

And finally finally, to The Voice. Whoever you are, whatever you are, thank you for saying to me, when I tried to argue, 'no! what you have to do now, is write a book about football.'

Craig T. January 2002.

1

In Bobby Keech's Arms

'In the beginning was the word, and the word was...............
..........floodlight.'

i
The Number 9

C lever, huh? My beginning was the North Middlesex Hospital,
Edmonton, my first home was just off the Seven Sisters Road,
Tottenham and because my cousin was an apprentice at Fulham
the only thing I was told about my time as a baby was that Bobby Keetch
once held me in his arms. Bobby Keetch played in the same Fulham team
as Johnny Haynes and Johnny Haynes played for England. All other pieces
of intelligence about my early years are irrelevant.

I nearly died when I was one, but seeing as I was very much alive by
the time this anecdote was related to me it was no longer that interesting,
though now I'm a father myself, I can see why this event was of real
moment to him. He was the one running in a state of total desperation up
to the end of Candler Street to find Doctor Wayne while my face was busy
turning blue. In my mind's eye right now I can see the sweat on his brow
and feel the hot panic spreading through his internal organs as he con-
templates the imminent death of his second son. I can picture this because
in what seems like lifetimes later, I almost killed the second son of a second son, allowing him to fall down the stairs before he was one year old.

When I go back in search of my earliest memories there is mostly just
a grey, swirling mist, but gradually the picture clears and the image
appears of a Spurs programme lying on a kitchen table. It has a white
cover with black writing, much of which of course I can't read, and there's
a cockerel on a ball staring out at me and suddenly in my mind there is
football.

I am aware that my Dad is taking my brother to a game and I know I
can't go because I'm not old enough. Then the picture isn't so distant and
sketchily focussed. It hardens suddenly and I am there behind the goal at
the Park Lane end in the seats - a debut treat, obviously, because for years

after that it was the terraces - and Tottenham are playing Burnley. I can tell you something about this game because it has always been stored away in my memory: the score was 1-1 and Ray Pointer who had a shock of blonde hair scored for Burnley and they played in fantastic claret and blue shirts. I was five.

Obviously, for me this was a watershed event: my first league match in the flesh. Without doubt that was the day my life as I truly know it began.

Well, that all sounds nice, doesn't it and very convenient when you want to reduce a life to a piece of storytelling, but my life wasn't like that. A life is a whole lot more than the one we see through our own eyes. I doubt whether my parents saw my life in terms of football. Sure enough though, my Dad, in the twelve months that followed, took my older brother Keith and me to a Charlton game, to Stamford Bridge to see Chelsea play somebody I can't remember and to Highbury for the Arsenal, of course.

At a more than half empty Valley I remember my Dad saying 'it's not like the old days is it!' to a weary old gateman who handed my Dad change, agreeing sadly, 'you're right about that.' Was this the moment when I realised that football had a history?

As for our lives observed from the viewing platform of my mother's mind, well, suffice it to say for now, she had plans for us which football could easily fit around.

My world when I was a child consisted of few places: places where there were shops, like Enfield and Wood Green; the streets that connected our house to the local main street and later to school. But the most significant was Tottenham where my Nan lived and where I more or less caught the football disease .

We went on Saturday mornings to visit my grandmother, 52 weeks a year. Dad dropped us off in the car and went to his office a mile or so down Seven Sisters Road towards the Spurs ground, while I tried to stave off three hours of boredom. I managed it by going round the corner to buy sweets or a comic or by tinkering with the untuned piano or my Uncle Len's drums. Lenny, who'd always lived with his mum when he wasn't in a mental home, must have saved for the kit out of his wages, unless my rich Uncle Victor, one of my Mother's three brothers, bought them as a compensatory gift after one of Len's 'episodes' way back when I was really young or before I was born.

The house was dark, dusty, had no bathroom and had an outside toilet with the company of spiders. We sat always in a small back room next to a scullery which housed a sink where everyone washed, a cooker, a

pantry and a coal cupboard. Upstairs, the front bedroom was shared by
Lenny and David, another of my uncles. Pity the estate agent trying to sell
this part of the property to a prospective client (and my God one of them
had to try ten years later when Victor moved them all out down to Surrey):
there was decrepit looking linoleum on the floor and the room smelled of
the piss the two men deposited in their conveniently appointed chamber
pots under the beds. There was always plenty of liquid in the tank to richly fill the thing because in Tottenham drinking was de rigeur. My Mum
called them 'po's, a word I still find faintly disgusting because of my mental association of the object with mid-nightly defecation.

Mind, I was fond of both of these men. Lenny, despite some strange
mornings when he paced around moodily - and in a house that small you
couldn't pace very far without everyone immediately noticing - or one
when he spectacularly broke into a streak of expletives Lenny Bruce
would have been hard pressed to match, was always nice to me. At least
he was in the few years I knew him before he was put away in an Essex
nut house for trying to settle a pub argument. Storming back home to
fetch an axe with which to make that telling last point was not the best
way to maintain his freedom. His interest in jazz, proof that his mental
instability couldn't have been his fault in my opinion, meant that he wore
jeans, a groovy item when it's 1963 and you're about to hit forty, and a
nifty denim jacket. The effect of being up with the hep-cats was somewhat
dissipated by his tendency to let go upholstery-ripping farts with com-
mendable freedom. On each occasion I was ready to burst into giggles
because everyone else in the room was faintly embarrassed and this, I
knew, was richly comic in a 'don't say bum in front of the vicar' kind of
way.

No, the only thing I had against this Uncle Leonard (my other Uncle
Len will swerve into the story in time) was that one winter Saturday morning he decided to light his first cigarette of the day with a large slice of the
front cover of the Northampton Town v Plymouth Argyle programme
which happened to be residing on top of the pile of some excellent reading matter I'd brought with me from home. I was predictably choked: I
was only seven. However, looking back on this from the vantage point of
considerable distance in terms of time, I'm rather proud of myself for a)
not crying and b) not wanting to take a leaf out of his own book and brain
him with an offensive weapon. I think even then I knew that Len wasn't
like other men and was, all in all, rather sad and helpless and very much
to be pitied.

He and his brother must have been tough too in their way, because living with my grandmother was like walking on broken glass in bare feet ten

hours a day. In all the years of weekend mornings and occasional all-day school holiday trips I never once heard my Nan laugh, nor my Mum for that matter, or saw either of them smile. There was always a family row going on. Always. It amazes me now as a fully paid up member of the adult world that I sat in the room with the pair of them for a huge number of hours all told and never once had the remotest idea what exactly was going on. The atmosphere was permanently like the inquest after an air disaster only with more attendant hostility. Sundry members of the extended family would drop by, accept a cup of tea and join in. It was a very inclusive family because anyone could get involved and make everyone just that bit more miserable.

What they were so miserable, tense and yet animated about was completely beyond the mere young likes of me, except my grandmother, Mabel Snr, always seemed to be at the centre of everything, like a Black Widow spider at the centre of an intricate but lethal web. My Mum was never the sort of woman who constantly radiated sweetness and light at the best of times, but at my Nan's she wore a face like the pool's winner who forgot to post the coupon. Or the woman who found out that my Dad had only been unfaithful once: with the Dagenham Girl Pipers, to slip in a weak period joke. In reality he had been unfaithful to my mum before they were married. He came home on leave from naval duties during World War Two and, presumably rather shamefacedly, announced to everyone that he had got engaged to a girl in New Zealand. At which his mother, Helen, apparently a wonderful Scottish woman from Stranraer who tragically I never met because she died of cancer in 1953, told him he had to the decent thing and marry Mabel Knight. Shamefacedly he assented. And the rest is my history.

Meanwhile, back on the N17* Wars Of The Mid-Nineteen Sixties, I do seem to recall my auntie Emmy from time to time being the cause of the vast, brooding Candler Street rain cloud. Even I'd worked out that Emmy spent more money than was rightfully hers down at Harringay Dogs and that Mabel Snr was anything but amused. Apparently her addiction to gambling was chronic enough for the bookies down there to club together to buy a wreath the size of Sheffield when she eventually died as a mark of gratitude for all the cars and foreign holidays she'd so kindly provided for them down the years.

Cousin Valerie was another frequent visitor and she intrigued me at first when she arrived on the scene for she had married my cousin Peter, the now ex-Fulham apprentice. He'd been good enough to play centre for-

*In the 1960s, N17 was the postal code for that part of Tottenham, the 'N' standing for North London.

ward for England Schoolboys, a fact that excited me no end, except it always used to clash in my mind with the only other piece of information my Mother ever added to the chronology: he'd got fed up after a season or two sweeping the terraces and painting the stands (or was that sweeping the stands and painting the terraces, I wasn't sure back then) and quit. This was a total mystery to me and tarnished what could have been a golden image of the man in my mind. When I became an apprentice pro' with whichever club would have me, I didn't care, the very last thing I'd do would be to walk off the job. I thought Peter incredibly silly to do this, but as the event seemed to mesh comfortably with the prevailing Candler Street madness, I was obviously not as outraged as I clearly should have been.

Emmy herself made an appearance very occasionally and the atmosphere immediately worsened, though this was scarcely possible. The very oxygen in the room seemed to brace itself against a possible outbreak of hot war. Perhaps the throwing of a few cups and saucers would have released a bit of tension, but whatever unspeakable event had precipitated this grim frost, nothing was ever going to thaw it. Naive as I was, that much I accurately sensed. Come the early seventies, though the Tottenham Knights had been moved lock, stock and worn out barrels down to Lingfield in Surrey, things were exactly the same only it now took two hours instead of forty five minutes to reach the row.

My Uncle David rose above all this like the totally decent geezer he truly was, to his dying day. He was a top bloke in my eyes even if it was a bit odd to be still living with your Mum way past voting age. Having said that, Tottenham was probably rough enough and sufficiently populated by criminals for this modern rationale to fail to fit the reality of working class London two years after the explosion of Beatlemania. Didn't Ron and Reggie still live with Mum in 1965? I really liked my Uncle David. He always called me 'fish face,' which I loved for the feeling of affection it implied, and ruffled my hair in a warm sort of way and fed me his bubble and squeak with a smile. This was my kind of uncle: never mind that he could never afford to give me extra pocket money. The only pity of it was that he always got up late on a Saturday and within half an hour was off to the pub again to play darts and organise a bet. David was also mad about comics.

You don't have to be remotely bright to appreciate the fact that there is something not quite right about a man of 43 still reading Topper, Beezer, The Hotspur and Victor: he wasn't a collector, you understand. I was too busy finding out whether Alf Tupper was going to recover from the grandmother of all fish and chip suppers at Toni's to up and win the three 'A's

1500 metres at White City to ponder the dysfunctional psychology of a favoured uncle. David had a wooden leg, replacing the real thing he lost on a Normandy beach in 1944. Perhaps there was a link.

ii
The Arsenal?

So Candler Street was grim but only in a way because when you're a kid, whatever it is you experience seems pretty normal and what everyone else's family does is strange. I remember my brother going round to a girl's house for tea when he was about eleven, a bizarre enough event in itself in the days when to talk to a girl was practically the same as being one. When Keith came home we were sitting eating our tea and when he told us with an expression of total incredulity that he'd been given fish fingers with only four chips, well I stared back at him in complete horror and even my Dad put down his fork and looked out the window rather bleakly, I thought. My Mum wore an amused look but I have no doubt that like the rest of us she found this both inexplicable and morally wrong.

In retrospect it's probably fair to say that 9 Candler Street was basically a place full of weird people but to me it was pretty unremarkable because I knew no different. I know now that the whole lot of them should have had a government order slapped on them so they could all be analysed, observed and treated with a view to eventual release back into the community, even though this would have meant that I'd have had to have grown up without a maternal parent. And I've yet to mention my Uncle Ted. He was as mental as they come. His never ending phone calls later on in my life where he tried to pin me down for hours talking without a pause about his two sons blighted my twenties and may have damaged me. No-one should feel a need to celebrate the death of their godfather unless there is some kind of physical intimidation going on or something, but I did; and because in the year before he died he was seriously considering a trip up to actually visit me, his timely demise felt like a release from prison. What I find unacceptably bizarre is that Ted was, I'm sure, a nice man too but his phone calls definitely represented psychological abuse.

However, Ted's role in this story is to me remarkable and it's this: nearly thirty years later I was talking to him at my mother's funeral, and he told me, 'Of course, your Dad was a big Arsenal fan, oh yes, he loved the Arsenal.'

Now, although Uncle Ted was as mad as a wildly barking dog, you could have an interesting conversation with him about things, especially the old days, and I've always been grateful for him telling me that Denis Thatcher was so thick he could hardly hold a conversation. So this genuinely shocking fact about my Dad may actually have been true.

And it was around this time that my brother confessed to me that his first game was Arsenal Reserves versus Shrewsbury Town Reserves, thickening the plot further. Father takes eldest son to first game: has to be something of an emotional event for father. Takes him to favourite London club, no? But why did he not tell me of the Arsenal connection? Was my father as weird as the Knights? What then?

iii
Mabel Jnr

I had a happy childhood, I feel sure, but Candler Street did its best to smash a hole in the side of it. I even had my own Candler Street nickname. It was a girl's name, naturally. They all called me 'Mitzi', because I was little and painfully thin. My Dad called me 'Muscles' with rich and affectionate irony, which was better than Mitzi at least. Normally something which could permanently damage the personality of a small boy, I survived this feminine branding because luckily I was fully fourteen before I found out Mitzi was what you called a second rate showgirl or a poodle. Also luckily, none of my friends ever discovered my secret so they couldn't taunt me with it. Working the same theme, my mother's pet name for me was 'my petite jeune fille' and as she was always in a good mood when I got this treatment I thought this was pretty nice. Again luckily, by the time I'd worked out the meaning of these words I'd been a grammar school boy long enough to be imbued with a sense of my intellectual superiority over an uneducated maman; thus I easily survived the Freudian implications of the matter, realising that this was mere language mangling caused by mother's lack of a grounding in elementary French. In the playground where real damage might have been done, Thomas The Tank Engine was the worst I got at primary school, hardly enough to leave me in puddles of tears wailing for a therapist.

The older I get, the more I entertain the notion that I ended up truly disliking my mother because she put me through the Candler Street years.

That is a terrible thing for a son to say about his mother, but it is nonetheless true. However, perhaps if it hadn't been for the evils inflicted upon her by her own mother, born in the same year as Adolf Hitler, 1889, she would have been a woman I could have been truly proud to have been associated with. For she had good qualities alright.

We lived in a nice, detached house thanks to my Mum saving the deposit of £300 through twelve years of marriage and possibly the five and a half years it took to finish the Second World War too for all I know. She was desperate, but desperate to get the family out of Tottenham and away from my Dad's side of the family who she thought were all drinkers and wasters.

And she did it.

Because of that I got to live way out in Cuffley, Hertfordshire, almost the country* where everyone around us had done exactly as my Mum had done. Mabel, or should I say Joan - my mum changed her name by deed poll before I was born - had been starved of education when she was young so she stormed into parenthood with the determination of a raiding Viking, aiming that Keith and I do the decent thing and make up for the strictly enforced failures she endured by being the hardest working children on the planet and woe betide us if we let her down. Times many as I grew up she reminded us of the fact that she'd won a scholarship for Tottenham Grammar School For Girls, had borne the stigma of a special poor girl's uniform and was forced by Mabel Snr to leave at 14 to take in washing. This scarred her mentally for life as you can imagine, and by way of compensation we were to share her burden in the opening rounds of life.

And yet, isn't life a mystery? Awful as my Mum could be, and I never forgave her for pushing my face into a plate of uneaten mince and mashed potato when I was four, she was right there in the blooming part of my youth, my going to football. My Dad must have said to her one evening,

'How about I take the little 'un to White Hart Lane on Saturday? He's nearly six, after all.'

And Mabel Jnr must have replied,

'Wilf, what a good idea. He's been moaning about not being able to go for months now. It's time we gave the little monster a treat.'

Or perhaps I'm being a bit slow; more likely it went like this:

'Have I got to take you to your fucking mother's again this Saturday? All you do is sit there and argue, the pair of you. And that little kid has to sit through it every week. Your mother's treated you like shit all your life and you, like a fool, put up with it.'

---

* and a mere mile from where Posh Spice, Victoria Beckham was brought up. The mother of my first serious girlfriend, Mrs Hardy, taught the young Adams and according to the claims of her daughter in 1999, was responsible for encouraging the future pop quasi-icon to pursue a career in entertainment. Take that with a pinch of salt, but that's what her daughter, Frances, told me.

'You can shutcha face. I work my fuckin' fingers to the bone all week cooking and cleaning and you don't take no notice. I don't know why I don't leave, see how you get on without me.'

'Tell you what, let's take Craig to his first game on Saturday, it's time we gave him a hobby that'll last him a lifetime and take his mind off all the family rows. It might keep him out of a mental institutions when he's grown up.'

Well okay, I'm sorry, that's the best I can do. The first two parts of the latter conversation are pretty authentic though. If I had nothing better to do than compile a list of the most stupid things I've ever heard of humans doing, just next to the release of Chris De Berk's 'Tart In Red' and the Treaty of Versailles, would be my mother's decision to dutifully visit Mabel Snr every weekend of her married life. 'The Duchess', as my Dad oft referred to her, seemed to have a supernatural power over her children. If Hitler had been given it, the result of the war would have been reversed, I know that. She didn't approve of my Dad, so when my parents got married in 1946 she refused to go to the wedding and wouldn't let my Mum get married from number nine. She was 27 years old.

If we were Mabel Jnr the last thing you and I would have done would have been to try to get a flat directly opposite Satan's alternative GHQ but that's exactly what she did. God, in the end my Dad must have been desperate to marry my Mum. Twenty years later during my Candler Street visiting years, my Dad used to deal with her in an impressively detached way. To her face he called her 'Rachel' because she had a jewish grandmother and there was much casual anti-Semitism in Tottenham in those days*. Perhaps her supernatural gifts only worked on blood relations. She didn't try any nonsense with my Dad. She affected a shy friendliness with him even, and they would exchange thoughts about Lester Piggot's chances that afternoon for a couple of minutes before my Dad would say, 'right, let's get going then.' My Mum should have taken a leaf out of her husband's book and grown a pair of balls, so to speak, but she never did. My Nan had The Power and that was that.**

---

*one of my uncles in fact joined Mosely's Blackshirts, allegedly because he fell for the uniforms as they marched down Seven Sisters Road one Saturday morning.
**I should tell you too that once we arrived at number 9 to find an old woman talking in a respectful way to Mabel Snr. To my bewilderment she kept referring to her as 'aunt.' Mabel would have been about 76 but this visiting newcomer must have been 68 if she'd been a day. Shows you that Mabel Snr had the power alright.

iv
The Toxic Seed And The Second Son

A Saturday morning in Tottenham - and I still dream about number 9 regularly, tossing and turning uncomfortably in my sleep all the while - was as tedious as watching live coverage of a Commons Select Committee discussing fishing rights, but now I'd turned six the four towering flood-light pylons of White Hart Lane beckoned: I got to go to matches regularly which gave me something to hold on to at least once a fortnight. Looking back at everything across this vast distance, I ought to recognise that without the Knights of Number Nine - in other words, without my mum - I might not have found football. Thus I owe her some gratitude. Or not, as the case may be.

From that first March afternoon at the Lane things began to expand seemingly exponentially. The first day of the 63-64 season we went to Highbury where as you will know, the Arsenal do their brand of work for Satan. The memory of walking up dark steps to crest the ridge which opened on to the top tier of the west stand, enabling my eyes to see the inside of a football ground for the very first time, is permanently tattooed on my brain. An absolutely incredible sea of magical, emerald green swam before me, and to the left in front of the North Bank terrace, the whitest of white nets. Whiter than Louis Armstrong's teeth (which I also saw that year, my Dad being the big jazz fan), whiter than the paper I drew on at school, whiter than the new fridge.

There was a buzz of excited anticipation in the air all round the ground. I didn't know it was exactly that back then, but I know it now. It was the opening day of the season! Looking back I can see that right there the devil himself was dangling me above the pit of boiling sulphur on the most anorexic of threads: here was the team I surely could have been tempted to support from now on. But they lost three-one, and it was probably that as much as anything which pulled me back from a sickening fate, as anyone who isn't a Gooner* will tell you.

The Gunners had recently signed a new player my Dad had told me to watch out for from Dundee called Ian Ure (he was passionate about anyone playing football with a Scottish birth certificate in those days). I have a vivid, vivid memory of him heading a ball away to my left and what has

---

*A Gooner is a supporter of Arsenal FC. By the way, they should have begun the season after the first world war in division two, but bribed their way into division one (and variations thereof ever since). The thought that had officials of the football league been less corrupt Arsenal may well have a history like Grimsby Town is both cheering and maddening at the same time, I find.

been left indelibly imprinted on my memory is the whiteness of his blond hair. Oh, the colour of football when you saw it live, when you were there! This was surely what won me to the game forever. If there is a heaven, the colours are those I saw that August day in 1963 at Highbury. Once I saw the coloured spectacle of football, I was well and truly gone.

But what I need to do here is try to grasp what it was my parents thought they were doing when they started to take me to football. Did they have any idea what they were about to do to me? When I took my oldest son to his first game when he was four, I had a clear plan. I wasn't trying to cram one of my own obsessions down his throat; I was trying to give him something that I thought would last him a lifetime: a love of football. I'm not sure my parents had a clue what they were trying to do with me and stupidly I never asked them to clear this up for me.

With a substantial measure of oddness, my Mum came to a lot of those matches, including one that season where the Gunners smashed Aston Villa 6-0 on a Tuesday night. A Tuesday night! What was my Mum doing at an Arsenal match on a Tuesday night? She claimed to be a Spurs fan, and was as far as I could tell because she enthusiastically would shout 'come on you Lillywhites!' at home games, so why did she want to watch Arsenal? To be with Dad as he watched his team? To me, she was never a proper fan, because sometimes the three men of the family went to a game without her and she didn't collect programmes (neither did my dad; he just craftily procured them from his mates for me whenever they went to a game somewhere).

Neither did she talk about football at home, never asking me why I thought her team were seemingly incapable now of recapturing the form that swept aside all opposition in 1961*. Didn't she want to work this terrible problem through until she could somehow live with it? No, of course not. Women don't generally get this illness. They're either too intelligent, too practical or simply too damned busy. To agonize about football you have either to be a dreamer or have plenty of time on your hands.

Dad worked hard but he had time for a hobby. But a dreamer of football dreams? I doubt it. He didn't like Tottenham though, I knew that. Whenever we were going to a Spurs game he always talked about the opposition, never the home team, even though in 1963 they'd just become the first British club to win a European trophy. They were massive in those days and crowds of fifty-odd thousand would pack the Lane to see them. But when Wednesday were coming my Dad would give me a miniature

---

*This was the year Spurs won the double, which is to say they won the league championship and the FA Cup in the same season, the first side so to do in the twentieth century.

run down on the opposition: the talk was of Bronco Lane, a swashbuck-
ling centre forward and Peter Swan the centre half. When Leicester came
it was Gordon Banks and Frank McLintock. When Manchester United
came that year it was already Law, Charlton and a new star called George
Best. Six years old I was my Dad's son alright, so as for a lifetime following the Lilywhites, forget it**. I didn't give a damn if I was in a minority
of one: I fucking hated them.

So if Dad wasn't taking me to the Lane to make me a Spurs fan and he
wasn't taking me to Highbury to fashion me into a Gooner, heaven only
knows why he took me so often. He just loved a game of football I sup-
pose+, and I also suppose, though this is not something you remember
doing when as a child, I must have badgered him every night when he
came through the door at 6.20 (exactly), as he strode into the dining room
to the drinks cabinet for his nightly dram, as all kids do when they want
something:

'Are we going to a match this Saturday, Dad? Can we? Can we?'

'Who are Spurs playing?'

'Everton.'

'Okay, we'll go: wait til you see Alex Young, great player. Plays for
Scotland.........'

Jimmy Greaves was the master craftsman, his little legs all a flurry as
he passed ball after ball calmly into the net, week after week. He was sick-
eningly brilliant. He wore slick Brylcreemed hair, he chewed gum and he
wore a look of cheeky arrogance all the while. Oh, how I would have loved
him if I'd been a Spurs fan. He should have been my first hero.

A lot of the time we did go, and I loved it, adored it, obsessed it. I collected football annuals, collected football programmes and sent to dealers
for them when I'd saved enough money, watched every result in the paper,
knew exactly who played for who in the first division, played Subbuteo
games on a board on my bed my Dad had had custom made. He even had

---

**In fact right from the off I always supported whoever Spurs were playing. This
was also because ever since I can remember I've always loved an underdog. All
around me at the Lane in those early days were rabid home fans baying for blood
and also, the great Lilywhites used to destroy most teams that went there daring
to dream about the possibility of getting a result. When they were attacking the
Park Lane end the half consisted of a tide of white and navy blue pouring towards
me. In the eye of my memory their moves were quick and destructive like sixteenth century swordsmen.

+He always was an odd bugger, my Dad, never saying much or explaining anything
in detail to us children, but in those days did anybody's Dad explain anything?
Isn't talking to your children a totally modern, post-Beatles, post-Led Zeppelin,
even, thing?

a friend paint numbers on the shirts of the different teams I had. Now that's love. I knew the name of every club in Scotland and I could spell Stenhousemuir before I could spell 'street'. I learned the names of all the English league grounds and the sound of them in my mind was like the greatest poetry imaginable: Old Trafford; Cold Blow Lane; Stamford Bridge; Ashton Gate; Eastville; St Andrews; the Hawthorns. My Dad tested me on them at the tea table on Sunday nights. I played football in the garden, at school, in the school team, in my bedroom and in the lounge, with my friends, with my Dad (sometimes) and on my own.

Is it any wonder then, that at the age of 30, after having been away from football for fifteen years, and thinking I'd left it all way, way behind me, I became obsessed and stuck like industrial glue to a lower division club in Derbyshire called Chesterfield? When you remember to plug Bobby Keetch into the equation, it seems obvious that I never stood a chance.

2

Dark Night of the Soul in the Boys Enclosure

' *I like the boy Cruft: he's movin', he's chasin'...'*

Joe Mercer

L ike a great many people in those days, when I hit my late teens I grew away from football. One watershed event took place on the opening day of the 1967-8 season, when West Ham United came down the Lane. The family went, up in the seats behind the Park Lane goal. The Hammers, Moore, Hurst, Peters included took an absolute pasting and with about ten minutes to go they were five-nil down. Suddenly, the strangest thing happened. From seemingly nowhere objects started flying through the air towards us: coins, bottles and stones mostly, but pieces of metal too and even lengths of chain. This was totally unbelievable. People I didn't know throwing dangerous stuff at me? What had I done? But one thing was immediately clear: it was absolutely terrifying. All the nerves around my stomach seemed to have contracted, causing most of my brain to shut down. The sensible and logical thing in the circs. would have been to start flinging the stuff back from whence it came. But terror collapses the mind.

Some people shouted down to the terracing below, 'what do you think you're doing?!'

'Bloody pack it in, you stupid kids!'

But most of us were too stunned to make any form of protest. Stupefied, in fact by this surreal event. We should have done another obvious thing: left but nobody did, as I remember it, we just sat there like proverbial rabbits trapped hypnotized in a set of headlights. The weapon shower may have abated somewhat after a few minutes, because the next thing I remember was being downstairs after the final whistle, waiting to move out on to the street, with an unholy host of voices were loudly declaiming, 'We are the Norf Bank!.. clagh-clagh, clagh clagh-clagh..We are the Norf Bank!'

We had suddenly entered the Modern Age of Football.

I now know of course that in front of me as I awaited the long walk down Tottenham High Road to the car were not just noisy young West Ham fans but a bunch of skinheads.

'I'm never going again,' said my Mum. And indeed, we didn't go much at all after this, the year I was eleven and starting secondary school. My Dad too must have seen enough to give him pause for thought. In fact it wasn't until I got to about fourteen that I remember going again with anything like regularity, so my Dad, thinking about it, must have come out in sympathy with my mum. Well to an extent. In fact he took up golf and played Saturday afternoons so that was that as far as family Saturdays up The Lane were concerned.

I reacted well to this, all things considered. If the football world was about to come crashing down, at least there was always music. The Beatles were as much a part of my childhood as my left foot, an experience shared by millions of other youngsters at the time of Beatlemania in 1963. In fact like life during wartime, it is impossible to truly convey what it was like to live in the years of The Beatles. Their fame dwarfed the country like a magical cosmic cloud. The England I understood was simply overwhelmed by their personalities, their style and their music and all the other forms of social changes they precipitated in their glorious wake: in art, fashion, hairdressing, cars, drugs, sex, conversation, television and dare I say it, football what with the Kop adapting Yellow Submarine of a Saturday afternoon. Theirs was a sublime ubiquity which seemed to contain everything in the world that was worth knowing. By comparison Madonna is a part-time waitress in a tea bar in Rhyl.

Following the apogee of their artistic and stylistic influence, the Sgt Pepper album, the year of 1968 saw the music scene opening out into further possibilities. This was more or less the start of the rock explosion and I was fortunate enough to have had a brother who was 15 and starting to bring records home.

I think it was when Paul Hemmings came round one Sunday afternoon with Wilfred and Mabel Jnr off at Mabel Snr's, sat there in desert boots and a beard, put an album on with these three angel voices singing 'Wooden Ships on the water, very free and easy....' that the penny dropped that there was something deep and more satisfying in the world than tackles, mud and aching feet from standing behind the goal.

So the house was filled with the sounds of Cream, Yes, Jethro Tull, the White Album, Crosby, Stills and Nash and Free. Keith would come home from the local youth club talking about impossibly cool bands with names like Chicken Shack, Black Cat Bones and someone called Captain B-Fart. I was wide-eyed with wonder. Then when he actually went to the Wake

Arms near Epping to see Yes and Genesis, I was just in awe of the experience he was going through. To me he had a ticket to a magic land of flares and velvet, forever unattainable to little me. But this was okay. It was enough to be the grateful recipient of the mystical backwash from his world: the music on 12 inch vinyl.

In fact the music revolution made football seem a very very small thing. But it had always been there in the house. My Dad loved Billie Holiday and for some unaccountable reason - he was a totally uneducated man, left school at 14 like Mabel Jnr - considered the age of six to be the right one to entrust a young son with the biographical details of the greatest singer of all time. It was as if he'd made the rational calculation of a Spock (and I think I mean Mr here, not Dr). I could grasp what he meant when he said she'd died young through too much drink and too many drugs. I knew what drink was because I used to drink the dregs from glasses whenever relations came round and bottles of beer were opened. I hadn't a clue what drugs were but I understood that there was stuff in the world that if you took it it would kill you. I knew her music was sad and I liked it. I also liked some of his old 78s that he'd get out of his 78 shaped box which were mostly blues things and ancient 20s jazz, when Mabel Jnr went out for the evening to something called 'Cuffley Wives' where I presumed the merry married ones of Cuffley made cakes or worked on their hoovering technique. One was 'O Didn't He Ramble.' There was another which began with eerie, disembodied American voice groaning, 'ashes to ashes, dust to dust, if the something don't gitcha, (was it 'women'?) the liquor must.'

I hadn't the remotest idea what these ancient sounding guys were singing about, but the sound of it was instantly attractive to my little sticky out ears.

All the Thomas men played the drums. Dad had a kit which my brother and I played practically before we knew how to spill a glass of coke all over the lounge carpet. Dad had played in dance bands after the war when M. Jnr and he would hump a huge bass drum and a heaving black lumpy case on the bus to the gig. There's glamourous. He still played the occasional 'band job' as I was growing up.

Full of Thomas genes at eleven I was drafted into the school orchestra because no-one from the older years could play a snare drum properly. Fine. I just read the simple rhythm line on the page and kept decent time and that was me for the next seven years. We played loads of concerts in the local area and even appeared on BBC's Nationwide. We were awful but we didn't care. When almost all your education consisted of sitting in the classroom copying off the blackboard and taking notes from text books, anything to do with the school band had the glamour of being on tour with Led Zeppelin. It was, I suppose, a spectacularly naff thing to be involved in. But it was one of the few good things about being a teenager. We got to go abroad: a week in Paris, a week staying with families in Germany, a week the following year to Rumania. I was with mates: when we weren't playing we were in hysterics about anything and everything or mooned dreamily and lustfully over girls. Nothing wrong with that, as the man said.

I played in pop groups with older lads always desperate for a drummer. But there are no stories to tell about brushes with fame or even aspirations in that direction. We were all boys of the new middle class, from families who had reached the moon just by dint of living in a house with a mortgage. We were being brought up to believe that success was a marriage and a safe job in a bank. And by and large we knew what space in the world we were to inhabit.

By the time the new decade arrived I had discovered James Taylor to be a demi-God whose music would rescue me from a hopelessly large case of early teenage melancholia and saw him with Carole King at the Festival Hall a little later. My first gig. A little later I saw Humble Pie at the Rainbow in Finsbury Park (formerly the Astoria where my Dad and Mabel Jnr had seen many a film if they weren't in the back row doing what young lovers do) then Zeppelin at the Empire Pool, Wembley, which, I can safely assure you, was brilliant and exciting. Led Zeppelin! IV had just come out and there was Jimmy Page with his violin bow and Les Paul, Plant with his tumbling curls and well, that was it. Who the fuck needed football now? Looking back, though, it was a slow divorce. So I did.

My parents didn't have the stomach for it after those nice Happy Hammers On Tour gave us a nice introduction to the future of football, so I kept in touch with the real thing thanks to Joey Smithers and his father allowing me to tag along to Tottenham games with them. For a couple of seasons, 1969 through 1971, we stood on the Shelf in a nice position watching the Spurs of the Perryman, Peters, Mullery, Gilzean, Chivers and Mullery years mostly take apart the opposition just as they had in my football baptism days. I still wanted them to lose every game, obviously.

Mr Smithers was a nice man. He was the only person I knew with a west country accent and a limp. He was tall, slim and cheerful which I liked, and I was very pleased that he didn't seem to mind in the slightest my being there which I liked even more. I can still see him in the dark green raincoat he wore whatever the weather laughing at some wry remark he'd just made about John Pratt or Jimmy Pearce and Joe, whose real name was Simon, being embarrassed in the way all teenage boys are of their Dad. This is normal. He'd be considering how marginal the chances were of Dad telling me,

'Did you know, heh, heh, that Simon used to rub his willy up against our next door neighbour's dog, heh, heh?'

Joey and I weren't proper friends because although we went to match-es and played with a ball in the street together he was in the year above me at school. Naturally this meant that from Monday to Friday we inhab-ited different universes although contact was made through Joey taking the piss unmercifully about my teeth - I had crowns on my two front teeth that were discoloured where they met. I won't say I revelled in being called 'Shit-Between-Your-Teeth' by my weekend friend but I understood the awkward position he was in: you lose vital cred points with your tough mates by even acknowledging a boy in a lower year in a way that suggests you might be muckers.

Slightly strangely perhaps, we often went up the Lane one week, Highbury the next, but on our own because I suppose Mr Smithers was a grown up and we were just boys. Either I went because something deep inside beyond my ken was compelling me or I didn't have anything better to do with Saturdays. I look back and think I must have been out of my tree. At the start of the 1969-70 season I saw the first 20 Spurs home games consecutively . The ones I didn't see with the Smithers, the ones in the Texaco Cup, I went with my Dad because he liked watching Scottish teams of course. It wasn't that hard a thing to do because my mum was always glad to give me the money to go- it bought her some peace and quiet for a few hours - and as all addicts know, once you get into the habit it quickly becomes a compulsion, so it's easy. I only broke it when my own team came down the Lane, threw away a two-goal lead and caused me to hate Tottenham so much I swore I'd never go again to their poxy, wretched ground.

So there we were, me and Joey, both with the addiction, though I'd - not boast, admit that mine was the more eccentric of the two. Joey had what for me was the luxury of seeing his own team actually play in the flesh, something I hardly ever did, and then the next week he could trav-el up to Finsbury Park station hopeful of his arch enemies dropping a cou-ple of home points. Me, I wanted the home team to lose every week. Unfortunately, Arsenal were building towards their first double win at that time, so most weeks we came away empty handed. One Wednesday night in 1970 we were buzzing with anticipation of the Gunners getting what their wingless wonders deserved when the mighty Ajax, complete with Johann Cruyff (or 'the boy John Cruft' as old Joe Mercer once described him on the telly one night, unforgettably - o how we laughed for years at that: 'that Cruft, he's chasin' he's movin' - no wonder he got Malcolm Allison in to do the technical stuff). Miserable night though: Arsenal won 4-0.

These are memories which lay deep under layers of geological memory. I never thought it would come back to me that Ajax had a famous group of supporters who wore long white lab coats and that we could see them up in the West Stand that night. But there, it has. So I can't be sure about this, but me and Joey may well have jacked it in after that and stuck to the two train trip to the Spurs where we bought programmes and ate delicious hot dogs with boiled onions at one and six a time (we did that at Highbury too, but it has to be said that Joe's appetite was just a bit sharper in the White Hart Lane area).

My non-football thoughts in those days were the usual churning maelstrom of the melodramatically over-emotional and the banal. I was in some ways, despite my nomadic wandering up and down the north London urban-suburban rail network, a typical teenager. I was must have been searching for something as I stumbled into my second teenage year in March 1971 and I tell you this: I wasn't finding it at the Arsenal. Football grounds still exerted a primal gravitational pull. I loved the way the winter afternoons grew dark under skies of slithering, mournful grey bringing with them the inevitable response of some ancient club lackey with flat cap, old coat and hacking Woodbine cough flicking the switch which turned the floodlights on deep in the bowels of the mighty stadium.

With each succeeding minute of fading daylight, the bright pale-gold floodlight picked up the colours of the shirts of the players, the pitch, the cinder track, the referee all in black, the red or navy blue scarves of the crowd, somehow adding romance and glamour to the occasion often when none had any right to exist. Put thirty or forty thousand people in a football ground on a winter afternoon and switch on the electric lights and the sight of a man counting paper clips at a desk somewhere near the centre circle would look powerfully alluring. The sky that half an hour ago had looked so utterly cheerless it was sapping your will to exist was now a rather fetching shade of indigo just above the top of the floodlight pylons. At the same time there was something wistful and sad about the players' striving, shouting and grunting in the gathering gloom of another awful English winter.

(I was only rising fourteen: could I really have picked up on these somewhat sophisticated (or male and arse-clenchingly self-indulgent) undertones of the best days of Frank McLintock's playing career? I think so).

The lifestyle couldn't sustain itself much longer though, not with Yes about to release Fragile. Soon an incapacitating ennui was sapping my ability to appreciate the silky genius of Charlie George. To me he was just a long haired poof in an Arsenal shirt. In football fan terms I was a freak: my team played their home games the best part of two hundred miles away so all I had was surrogate football, a placebo. When I should have been stepping out gleefully, salivating with anticipation at the prospect of how my favourite players were going to play, of two points in the bag, or plodding there sick with worry about losing one-nil to a last minute breakaway, I was empty of the emotions that make up a normal, true football fan. No wonder I was unexcited about Peter Simpson's ability to put an opposing striker off his game with a sharp kidney punch in the opening minute. No wonder Stevie Perryman's effortless ninety minute scurrying about the pitch like a whirling dervish after a frontal lobotomy left me moodily reflecting upon the possibility of my having to find meaning in a God-less universe.

However, honesty insists that whatever pretentions I might give myself in terms of being stuck in those agonising twilight years between being happy in short trousers and being able to drink, smoke, drive and snog girls, I was simply one sorry teenager. Maybe my doomy Neil Young albums were dragging me under. Possibly the fact that I also idolised Cat Stevens, Paul Simon and any bloke with a guitar and a miserable song to sing meant that I was just a hopeless, pubescent prat.

Or am I being too hard on myself? Was I even then beginning to pick up on one of my key neurological sensors the complete pointlessness of all this striving, all this commotion, all this walking to stations, all this paying good money to get in? Was my own now considerable programme collection just a heap of printed paper?

One grey Saturday in Goonerland I went home half way through the second half because I was so fed up. In the end it's better and safer to argue that it wasn't at all because I was going through some sort of teenage hormone-explosion crisis. Not because of obvious girl problems. Not torrential emotional torment because of an acne outbreak brought on by an overexposure to Bob McNab. No incipient parental breakup already beginning to scar me and forcing me to contemplate an uncertain future. It wasn't because I was so mature somewhere I had recognised that this massive slab of our nation's culture boiled down merely to twenty-two grown men kicking a ball round a field as almost all the women of that age averred. No. Let me believe this:

I just got totally bored with seventies football.

3

'I gave up football for snogging' (a young fan confesses)

'*O'er ladies lips, who straight on kisses dream.*'
William Shakespeare

I asked Lorraine White out when I was thirteen. I was crazy about her and had been since our first English lesson in secondary school when she had to come out to the front of the class to do the opening scene in Toad Of Toad Hall. If you don't know it (and why should you), it begins with Mole soliloquizing about his petty problems of trying to find his glasses or trying to pick a winner in the 3.30 at Kempton, I forget exactly which. The important thing is that I'd have been shitting myself right there in front of 25 new classmates if that were me and already needing to find a new school for the next day. I watched agog as Lorraine carried the part off with considerable aplomb, I thought, for one so young, and I was immediately smitten. She was a bit of alright to look at too, I might tell you, but that could just have been me.

Eventually our affections were focussed in such a way as to suggest that we might begin to shape a future life together. This state of play came to pass only a year later so I reckon I'd done pretty well for a callow youth. All along I had known that time was on my side. Lally, as we called her, couldn't leave school until she was sixteen. I'd reel her in one way or

---

* I should perhaps share with you the fact that when we were on the doing games at school in July, the Spurs first team squad, back in training for the new season, used to run along the length of the fence at the edge of the field. I'd like to relate to you the fact that lads awaiting a tilt at the long jump pit would shout 'Chivers! Your a big wanker!' and other examples of original thinking (we were a grammar school after all). However, we didn't because our games teacher would have killed us. Even if we could have got away with anything, the bravest our lot would have been would have been to have shouted out 'Arsenal!' hardly the thing to get Alan Mullery shaking an angry fist at us, or better still, jumping over the fence to thump the culprit. Spurs fans will obviously be pleased to hear that Alan Gilzean was always the back marker, some two hundred yards behind, walking, with, I think, Martin Chivers and a.n. other not far in front.

another.

I was ready to pop the big question. She'd been passing me notes in Chemistry for a while (and they weren't to find out the chemical properties of manganese sulphate) and demanded to know from my mates when I was finally going to get round to escorting her around the luxurious bars, restaurants and theatres of downtown, turn of the decade Cheshunt (home of the Spurs training ground*).

The big problem now was not her saying 'yes,' I had all that nerve racking anxiety still to come - at 13 I had the supreme confidence only complete ignorance of the ways of the world gives you - but where to take her. There was the pictures, the obvious first choice, and the activity Lally was obviously expecting, but my mum would have killed me because she thought I was too young to go out with girls and I was in total fear of lying to her. Thus, my options were narrow. To be frank, they were practically non-existent. I could go shopping with my new love. What were we, married and in our forties? We could hang around the streets or go to the park. Out of the question, it was winter. So, go hang out in a coffee bar or something. Nope, such things didn't exist where I lived. Well then, take her to a Wimpy Bar and a plod round the shops, perhaps. That should do the trick. Actually, thinking about this thirty years later it might well have done. But I asked her to come with me to Tottenham-Newcastle.

This turned out to be a complete and utter disaster. Oh, you're surprised? Yeah, so was I. I felt sure that my irresistibly boyish good looks and winning sense of humour would smooth the way past any ideological objections she might have to this somewhat unromantic backdrop to the opening night of our fledgling hot love affair. I mean, she loved me, right? I had wonderful visions of us walking together along Paxton Road sharing a hot dog with onions, smothered with tomato sauce, and me perhaps kissing away a smear of watered down Heinz ketchup from the side of her delicious mouth. We'd watch the match hand-in-hand and we'd both be laughing at my cruel jokes at the expense of Bobby Moncur's hairy back and Joe Kinnear's poncy haircut. We'd walk to the station after the match and Lorraine in my mind is still laughing at my constant flow of wit and then waiting for the train to Cheshunt.

I'd take her round the corner of the waiting room up the far end of the platform and plant a generous handful of wet kisses on her pert and luscious little lips and the world for once would be absolutely perfect.

So I wrote Lally a little note of invitation and to cover the possibility of being a total laughing stock with all my friends when she turned me down - which of course she wouldn't - I worded the thing as casually as I could. After I'd spent an hour at home drafting it, it was ready. having successfully drained it of any recognisable human emotion except an extrav-agant Wildean boredom. Thus I could laugh off any attempt my so-called mates to destroy me:

'Aaagh, you asked Lally White out and she doesn't want you! Haaarrgghh!.'

'Lads, lads, calm down, I felt sorry for her, I was going up the Spurs anyway so I asked her along: I wasn't actually going to talk to her.'

Nothing happened. My pals didn't rip me to pieces. Lal hadn't put the word out about it, obviously. Brilliant. Thank Christ for that. I got away with it. Trouble was, next day Lorraine pretended to deny my very exis-tence on the earth with a vehemence Margaret Thatcher herself would have envied. You'd have thought, the way she was carrying on that I'd invited her to a guided tour round a sewage farm. I was indignant and hurt: what was wrong with football? She didn't, in any real sense speak to me again. That was the way things were with teenage romance in those days.

I refute entirely the idea that this scarring episode in my fairly uneventful romantic history had anything to with my leaving the game. In the end it wasn't the competing charms of the rock and singer-songwriter revolution either. No, I'd found that there was more than enough time and energy for being fanatical about music in my spare time and popping off to see a game three weeks out of four. For a start, the weekend is long enough for a myriad of pastimes if you think about it; second, the rest of the week we were home from school by half four and we had thirteen weeks holiday on top of that. The final nail in the coffin of my taking leave of the great game was finally and simply, a girl.

No big deal there. There are millions of us who have suffered or enjoyed this same experience down the last thirty British years and women have been the prime cause of the divorce time after time, after time. The name of my causal trigger was Frances Hardy, but not, I hasten to add, an anglicized version of the sultry French singer-actress. Getting to this point was fraught with difficulty and ineptitude, as it is for many hopeless teenage boys, but I got there. I say 'girl': the word is laughably inadequate to describe her. She was totally beautiful and completely love-ly though I'd never spoken to her. A third party set the thing up but wouldn't you know it, practically the night before I was going to ask her out - and not to football this time - when I got sidetracked by the local youth club. This was a brilliant purpose built thing with great music, pin-ball machines, snooker, table tennis (which I adored almost as much as shimmying my way to some sort of glory along with the other, whoops, here we go again, pinball addicts), really decent gigs on a Friday (Slade!

America!!) and o blessed relief, no fighting thanks to a local chapter of greasers who insisted upon pain of being beaten to a pulp on a peaceful, easy scene.

I digress. The night before my big day so to speak, I got talking to a girl I knew from school there and I got on with her so well that a sudden thought entered my silly little head. Naturally, at 14 years of age, I was an idiot, loud mouthed fool with verbal diahorrea. But let me tell you, the human being is a marvellous piece of work and if you want a reason for believing in God, it's right here. I was talking to this girl Patricia, and she wasn't at all bad looking, and a sixth sense started to work inside me for the very first time in my life. It suddenly dawned on me that some heavy grey clouds were beginning to pull apart and that in about three more conversational moves, if she said the right things and I continued to deploy my mental and verbal forces appropriately, I could be going out with her in about, ooh, four and a half minutes?

This practically unfathomable and rather predatory sense, ability, without a proper name as far as I know, only worked about another three times in my entire life and perhaps way back then I appreciated its rarity value. Because once I recognised it I was like a mad dog and all thoughts of Frances disappeared out the window and off into a distant blue yonder. In two hundred and seventy two seconds - the two extra I needed to break off and deal with a tickle in my throat which I hadn't foreseen - exactly, I was almost simultaneously asking Pat out and moving in for my first proper kiss with a real live female type person.

Four weeks later it had fizzled out for reasons I don't even remember. Probably we just happened to be at exactly the same point on the learning curve of romantic and sexual love and both felt that Neolithic mating urge at precisely the same moment and acted on it unthinkingly. Before realising that we had absolutely nothing in common and that being together had about as much point as an ashtray on a motor bike.

However, the episode had an explosive residual benefit for young me. Come the season of the Christmas party and school disco, I was snogging schoolgirls like they were about to ban it. Come one, come all, if they had lips and weren't totally bestial or smelly, spotty or fat, I was there, mouth working with a level of commitment previously unsuspected in one to whom laziness and lack of drive were second, third and fourth nature. Quite what was wrong with the girls of Goffs Grammar School, Cheshunt I didn't stop to reflect upon less they stop accepting my advances. If there is an explanation for my success, it can only have been the total and utter belief that if I said 'do you want to dance', moved in close and shaped to kiss, I would not be pushed away in disgust. And the possession of that steam hammer self-belief I can only put down to my brief dalliance with Pat Dixon. Amazing. Oh and a gizzard full of rum and coke, it goes without saying.

The crowning moment of this high summer of lip wrestling came at the school Christmas bash where after many rounds of serious oral fluid exchange with a satisfyingly numerous cross section of my female contemporaries, I managed to summon up the bottle to attempt my moves on Maureen Lodge.

This for me was really a step up to the big league. For all the boasting going on round here I ought to tell you that there were certain girls I daren't contemplate approaching. I mean, come on, this is me we're talking about, not the likes of Dave Mutter or Pete Rooke. Mind, I'm presuming these unattainable Goddess-cum-vamps were actually present at a mere school disco, which may be quite an assumption seeing as the Wendy Moons of that world may well have had more exotic fish to fry in rather less un-cool parts of Cheshunt (stamping ground of Cliff Richard, no less). We were all grammar grubs from the posh end of the catchment area; it was axiomatic therefore that we were as soft as shite. I therefore rather fancy that the upper classier reaches of our potential mating habitat, so to speak, were already riding around in the Capris and Minis of the local seventeen year olds. This was accepted as the natural order of things. Fine. Well, pretty much.

But for some reason that night, there, over to one side of the dance floor was Maureen Lodge, I thought she was gorgeous, that although a year younger than me, she was Premiership. But I landed her. It came to pass that she was swept away on a tidal wave of my outrageous confidence and heady pre-vomit alcoholic bravado. She may have had a drop herself. Whatever, by the time the evening was winding down towards the slow dance phase, twenty minutes to go, I found myself kissing the most soft, moist, yieldingly full pair of female lips you could possibly imagine. And she had breath that could fell an empire - it had a taste that would have tempted Gandhi. In the middle of the first kiss I was floating above the madly dancing throng enjoying my first ever out-of-body experience. By the beginning of the fourth my face was melting. It should be said that Maureen's, shall we say, figure, had, at the age of 14, begun to expand in all the right places in a quite sensational way, which added something to the majesty of the event, let me tell you.

So taken all in all, I was mid-way through one of the best experiences of my life, and I say that from here, not just back then. I'd hit a real blue streak right enough, and for one of the few times in my life managed next to do a truly intelligent thing: I quit while I was ahead. We had the last dance, made not a single arrangement - as if she would have anyway - and I fled. If I could remember things really clearly I might be telling you that I ran away to get the last bus or left before she could dismiss me with some withering insult. This may have been the case but I'm clinging on to my moment of glory and you're not going to stop me.

In the day or two before Christmas I made a token effort to prolong the entanglement by passing her my phone number and saying to her get in touch if you like, hey, you know, if you get fed up over the holiday but, the world order settling down to its normal distribution of natural forces and rhythms, checks and balances, I heard nothing.

I was relieved, if truth be told. I wouldn't have known what to do with her, where to take her, what to offer her. Most important of all, she lived in a rough part of the area: I'd be waiting for the last bus home crapping it in case some tough eggs came along and beat me to a wet mess. Or looked at me funny. No, the Maureen Lodge Disco had all the hallmarks of a giant killing in the FA Cup: my Yeovil to her Arsenal. I'll grant you I may have been a Swindon, I don't want to over-egg the pudding. I went back to the second division and she went back to playing Leeds and Chelsea. I was happy for the brief moments of glory I'd won and I don't think I have ever felt quite the same way since.

I don't know whether Frances was there the night of my European Cup final triumph but if she was, her dubious taste in young men may have been intensified by my roaring around all night like a deranged Rent-A-Snog representative. You know what they say: treat 'em mean to keep 'em keen. She perhaps should have been disgusted by me putting myself about on such a broad scale, but as I say, she may have been home watching the telly or been in the midst of a romantic encounter of her own somewhere. I quite hope she was.

Anyway, the point is this: the new year turned and a fraction under two weeks into 1972, the phone rang one Friday night and I had another result I was never to experience again: I was head-hunted. It was Frances herself. One of my alleged friends named Jamie Crompton* had revealed one of my secrets, to wit, that despite my fondness for getting my hands on anything in a skirt, I would have practically paid hard cash, and lots of it, if she, Frances, would go out with me. Was I interested? Was Picasso a painter? Was Roy Tunks a Wall-Cavity Insulation Specialist?

The night before our big date on Saturday afternoon at the Embassy, Waltham Cross, to see the film version of Please Sir, I had one for the road with Jackie Jones outside the youth club, just to prove something male

---

*Jamie was later to find some sort of fame playing guitar with the Suzi Quatro band. Frances now writes features for the Daily Mail. How about that.

and fairly pathetic to myself. Come the day, I prepared myself in the time honoured way: bathed myself 'til my skin was peeling off in handfuls, covered myself with a notional male after shave (it's really perfume, let's not kid ourselves), dolled myself up to the nines as if my life depended upon it - which it did, really - and tramped up the hill to the bus stop in Goffs Oak hoping for the best and feeling manically excited.

By the end of the film, which was quite good, actually, I was already morphing into a new and different kind of teenager. I'd fallen hopelessly in love. She smelt like all fresh, newly minted teenage girls should: a waft from her fragrant neck and it was like I'd been drugged by some fairy from Never-Never Land. I would have barked for her like a dog right there and then on the front platform of the 242 to Chingford if she'd asked me to. I'd have converted to Islam. And later there was all the jealousy, pumped into my nervous system by the inhuman thought that she might leave me and go off with someone else. Ah well: we might as well be honest about teenage love. There were nights to come of howling in silent agonies of existential pain as well as blissful evenings of total, soul-drenching ecstasy. How on earth was football supposed to compete with these sorts of human emotions?

We stayed together for eighteen months. I gave up even trying to snog other girls. All other facts about my life during this time apart from an obsession for the next Yes album are irrelevant.*

No caveats.

At the dawn of day one of my first love affair I finally left football behind me. It had to be a Saturday afternoon, didn't it. How could you beat that for symbolism?

**Close To The Edge was released in early September 1972, for the first 9 months of this period I didn't even have that to distract me.

4

The Great God of Football

Do not bow down to any idol and worship it, because I am the Lord your God and I tolerate no rivals.

Exodus ch 20 v5

I was gone a long time. Permanently, in fact apart from a few meaningless lapses which I'll tell you about later. It was nothing personal: it was simply the shedding of a skin as I grew from a child into a writhing mass of the moods and moroseness better known as adolescence. And it practically goes without saying that anyone indelibly marked with the football addiction who reached the age of thirteen after about 1960 tends to ditch footer not only for girls, but also for music.

Naturally we round ball addict-casualties from the sixties were totally assured that music and football inhabited parallel and distant universes. Did Jimi Hendrix look out for the Everton score when he was making Electric Ladyland? Did Eric Clapton think out his rock n blues future down the Shed? I don't think so. Jon Anderson, Yes's lead singer, sage and mystic was from Accrington but did he shed tears when Stanley folded?*

Mind you, there was Rod Stewart, who never did and never has made a secret of his love of the game (there's always one maverick around to spoil a neat theory). The inside sleeve of his Never A Dull Moment album, contains photos of the musicians on the pitch at a London non-league ground for example. Furthermore, I actually once saw him play, back in '72, an event I've tried unsuccessfully to dine out on ever since. On Saturday afternoons back at the start of the Seventies and being diseased in the mind, I used to occasionally walk the mile to the edge of our village to watch my brother play football for the local men's team, Cuffley FC. One grey autumn afternoon they'd kicked off when I got to the touchline, and my brother, who I hardly spoke a civil word to at home, and neither he to me (why was I watching him play football then? Don't bloody ask:

---

*Stanley refers to the late professional league football club Accrington Stanley - has there been a club with a better, more alluring and evocative name in the game's history? - who fell off the league ladder in 1962. The Shed refers to a popular 'end,' area behind the goal, at Chelsea's Stamford Bridge.

call it a residually damaged Knight-inherited gene), was looking straight at me, pointing stage left and mouthing what appeared to be the words 'Rod Stewart.'

Uuughh? I swivelled my eyes around the pitch and sure enough an emaciated little thing in an all red kit was indeed The Mod himself. You could tell because he had the most belting feather cut you ever saw in your life. He played football like a pansy, much to my disappointment, and held his cuffs over his shirt in the style of his hero (and mine) Denis Law. Prat. He drew further attention himself by seeming to have taken a vow of silence to The Great God Of Football, whereas practically everyone else was shouting every five seconds: 'Mickey Roberts, on your bike!' etc. 'Aw-wight lads, keep the information goin'!' He could only have got a pick because at the time Maggie Mae had just been a monster first hit for the lad, because Highgate Redwing were a decent outfit. But I'll give him this as well as his immaculate barnet: he left the changing rooms with not one, but two extravagantly good-looking women on his arm(s) and smoothed off in his celebrated yellow Lamborghini back up to London and heaven only knows what good times. I trudged off home in a terrible herringbone double-breasted coat to tea with my mum. You have to say, for all the mess he's made all over his career since: he knew what he was doing when he started out.

As the years rolled by and my youth became what nominally might be called the first flush of adulthood, I had gradually joined the massed legions of a community lost to football, who didn't want to take the risk these days of taking a boot or fist of a suedehead in your face. Or in the mid-Thatcherite days, find yourself in the middle ruck between warring 'casuals,' fighters and glass throwers who had given up coaches and scarves for trains and Lacoste t-shirts.

Since moving my heart on from football to the fair maids of England (I never did manage to pass off such charms as I possessed on any young foreign women) and Rick Wakeman, it should be said my poor, miserable mother country had seen hooliganism become not only endemic at home but one of its chief exports of the 1980s. For millions of lost souls, the sweet pain of pursuing girls was infinitely preferable to the grisly pain you suffer as some inferior outfit shows up at your ground only to nick three points off you. Or if you weren't a partisan, just popping along to a game to see the stars of the day (who, I might add, were disappearing faster than flesh off a supermodel's backside). Added to that, in the process of reaching man's estate I had come to be such a total coward I could have been lecturing at Harvard University on the subject. When my University team played in our change strip of yellow, I didn't need to put a shirt on: I played in skins. Music, women, cowardice: a mightily powerful enough brew to keep me clear of the game we were eventually told was beautiful. Year after year after year.

And yet, through all this time, twelve years in all, almost half my then life, there were still football rituals. These were observed with the ease of the long time Sunday Anglican worshipper who chants the liturgy and sings the hymns in a state of semi-hypnosis week after week. Actions and habits so natural that they're completed with only the most minimal level of self-awareness. Saturday 4.40: teleprinter. 4.50: results. If out shopping, find a Radio Rental shop window. Sunday morning newspaper: league tables, scorers, crowds. Even when going to a match was the next to last thing on my mind; when playing cards with friends, trying to sleep with girls, considering when would the most judicious time for Prefab Sprout to release their next LP and wondering how big a glorious but messy terrorist explosive advice to get rid of the entire Conservative government were way way out in front of what passed across my brain in those early adult years, I would still notice that Wrexham's crowds weren't getting any bigger.

The thing was though, apart from the prospect of Saturday afternoon leisure activity seeming to be about level with the experience of going over the top in World War One, there is also the salient fact that the Seventies and Eighties was the era of crap football.

A suitable managerial name for us to conjure with here and to represent this period for us is Ron Saunders who stamped his mark on the contemporary game wearing the expression of a bankrupt undertaker. He was less a man who had taken Sophocles' line about 'life without life's joys is living death' to heart than a Munsters lookalike determined to abolish Christmas. A quote from another manager of the time, Alan Durban might easily have come out of the mouth of the large Ronmeister himself, Atko.* Indeed for all we know Durban might have stolen the line, only I haven't the proof just now. 'If people want entertainment,' he said after masterminding a 0-0 draw at Highbury, doubtless by way of playing none up front, nine at the back and two on the goal line trying to brick up the goal, 'they should go and watch a circus.'

Is it any wonder that with attitudes like that dominating the game crowds stayed away from football in droves, like the massed throngs in recent times who made suicide pacts with partners and wives if they should ever lose their minds and visit the Millennium Dome?

Villa fans and football addict freaks can rail at me here about Saunders winning the championship in 1981 but how many players can you name from that team and more, from those three, how many neutrals would have crossed the road to watch them playing in a public park? The fact that a Saunders team won the league simply tells you how awful the competition was. And then there was a Norwich-Coventry 0-0. I saw this game sometime in the late seventies and it was about as useful an exercise as watching a broken clock in the hope that Uri Geller might be somewhere in the vicinity about to spoon-bend it back into life. I'd have flung myself over the terrace back wall to join a circus if one had been passing along Carrow Road that day.

So there's another nail in the football coffin for you: the reign of the philosophy of the killjoy. Which brings us back to what on earth I was doing going back to it at the end of 1984, even allowing for the fact that I needed something to do the day after Christmas. The thing about football attendance is that once you're in the habit you go to a game as easily as putting milk bottles out. Then when you stop going, doing other things and not even stopping for a second to wonder why you're not getting your coat on at two o'clock to get to the ground in plenty of time becomes completely normal. You'd no more think of going to a football match than of taking heroin.

So how on earth did I go back to football? Did I believe that it would be a safe, benign event without any future implications? I believe I did. Did I think I could go to one game and then leave it? Uh-huh. Should I have known better? Well.....just let me tell you about the watershed day

---

*An appropriate time-out here in honour of Mr Atkinson, perhaps rightly maligned at the time for being the archetypal good time Charlie soccer manager with his Champagne and chunky gold bracelet lifestyle. He went on to fully flower as a professional man as a television pundit who, apart from being the first to spot the fact that the German national football side were the biggest bunch of cheating divers of the latter part of the twentieth century (take a step down from your lofty pedestal Bobby Charlton) during the 1990 World Cup final, added to the language such riches as: back stick; crowd scene; putting it back into the mixer, Hollywood Ball and spotter's badge. PG Wodehouse, the best writer in the English language save Shakespeare, would have called these 'nifties' and, I think, would have been all too happy to have patted BFR on the back in approbation. There can be no higher accolade. My favourite, from Ron's nothing short of immaculate collection. was from a couple of years back, it might even have been 1999 when Manchester United snaffled a whole European Cup from under the noses of Bayern Munich. Roy Keane wafted a ball into the air from way, way out which ended up going just wide of an upright. Ron analysed the situation, decided the United captain's attacking gambit was deliberate and gave the audience his deadly earnest verdict thus: 'tell you what you know, that could have been a nomination!' To have the verve and invention to describe a shot at goal a 'nomination' makes the mind reel in wonder.

that was 26.12.84.

It was the day after Christmas in George Orwell's year and I was quietly marooned with my wife at the in-laws. There are worse places to be. The previous twenty four hours had been devoted to the pleasures of quiet and substantial eating, which is just how I've always liked it. You may know exactly what I mean: shoving turkey, potatoes, stuffing, bread sauce and gravy down your throat til your stomach's in love with your mind and then anticipating the arrival of a satisfying snooze in the chair while your digestive equipment prepares for the traditional pud and custard. I love every second of it. By the time I'd got to about fifteen I'd mastered the art of impersonating a fois gras-ed duck at Christmas day lunchtime and had no desire to be cured.

However, add a turkey sandwich and trifle tea and a comforting fry-up next morning and you get a man who begins to feel you can stretch the holiday feasting a mite too far. In this situation, a claustrophobic too-much-central-heating feeling can steal upon one and on this fateful day, did. I just had to get out of the house and do something. Something useful even, perhaps get some sharp, cold winter air into my lungs. Then, out of the murky backwaters of a mind on holiday comes a sudden idea which surprisingly, looks full of promise. A look in the paper: hmm, 11.30 start, take about a quarter of an hour to get there, no need to worry about parking for a fourth division game. A case of 'how about one for old time's sake?'

'Um, do you fancy going to the match, dear?'

Whatever faults my wife Louise may have had when I managed to bribe and generally coerce her to shackle my rusty old wagon up to her pristine, freshly-painted royal coach, an aversion to football wasn't one of them. Not that this was an issue in 1982, the year of our sacred union when no-one I knew went to football matches, apart from my pal Frankie Glasser whose family had had a couple of season tickets in the West Stand at Spurs since the early Renaissance. She was up for it (an amazing woman, my wife) and so was Perce, her father and before anyone could come up with a sudden reason why not, - 'if any man knows why these three should not be joined in pursuit of enjoyment at a Boxing Day morning football match, speak now or forever hold his peace' - we were off to Saltergate!

Many or perhaps none of you will know this word as the name of the home of Chesterfield FC, of Football League Division 4, today hosting hated rivals Mansfield Town. I don't remember walking to the ground (one of the most delicious joys of football supporting) and I don't remember paying to get in or buying the tickets. But I remember what I looked out upon when I took my seat in the centre stand and what I stared at for the next two hours and above all, how I felt. Because you feel a football match, you don't just watch it. You absorb it all, not just with your six senses, but through your skin, and up through your body from your feet like capillary action.

I felt the chill that morning, it being cold enough for the frost still to be clinging to the touchlines. And the noise. There were nearly seven thousand in the ground (I just looked it up) which won't seem like much to you, but there was much raucous chanting, mostly where two opposing sets of keen lads shared a long terrace along one length of the pitch, separated only by a narrow empty pen and two metal fences - so they could work up a good honest modicum of hatred to spit and spew at each other. And it was then that it dawned on me that this was a real local derby. That stone me this was proper football.

Then again your eyes pull together your other senses. What quickly struck me was the smallness of all the stands but still how lovely they looked. I could see an attractive line of coloured advertising boards just below the roof that framed the crowd along the touchline opposite me. This was an area of terracing, only around twenty steps high called simply 'Compton Street.' To my left behind the goal was the most important area of any football ground at that time, the standing area which attracts the thickest concentration of fans, or at Chesterfield it is when the Blues are kicking towards that goal. It had a neat grey pitched roof and this being a good year for the team it looked solidly full. This space was known locally as the Kop.*

To my right was open terrace - the Cross Street end - populated by

---

* 'Kop' is an abbreviation of Spion Kop, a hill in what is now South Africa. On Spion Kop a well known battle of the Boer War took place, so it was a spot well known to the British public at the time - 1901 - via the newspapers. Soon afterwards, one set of fans nicknamed its high terrace behind one of the goals at their ground 'the Spion Kop' and the name not only stuck in one place, but was adopted by the rabid supporters at a number of clubs. Liverpool's became the most famous, though through the ignorance of commentators at both main TV stations through the 60s, 70s and 80s the mass of the football following public thought Anfield had ownership of a unique, special name for its main end. Chesterfield's is one of the smallest in the history of Kops, but certainly not the smallest and lowest: that ironic accolade belongs to Northampton Town's old County Ground. The other clubs to name an end 'Spion Kop' are as follows: Tranmere Rovers; Bradford City; Chester City (at their original Sealand Road ground); Blackpool (along with Sheffield Wednesday, one of the two highest); Barnsley; Notts County and Birmingham City. The Kop phenomenon is unknown in the north-east and south of the Trent apart from Northampton for reasons unknown to this author.

more Mansfield fans, and though atmosphere and intimacy is always lost when an end is open to the skies, at least it had an unusual back wall designed like a castle balcony, with evenly spaced cut out squares for look-out and firing arrows. The stand I was in, all seated, with a tiny enclosed terrace below us, was small and obviously showing its age. Neutrals would have called it shabby, grey and easily improvable by one or two cosmetic changes, such as outright demolition, but to me it was cosy and real. There was so obviously something different and special going on here, a different football world from any I'd previously inhabited. The whole place was a living slice of northern history and I both sensed it and fell totally in love with it the instant I sat down. It had a quality only the very best of places have: it was homely and it said 'come on in and I'll make you a nice cup of tea and get you some toast. How many sugars do you take?' It gives me an ache in a deep and tender spot inside me just to write about it now. I knew that whatever happened in front of me for the next two hours I wanted to know everything about this world and become a part of it. This was the world my father had been brought up in, the one I'd always felt empty about missing out on.

The teams soon came out, always a great moment at a football match, all men whose names I hardly knew, except for the few Town** players who scored regularly enough for me to notice their names in the paper. Then we kicked off. For virtually the whole hour and a half, the ball whizzed to and fro, thumped unmercifully from one end to the other by defenders who were told by managers not to do better. The players whizzed about too, chasing useful balls and lost causes both, in their frantically concerned attempts to score goals and win points. I knew that Chesterfield under their manager John Duncan were not big scorers of goals and it wasn't too hard to see why. They had a great defence, and a tough, battling midfield, but there was no-one really to attack down the wings and the two strikers weren't quick and weren't overly skilful, though one was amazingly good at shielding the ball from opponents with the biggest arse I'd ever seen on a football pitch.

** Chesterfield FC have been through a few different names in their time, such as Chesterfield Borough (though not a name to fire you with romantic enthusiasm: why not go the whole hog and call it 'Chesterfield Borough Council FC'). Around the turn of the century, the club called itself 'Chesterfield Town,' and though it was only officially thus for a short time, it stuck like industrial glue and is the local nickname among the faithful to this day. Locals don't ask their mates if they're going to watch the Spireites or the Blues, the two 'official' nicknames, they ask them if they're 'going to watch Town,' or 'Tarn' if pronounced in a Chesterfield stylee.

Strangely, it seemed to me, incredible even, he seemed also to possess what seemed to me to be a beer drinker's paunch*. I knew that in the lower leagues the players' fitness levels might not be as butcher's dog sharp, but a beer gut on a professional footballer? What the blazes was this all about? I have to say it added to the romance of the occasion but I was still scratching my head about this months later.

There was another reason too for the lack of pretty football on show. Anyone who has watched Match Of The Day and has heard pundits, players and managers regurgitating the same old cliches about derby games will know that we should have expected little to warm ourselves over that morning. The soothsayers were right about these games being all scratch, bollock and bite, though they wouldn't have known about the John Duncan method of trying to score goals by hoofing the ball long to the strikers and hoping Ernie Moss** would flick the ball on to his partner.

So there were no goals to jump out of your seat to or cause your day to be threatened with ruin. No penalties, no sendings off and no balls hitting woodwork. I don't recall a near miss or a single shot. I do remember a grey haired man in the vintage, the classic 1980s football manager's camel hair overcoat on the touchline down in front of us, because that was Ian Greaves, Mansfield's manager and managers are always important and anyway, he used to play for Manchester United.+

I remember a blonde, long-haired striker in a yellow shirt but that's because he was Dave Caldwell, an extravagantly fiery Scot who comes back into this story a little later on. I remember Sean O'Neill, his white socks and his patch of icy-white turf, probably because he took about twenty throw-ins in his forty five minutes in front of us in the main stand.

But most of all I remember sound and light and air. The sound of a crowd of football people on the pitch and off it: fans chanting obscenities in packs, the single raucous shouting of 'get rid on it!' from gruff, no-nonsense Derbyshire men who had no time for fancy farting-around-wit'-ball from fourth division defenders, and the grunting, moaning and calling of

---

* This was Bob Newton, good player and local hero. Think how good he'd have been without the gut.

** Ernie Moss is the Chesterfield legend of modern times. He played 535 games (in all comps) and scored 191 goals in three spells at the club and despite being unmercifully pilloried in his first season by the fans, ended his days loved totally and unconditionally. His name was later borrowed by Steve Coogan for one of his comedy programmes, though as 'Ernest' not Ernie.

+Though his real claim to fame has to be his gift to us of the magnificent phrase 'fagging it like a maniac', referring to his preferred method of stress reduction in the managerial dugout during a game.

footballers just toiling away in the unglamourous process of simply trying to earn a living. The clean light of a late December Boxing Day morning where all outside is quiet and seemingly contented. The winter air which had that crisp, winter tang which makes you feel connected to the rest of the human race. You were out there. You were doing something. You were participating in something.

On the way home I was already thinking like a fan, disappointed that the team hadn't won. As yet this was only a slight thing. For the moment I was just in a pleasant dreamworld having found a new lover. Ever the obsessive about the irrelevant, I was about to grab hold of supporting Chesterfield like a man going under for the third time suddenly spotting Kate Winslet bobbing up and down in the water. I climbed into Percy's car watching the crowd go home to their lunch, central heating and telly and everything in my winter garden was rosy.

Occasionally, well, if I'm brutally honest, just now, I wondered whether my life would have been different if Chesterfield had not been at the top of the league that Christmas. Had they been sixth bottom, would there not have been a greater chance of me going off to applaud the local hunt than me making my home debut at the residence of Derbyshire's footballing finest (and I would no more go off to applaud a hunt than I would pour warm gravy over my own gonads and go among a pack of baying hounds naked)? It shows you, I think, that even when you have the toxic seed, it takes a bit of success to get the blood up. (The Spireites, to be precise, were second behind Darlington at the giddy peak of Her Majesty's fourth division).

In truth, it had nothing to do with this. Fact is, with my hankering for the past my father knew somewhere deep in me - why else had I wanted to go north to university after leaving school? - I knew Saltergate was lying there in wait for me.

However the cause of my return to football, likely as not, was simply that the great God of Football Himself just twitched the thread to which I was connected to him for the sheer pleasure of exercising His power: said, 'you have the affliction, I control the afflicted, it is time for you to serve me once again.'

Daft as it sounds, that may be it. Who in the end knows? Who in the end really knows anything?

5

You Can Call Me Al

'But the father answered never a word, a frozen corpse was he.'
H. W. Longfellow

Alzheimer's Disease is anything but funny. The victim - and yes, like an innocent child tortured and strangled by a psychopath sent straight from the underworld, an Alzheimer's sufferer is a victim alright - begins their lonely journey to the grave by feeling an inexplicable confusion and seemingly trivial slip of the memory. Where did I put down that important document? Have you seen my car keys? This stuff can happen to anyone. But when this starts to happen every day, three times, six times, ten times, twenty times a day, even the victim begins to appreciate that there's something wrong.

Perhaps it's not serious, think members of the surrounding family. Dad's been working too hard, he's been stressed for years and at last the chickens have come home to roost (o you bet they have): it's some sort of breakdown. Or maybe it's a tumour (if only). Perhaps Dad just needs to see a therapist because it's all got too much for him. I'm not surprised, he's always been a worrier.

It starts out like that but two years down the line you've sat in a consultant's office in a large, intimidating London hospital hearing about a disease you've never heard of before. He's a lovely man, the consultant. Yes, it's true, he really does care. 'It's as if his brain has just worn out,' he says to the other victims, the immediate family. And he shakes his head in genuine disgust, firstly because he finds it hard to work out how a world with or without God can be so cruel. And secondly because despite his brilliance and his international renown, he can do nothing to stop this disease from killing the sufferer, and, if that isn't bad enough, slowly. He can do nothing either to stop this thing destroying the spouse who carries a perpetual look of love and soul-darkening horror she finds herself wearing on each of the four occasions he will see her. She will die broken completely by the effort of carrying ten years of grief and heartbreak five years after the original victim.

My Dad.

I am part of the immediate family. But me, with my heart of granite, or rather, with a single-minded selfishness that would do justice to someone in a long leather coat and a couple of swastika armbands, gets away with it. Or at the least I get off lightly. There is an older son, and when you are the oldest son you are a front line paratrooper. When the whistle blows, it's you who's going over the top into the machine guns, brother, not me. Brother lives near victim, so he gets to visit and witness his father's incredible, miserable decline, disappearing from the world inch by terrifying inch. Me, I'm insulated by 40 miles of M25 and a couple of dull suburban A roads and a job. I also have a wife to consider. Me, I only cop it at the odd weekend and in the school holidays. I walk through the door hoping I can cheer my mum up by being supportive and just being there (heaven only knows what I can do for my Dad now he can't speak and spends most of his waking hours sitting on the downstairs toilet switching the light on and off - at least he hasn't got to the stage where he shits his trousers: no, that happy day was still to come).

She's in the kitchen looking not so much depressed as terminally bleak, as if she had two days to live. Hello, how long are you staying. I am with Louise. 'Two days. We have to get back to....' But her face has dropped like the bombs she had to dodge in Tottenham during the war, dragging the flesh on an ageing face down towards the floor. She looks at me as if I have knifed her.

How do I cope? By pretending it isn't really happening and by continuing to absorb myself in the rich textures of my personal life, my leisure time. Despite this evil wind howling at my door, while over the way it's fully destroying the people who sacrificed themselves by bringing me into the world, I continue to satisfy my lust for pleasure: nothing interesting, you understand, just films, books, music, TV, talking to my friends who happen to make me laugh for hours at a time or who enable me to indulge my cravings for passively, self-indulgently wasting some of the best years of my life.

Yet I now find that when I go stay with the victims, I have excruciating pain in my nob when I need to urinate and I have to spend up to half an hour waiting to pass urine and for the agony to subside. I assume that there's something in the water over at my Mum's house that doesn't agree with my urinary tract. That's 'my Mum's house', you'll notice, not 'my parents' house' seeing as my father, who was once Wilf Thomas, has ceased in any meaningful way to be a parent.

6

'My name is Craig Thomas and I am a Manchester United supporter...'

'Real rings revealed, the heartspoken khatru.'

Jon Anderson.

So I had to go away again. My father went into hospital with suspected pneumonia in November 1985, a Saturday. I remember that because at about half past four that afternoon that day I was looking up at a TV screen on the ward watching Grandstand. I was somewhat concerned at the time as a progress report from Filbert Street gave out news that Manchester United's magnificent start to the season was beginning to falter: they were on the way to losing 2-0. That league championship title, not won for eighteen long, desperate years, had seemed at last to be sailing like a long lost boat, up the Manchester Ship Canal to Stretford. They'd won their first ten games of the season and were miles ahead at the top. But now, a dip in form. Only a lock gate? Or the Government officially declaring that all eighteenth century forms of water transport were now banned? Whatever it represented, this was depressing news.

Yes, it's time for me to fess up: loath as I am to admit it to you, for twenty years I was a Manchester United fan, and I suppose it would be better for both of us if I explained how it happened.

Covering emotional allegiances and aversions to football teams must run in the family. My brother kept his antipathy to a football club a dark, dark secret from his girlfriend (later second wife). Like you do, or at least, as Thomas's do, he was ingratiating himself with her something stinky because he was so enamoured of her abilities as a cook, or whatever it was among the many attributes she possessed. It so transpired that not one of these was her strong feeling for the Arsenal.

Nonetheless, too much of a good thing not nearly being enough, Keith was quick to point out to Tracie that one of his good points was a strong feeling for the Arsenal; which is about as true as the works of Matisse having been painted by Bob Monkhouse. Come the morning after the night before their, that's the Arsenal's, not Keith and Tracie's, big night at Anfield' in May 1989, they're in bed thinking about getting up, or whatever, and over the bedroom radio comes the earth-cracking news for all those steeped in the bouillon of the game, that the said Arsenal, have against more odds than you could shake a large stick at, beaten the Mighty Reds of Liverpool 2-0 to take the title.

'Shit, no!,' ejaculates Keith, deeply in tune with 98% of football supporters in southern England (and outlying districts).

'Keith? What do you mean? It's fantastic news! I thought you said you were an Arsenal fan like....'

'Yeah, well,' says Keith, 'I told you that, but..........'

It took him two weeks of serious thinking and many consultations with friends and acquaintances before he dug himself fully out of the landfill he'd dug for himself for not being honest about his relationship with football.

His relationship with Tracie, I might add, must have been some love affair in its early stages here: if she was fond of the Arsenal, and I can testify to this fact myself, why hadn't they been watching the game live on ITV the night before like everyone else with a red interest and millions of others besides?

Exactly.

I am relieved to be able to tell you that my falling for Manchester United had nothing to do with such adult tomfoolery and was only marginally connected with my being a glory hunter and at six I hope you'll forgive me. My good ol' Dad is mostly responsible, so I plead that in my defence too. It was the week before the 1963 Cup Final when one night he said to me,

'Son, you wait til you see this player called Denis Law.'

The rest of his sales pitch I forget exactly, but the gist was, this feller is a genius so if you know what's good for you, sit up and take notice when the game's on.

Yes, Dad, said my dutiful, loving eyes.

Again, what would have happened to me if Leicester had won and Law'd had a total mare of a game I dread to think. Fact is, he gave a bravura performance, scored the opening goal in his own inimitably electric lightning style. United won 3-1 and that was me, a Law and United fan from then on. And why not? they'd just won a trophy and I was only little*. Dad had said Denis was a character and he wasn't wrong. When the

---

*For those of you snorting with derision at my claim to not being a mini-glory hunter, I should tell you that they finished fourth bottom of the first division that year and were still, until the cup win, in a deep post-Munich cycle of failure which at this point had lasted five years.

third went in, not scored by Denis but by David Herd, he grabbed the available limelight by trotting into the net to pick up the ball. Now picked up by a TV camera, he walked towards the penalty spot for a few yards holding the ball in the air as waiters used to carry a plate, and slapped it back into the net, wearing the grin of an imp with a degree in audaciousness. I was immediately entranced.

'And the best thing of all, son,' and I'm paraphrasing, but again the gist is there, 'is that he's a Scot.'

Well that would have cemented it: I was my father's son alright and already I was a little Scot manque. Did I not tell you my Dad was born in Glasgow and his mother a Stranraer girl? You know now. When England were playing anybody, I always wanted them to lose: still did, in fact until Sven Goran Erickson took over. An even then because this and his subsequent success is a slap in the gob with a large halibut for anyone calling themselves a true Englishman.

Though the tendency was fading somewhat by 1985, I measured out the next fifteen years of my life in Manchester United trophy chases. It was love: I was besotted. Undoubtedly, my childhood was a largely very happy one as the so-called Red Devils - a proper nickname that long since seems to have fallen out of favour with the media - won the league in 1965 and again two years later. What I loved about supporting them was not that they won an awful lot of games in the mid-sixties, though they did, but that they were considered to be the great team of the sixties and an aesthetically superb. The magic words 'Best, Law and Charlton' meant a team that entertained the people royally. Huge crowds turned out all over the country to see not only stars, but men you gladly paid to watch because they did things that made Arsenal fans, Spurs fans, Liverpool fans even in those days turn to their neighbour in the crowd, a stranger maybe, and say, in wonder, or respect,

'Did you see that? Best - what a player!'

Law was fantastic at whipping the ball into the net if a chance fell to him in the box before you could blink. He could also leap like a ballet dancer to score with headers, outjumping massive centre halves in the process. He has no modern equivalent and in 1964 or 5 he would have been transferred for a fee of at least 25 million pounds, possibly more. Of that there is no doubt.

Which would make George Best at the same time practically beyond price. 40, 50 million, let's say. He was a Mozart, a Shakespeare: a person so stellar, so colossally possessed of talent in his own field that he was unable to cope with life as the rest of us, we mere mortals, know it. Ryan Giggs is a similar player and a vastly talented one, but here's the difference: that wonderful goal he scored in the cup semi-final against Arsenal at Villa Park in 1999: if George Best had scored that goal, he wouldn't have run halfway up the pitch on a sonic, adrenalin-charged rush of hysteria at having done something brilliant - and what he did was brilliant. Best would have grinned and run away in triumph somewhat, because he would have put United 2-1 up in extra time in a hugely important game. But it wouldn't have stayed in our mind because this sort of fabulousness was his stock in trade. And I know what you're thinking: nostalgia. No. I absolutely promise you, even as you see the George Best now, a physically damaged man, old before his time, this man really was mesmerically brilliant.*

Furthermore, there was the residual sentiment left over from the Munich air disaster of February 6th 1958 which in historical terms in the mid-sixties had only just happened. Terrible as it was, it helped create, or allowed the media to create an aura of legend around the club and their manager Matt Busby, who for a week after the crash had one baggy-shorted leg practically past St Peter before being flung back to his oxygen tent on earth. So to support Manchester United back then was to make a rather grand, not to say somewhat monarchical gesture, and you walked around with your head in the clouds or with an imaginary crown on your bonce and you felt rather wonderful all the time. Which made their decline in the early seventies so unbearable for all their fans.

The high water mark of my Manchester United years was that pseudo-emotional Wembley European Cup Final triumph in May 1968. Dad had somehow got tickets to The Big Game, but on that historic day I was on a school holiday in Swanage. My brother - who supported nobody - went with what was so obviously 'my' ticket instead. I was met off the coach at the end of the trip by my Dad, he clutching the programme from

---

*Bobby Charlton was the lesser of the three United greats of the 60s, which only tells you how great were the other two. Not that this matters much as he was still as close to great as makes little difference. His shooting was better than anyone in the game before or since with the possible exception of Peter Lorimer: as accurate as a computer most of the time and at its best, totally devastating and match winning. I saw two live. The first was at Old Trafford in a 3-2 win against Southampton where being fed a pass thirty-ish yards out he unleashed this shot: the ball became a shell which angrily screamed into the net in a vicious curving arc while the goalie made a token gesture of a dive to try to save face. The second was at Tottenham in 1965 in the famous 1-5 game when J. Greaves scored that goal of the mesmeric dribble. Later, the score 0-5, Charlton crashed one past Pat Jennings from far out, a thing of beauty though never shown on TV. He did this with such ease and so often at that time that the crowd merely cheered ironically, when it would have drawn considerable applause in those days from any other player.

the game in his left hand, no doubt hoping this would prevent me from throwing the mother of all tantrums when I found out what I could have had instead of trips to Lulworth Cove, Tilly Whim Caves and seeing Ruth Gardiner accidentally expose her pudendum on the beach. Fortunately for all concerned, I was so deliriously happy my team were champions of Europe, I wouldn't have cared less had my brother been allowed the privilege of doing the lap of honor round Wembley with the team.

I had also just had the ghastly experience of the traditional last night Fancy Dress Competition back in Swanage where I not only came last, but completely humiliated myself by being the worst Arab in fancy dress history. The actual competitive denouement required us all to stand up one at a time in front of a tight circle of our teachers and peers and declare who or what we were. I knew before hand that I was going to be as inept as it was possible to be at this but to my abject horror, some of the contestants, before the grisly ritual saw my turn to get to my feet, were doing little speeches and even, in the case of Stephanie Heath and one or two others, were actually doing an act!

Without a shadow of a doubt, mothers had been preparing their children for this for weeks. Even friends seemingly preparing at the last minute were producing Charlie Chaplin bowler hats and clown red noses from suitcases. They'd all been told about this event a long time back: why not me? Unfortunately back then I didn't have the presence of mind to blame this imminent disaster on my mother, as I clearly should have done, but just sat there shitting my pants in dread. Sure enough, when my turn came, I duly stood there pathetically, mumbled something almost inaudible about what I was and was laughed at - not with - and sat down feeling relieved, overwhelmingly inadequate and bitter. If I hadn't had my team's shortly expected Wembley win to think about - there was no possible way we could lose - I think I'd have thrown myself from a second floor hotel window and put myself out of my misery that way. How could I go on after managing to be, as well as look, a total fool, prat and idiot in front of all the people I'd ever gone to school with, a group that represented around ninety five per cent of all the people I'd ever known? (This also would have been useful as I would have ruined the trip for the insensitive berk of a teacher who thought up the stupid idea of a fancy dress competition in the first place.)

Three hours later Manchester United gave me back a healthy slice of my self-respect: all the boys in the fourth year watched the game and I was the only one wearing a long red and white scarf. I even managed to smile a big smile at my teacher, the wonderful Mr. Joy, who took the school team and knew all about football before I went to bed now a supporter of the

European Champions. We were the only fans in England then that could say that.

As I sat on top of the world at 11, I wasn't to know that football superiority does not go on for ever. In the case of United it was over in a short space of time. Two years later they were in serious decline because ageing players weren't replaced and as George said, because, fatally, the players felt that winning the European Cup had been an ending, not a beginning.

This devotion to my first love receded gradually like an ice age, though the change was so imperceptibly slow I was hardly aware of it. How I coped with their relegation in 1974 when only seventeen mind, I have allowed myself to forget. Perhaps like my father's illness, I denied it was happening or fell more deeply into another pathetically juvenile infatuation with a schoolgirls or bought more albums.

The emotional attachments you form at the age when you're learning to ride a bike don't enable you to just get up from the table and politely excuse yourself. It isn't that easy. I used to naively theorize that with a serious girlfriend, it took as long to get over her as the time you spent going out together. I realised later on that this didn't work at all. It took me half a lifetime for my emotional wounds to heal over from my relationship with Frances, and it took about the same for me to come to my senses about Manchester United.

It was a long, long haul. In the end, though, you can only read the women's page in The Guardian for so long before you are brought to the conclusion that becoming an adult, something I definitely had begun to aspire to by the age of twenty-five, is a state of grace you can only reach by leaving behind football as one of the childish things St Paul talked about (and I don't mean McCartney). So to a large extent I did. Eventually a home defeat would no longer cause an inexpressibly painful throb of electrical pulses in the central cortical area of the brain, throwing me into witless depression.

My enthusiasm for the game went the same way. After 1979, the year I had to go out into the world to earn a crust of bread, I saw, aw, five matches? Four at Spurs and one at Old Trafford. Friends dragged me to the games and I must have gone for the novelty or the nostalgia. I remember registering shock and dismay when in 1983, my first game at the Lane for over ten years, I recognized faces and voices still selling roasted peanuts along Tottenham High Road. It was terribly depressing. Is this what some people still had to do to eke out a meagre existence? And in what dank, dingy places in this grotty inner suburb did they live? I was also somewhat taken aback, though immensely cheered up by a fight that broke out behind my friends and me up the Paxton that day. The mid-first half air was pretty subdued with Tottenham one-down to lowly Everton when it was rent by a raucous, working class voice intoning, amid much commotion, 'You cunt! You striped me up for a fuckin' beer..........' (striped? this was refreshingly colourful departure from the word's normal meaning!)

I'd been very uneasy about coming back to football then, what with hooliganism being in the news all the time, but I'd expected teenage hard nuts in designer labels to be making up the danger element, not over-grown short-trousered playground scrappers. The law had to come in to mediate this grave dispute, one which was so fraught with serious reper-cussions for the future that late in the second half another round of 'you striped me up for a fuckin' beer' chimed behind us as the tenacious man-child, having once been thrown out, snuck back in to restart the post-event analysis.

There was another game against Leicester at the same time which had me going back to work warning everyone I could about a startling unknown scorer Leicester had called Lineker, and one later when Wimbledon handed out a three-nil thrashing to the old Lilywhites with their muscular brand of football, to my absolute delight. And it was great to go back to Old Trafford with some bored weekend workmates who wanted a road trip. The Reds won 2-0 and I was well pleased, but it was nothing remotely like going there in the old days when just to be near the ground was to be like floating on a magic carpet, and to sit among over sixty thousand people and actually see men who even now are icons, play-ing on what to me was the equivalent of Mount Olympus was like reach-ing nirvana. It was pleasure beyond any words I can use to try to describe it: a state of rapture greater than anything I have experienced since (though one or two things I could mention run it fairly close). Being back was just nice, very pleasant. I was a child back then when every day is like Never Never Land. Now I'd grown up. I taught the nation's youth, for goodness sake. Football now was just, well, football.

Or even less. The game was about to go into the pit of its long dark night of the soul: we were then a year away from the Bradford Fire, two from the Heisel Disaster. Serious pundits wondered seriously whether football was worth carrying on with, remarkable when you consider the fact that football was the national sport with a recognizably organised his-tory going back a hundred and twenty years. It was like Italian journalists suggesting pasta wasn't worth eating anymore. Even in 1984, in the pop-ular mind football meant fights and fences: mechanical, cheerless football played mostly by journeymen in crumbling stadiums which had become slums. And all this played out in front of a backdrop of the nation's economic misery. Fans were steadily becoming stay-at-homes and Saturday shoppers. This made the withering of my new found enthusiasm of the previous winter all the more likely to be a permanent thing. No-one I knew went to football any more. None of my friends talked about it. We all had more fruitful and positive things to dwell on. Everything was more interesting and more fashionable than football.

However.

If you'd asked me that Saturday afternoon in the hospital visiting my Dad what was hurting me more, United losing at Leicester or my father contracting a possible fatal infection, I would have been hard put to answer you if I were being totally honest, although of course I knew what the answer was supposed to be. My Dad was about to expire and I was getting annoyed about losing at Filbert Street? Football should have been nowhere in my mind. If I'd have mentioned my concern about the back four being too brittle to sustain a true title challenge to my mother she would have written me off as a human being completely and scratched me as a fixture in the family inheritance. And rightly so.

Naturally a psychologist would rubbish these musings and tell you I was submerging my grief below a cushion of harmless escapism. Clearly, though, the said shrink wasn't taken to their first game of league football at the age of 5. Once you have been nurtured in an environment where football, axiomatically, is considered to be important, the affliction is still there nestling deep inside you rather cozily, like the propensity to contract cancer, waiting to be triggered by a chance event or shifting pattern in your life. And who was it gave birth to and then suckled my obsession with the game? My Dad. Lying there a hollowed out shell of the man he once was, was still the one who'd got one of his friends to make a neat wooden box for me to stand on at the very front of the Park Lane terrace in 1963; the one who had queued up from a quarter past twelve outside the ground so that I could go to my first matches. Knowing he did that, and for love, both for me and for football, makes me forgive the man I was in Chase Farm Hospital that day. And when I'm on my back in a similar place one day, and it's a Saturday, and Spurs are losing at home to Chelsea with fifteen minutes to go, I'd rather they fretted about that than worried about me. Because I'll be okay.

As my bewildered looking father was undressed and manoeuvred helplessly into a bed, perhaps for the last time, it turned out that at that very moment when I look back, even as the whole game itself was about to enter a period of near freefall disintegration, I was nursing a trigger that would cause the affliction to explode. But because of what was happening to this family of Alzheimer's victims, not yet.

7

As Good As An Anorak

'When I eat a biscuit, it stays eaten.'

Arthur Dent

United did indeed fail to win the league in the spring of 1986. We buried my father in the spring of 1986. I coped with that, too. In fact, I have often boasted about how at his funeral, I almost wet myself trying to stop myself exploding in raucous laughter in the middle of The Lord's My Shepherd.

One of my old school friends, Steve Perren was the one who caused me to break the world record for the most laughs laughed in a calendar year, though you won't find it in the Guinness Book of Records. And he had always found my Uncle Len the funniest bloke on the planet. If you can imagine the face of Ray Davies merged into Terry Venables you have Len's looks exactly. He wasn't tall, but was well built, with the classical swept back Brylcreemed hair of the fortyish early-sixties slightly modish middle aged male. Len, aspirant upwardly-mobile working class boy made good-time Charlie if remotely possible, tried constantly to be funny, and he was almost always successful, though the loudness of his generous bonhomie was a bit much if you weren't quite in the mood.

To Steve and I he was nothing less than a legend. He was more than just larger than life: a cloud of charisma always entered the room before his body. His crowning moment, in my life anyway, probably came at the party we had at our house the night my brother set off on Day One of his doomed first marriage. He'd have been better off at our party, as he now knows. Len, at about one in the morning when the gathering still had plenty of legs decided he'd had enough drink, and enough fun. So he got his camp bed out and placed it emphatically on the floor in the middle of the living room and began getting undressed. To the complete astonishment of many of the assembled multitude who were having a gay old time in the immediate vicinity. The last guest was cheerfully waved off into the night about twenty minutes later.

The first time I ever told Steve this, the physical manifestation of his mirth made such a commotion that a neighbour anxiously knocked on the front door a few minutes later wondering who needed fetching off to hospital.

It also delighted Steve hugely that one of the loves of Len's life was crooning. The memory of a very tired and emotional uncle belting out Blueberry Hill at my cousin Ian's wedding, shirt unbuttoned, jacket and tie long since discarded, eyes closed in a paroxysm of ecstatic concentration, is one which etched itself on a eight year old boy indelibly. Twenty-one years later Len seemed to think he was a sensitive amalgam of Frank Sinatra and Tony Bennett, with just the merest touch of Perry Como on the side at Northaw Parish Church as he leaned into that most famous of hymns with great care and respect - the register was a little low for his mellow baritone. He was immediately behind me, and the moment I picked up on it I began shaking at the shoulders. I had never heard a hymn being crooned like this before and the whole notion of it tipped over the part of the brain where the proclivity to helpless laughter resides and I was a goner. I have never felt bad about this either: if my Dad could have been there in my head, he'd have been laughing fit to bust too. My mother, beside me in a state of terrible grief and other dark emotions, thought I was crying and squeezed my hand with only the tiny shred of supportive energy she had available to her.

You might well ask at this point what Uncle Len's vocal performance at my father's funeral has to do with football or indeed why I have just explained how my father died when I was 29. Good point, but I can explain the latter at least: after discovering at Christmas 1984 that, to my surprise that trips to football matches at Saltergate at some point in the future offered the promise of a considerable amount of pleasure, my father's slow, but inexorable decline kept me away. I'd worked out an accommodation between my waning ardour for those Red Devils and the green shoots of a new infatuation for the Spireites in my mind without any real difficulty and basically, I was ready to get going. But it was not to be. Holiday times, if you could call them that, meant trying to prop up my Mum. I got to Tupton, the ex-mining village four miles out of town where the outlaws lived quite seldom. Often Louise would drive up to see her parents alone while I grimly faced the Cuffley music by myself.

As for Len, suffice it to say, the world is a much cheerier place for having such people in it and they're sayings and doings deserve preserving for all times, such as his passing of sagacious judgement, sat in an 11 Bacons Drive lounge armchair one night, in pink cashmere sweater, chunky Rolex - this was Len in his successful businessman days as a furniture maker - nursing a brandy, upon the career plans of one S.J. Perren:

Len Parrish: what you goin' in for then at university, Steve?

Sheepish S.J. Perren: um, history.

Len: History? Magic.

Expansive, especially when compared to the reaction of a celebrated local milkman.

'Wot you layabouts doing at university, then.'

'History, Bill'

'Just what the country needs, another couple of fuckin' 'istory teachers.'

I did in fact get to one more game that 1984-85 season, after Easter when the Champions soon-to-be scraped a 1-0 against a far superior Swindon Town under Lou Macari. They were to go up the following year, to no-one's surprise. I was somewhat mystified as to why it was that my newly adopted team were being outclassed and passed-to-death by a team only half way up the table. There was a blank in my Explanations Inbox when I switched my brain on, so I just shrugged and watched the match. It niggled me though. We sat in the main stand this time, Perce and me and although we'd lucked it, I left satisfied by the knowledge that I had seen my first home win. But that, for the time being, was that. Thanks to circumstances beyond my control the embryonic new Chesterfield fan in me was put back in its pen and covered with tarpaulin.

Boxing day 1984 might easily have just been a dry run for the same feast day of 1986, because two years later I was back at Saltergate for the same reasons with brother in tow between marriages and with nothing more exciting to do this Christmas than spend it with Louise's parents and the reduced forces of the Thomas nuclear family. Only this time it was different and the damage or should I say, alteration to my system was to be more or less permanent. This may have been something to do with the fact that this time there were goals, five and four of them to the Spireites*. This time we weren't in the main stand, where the inhabitants tended mostly to behave in a manner that would have been well received at a gentleman's club, but on the terraces, which at Chesterfield was the equivalent of the docks area of a seaport. It was rough, in terms of language at least, it was exciting, it was noisy, it was throbbingly alive. Like the docks, if you knew what you were doing, it was safe, very safe, in fact. If you wanted to get a slap, it could be arranged easily enough for you: all you had to do was to turn round and tell the big feller stood behind you who looked like he

*Chesterfield's 'official' historical nickname is 'the Spireites' because of the peculiar spire of the parish church which rises above the centre of the town: it is twisted into a curve, bent as if permanently on the receiving end of a gale. This was caused way back when by its being built from immature wood and is a feature that is unique in the United Kingdom and quite possibly the world.

hacked coal out of the ground for a living with his teeth that he was talking rubbish.

It might well have been a hairy-arsed collier - oh yes, there were pits still open in the area then - who was giving on loan striker Carl Airey a right load of stick that day. And his mates. Moaners come in all shapes and sizes though and it was more likely a boring looking bloke in a flat cap and a fawn British Home Stores rain jacket, out on leave from being henpecked half to death by his wife, who was telling Carl he was 'bll-oody yoooselless, Airey' for the twentieth time that half. It may well have been what happened next that shaped the next ten years of my life. Big, his hair featuring blonde highlights, slightly overweight and waiting to receive a throw in five yards in from the touchline and ten from his critic, made a deft and mobile wankers' sign in the direction of the voice. This is a move which can and doubtless has prematurely ended many a career at lower division clubs down the years, and may indeed have ended Carl's league career a few years later. But as he made his views felt he laughed and grinned a big grin and all those around me and the critic laughed too. It was a moment of pleasure shared by a group of people with a shared sense of belonging and of common identity. Suddenly, I'd found something I'd been denied all my life: I was part of a genuine family who all shared a common bond, if only for ninety minutes at a time. Not watching it: a part of it. It was a very nice feeling.

Airey was laughing even more minutes later after he tidied up a spot of inept defending in the visitors' defence by slapping the ball under their keeper to make it four-one. What the critic said on the way home to his companions (if he had any) isn't recorded, but knowing football fans it may well have been, 'I always said 'e were a good 'un, that Airee.'*

Goals and points and laughs, a feeling of being a part of something greater than oneself, this time I was, as the poet put it, real, real gone this time. Back home I was nose deep in my souvenir programme (Christmas double issue, one pound and a picture of Santa on the front just in case any of the fans needed reminding what time of year it was) trying to work out how many other games I could get to in what remained of the season. By the time winter turned to spring, I'd only got myself to one home game, a stupendously uneventful goalless draw against Bolton Wanderers. Still, disappointing as this was, I knew that if I was to become a real fan of the

* It was this sort of supporter, the stereotypical cloth cap northerner, who, when there was a Chesterfield booking in the offing right in front of us on the Compton, added to the pile of abuse the ref was getting by shouting, when he'd waited for a momentary lull in the air and got it, 'Roob 'im all over wi' a wire brush.' I've never quite got over hearing that one.

club I would have to suffer not only the gifts of pleasure and pain that victory and defeat bring, but games where all you feel is a small and insignificant disappointment because nothing happened and there was nothing at stake. I knew this was a necessary part of the initiation process.

However, before the 1986-87 season was done, the onset of reviving, resplendent nature and balmier air also saw one of my most important rites of passage: my first away game. Living in Orpington, on the southeast edge of Greater London it would have to be a game in the capital, what with the Gillingham and Brentford matches having come and gone by early January. And though the latter had been a possibility, I wasn't sufficiently adventurous yet to explore the uncharted waters of south-west London; I was from north of the river: you Londoners out there will understand this, if you come from the Enfield district: Brentford might as well have been Exeter or Arbroath - people from my part of the Metrop's outer reaches just never went there.

So it was then that on a bright April late morning I set off, feeling much as Scott must have done on his first trip to the far north, only he probably knew it wouldn't involve a ride on the tube. It felt great but I was a little nervous. All the newspaper horror stories of thuggery at 'soccer matches' over the previous ten or fifteen years had left me feeling as though a bunch of ruffians might still be keen to mug an unsuspecting lone adult in the park my A-Z told me I'd have to negotiate between the tube station and the away turnstile.

This is an entirely natural and, I hope, forgivable fear given my feats of cowardice in my past, though it's possible that the thought of this solitary walk to the ground was automatically causing my memory to throw up another of those painful memories. Back in 1970 my friend Martin and I went to see Spurs play Coventry. Foolishly departing from the main road outside White Hart Lane station to take a short cut we'd been set upon by what seemed like a small army of cropped-haired kids our age. They started by innocently asking to borrow 15p to get in the ground, which I thought was a little unusual though not totally unreasonable and ended by my getting thumped in the ear and losing my programme.

Martin, I thought after having known him for a couple of years, was a lot more streetwise than me and I admired him for it. But the clout he got from the splinter group of this little firm of monkeys somewhere in the region of the breadbasket had punctured whatever joie de vivre he'd set from home with that day. Noticing that he'd copped it in a similar way to me was about the only thing that gave me the will to live at that moment in time. Naturally the afternoon was ruined. The allure of watching Martin Chivers toying with the Coventry defence like a street urchin torturing a cat had totally evaporated for Martin, and my appetite for a shock Sky Blue victory had taken a fatal knock.

Of course, I was also totally appalled that such a thing could possibly happen to me. Where I lived, in the tranquil suburbs of Hertfordshire, you only got punched if you were totally stupid and went up to one of the three tough kids in the village - and that's tough for Hertfordshire country, mind you - and told them they had rancid breath or couldn't get girlfriends because they wanked too much, or something. Of course, I had tried this once after I'd read somewhere that if you were a teenager you had to face up to the fact that sooner or later you'd end up having a fight with someone so you might as well get one sorted out quick so you could start toughening up. And if you didn't fancy it: bloody get used to the idea anyway. So being a complete idiot I was listening to a lad a year above me at school saying that this local hard nut, known to the cognoscenti by the soubriquet of 'Dimble,' wasn't so hard really and that anyone with a reasonable amount of spunk and get up and go could take care of him. Well, to young four-eyes here, this was music to the ears and I became convinced that as soon as the opportunity arose, I would do the manly thing.

The coach we all shared to and from our schools, both the grammar and the secondary modern (which the supposedly slow, the socially disadvantaged and the left-handed who'd been forced to write right-handed at the age of four and a half by the visionaries who ran the British educational system during that golden age in our history, went to) kids, pulled up in its usual stop the next afternoon back home in Cuffley High Street. As he went past me, Dimble lovingly rubbed his favourite metal comb against the top of my head, causing me predictable discomfort. Here was my chance.

'Pack it in, Dimble.' (a useful opening gambit, I'm sure you'll agree)

'What are you going to do about it?' (a decent, if predictable reply, I think)

'Hit you, that's what.' (looks promising on paper, but the only boy I'd ever hit was the local creative genius in the year below me at primary school who wore girls knickers, played the recorder and wanted to be a ballet dancer: everyone hit him.

Looks like it's shortly to kick off between Dimble and Dimbo.)

The next event was the sound of Dimble's raucous laughter.

'Hah, hah, Thomas wants a fight!' he told the small crowd of admirers who were beginning to cluster round, interestedly. There is nothing that beats a fight for entertainment value when you're young.

Of course, I realised I'd dropped the most enormous bollock straightaway. Dimble's implacable certainty that he was about to hand out the easiest duffing over of his career as a prospective hooligan reacted on my thought processes with total immediacy: my stomach hit my shoes in less time than you can blink, and I considered my options: Dimble might leave a respectable amount of blood on the high street pavement, but I was confident I could outrun him. For a change I was right: I ran home. Crying.

The final installment did not produce a happy outcome for those in school uniforms who enjoy the sound of crunching bone first thing in the morning. At the coach stop next day I was predictably jumped by a gleeful Dimble, who'd no doubt awoken with a song on his lips and joy in his heart at the prospect of catching up with me at last, but was saved by an amazingly generous acquaintance of the both of us, one Andrew Barnes who, being both bigger and mentally tougher than Dimble, put a stop to the slaughter before it really got started. Either the sight of blood didn't do much for his digestion at such an early hour or he couldn't bear a totally one-sided contest. Whatever, I could have kissed him then and I could kiss him now for saving me. Humiliation was something I could deal with. I'd only confirmed what everyone already knew: that I had a yellow streak down my back wider than Bessie Bunter's underclothing. The awful, chronic reality of a fist crushing into my face causing me immense pain, bloody clothing and a feeling of total confusion was something, I now realised, I would do anything to avoid. Lucky for me Dimble wasn't the type to bear a grudge and it all blew over. Perhaps he was smarter than I thought and realised that there's no sense of challenge in beating up someone who was as soft as a girl.

So that's why I had violence at the back of my mind that day on the way to Craven Cottage. I needn't have worried. There was nothing in the park but newly sprouting trees and bushes, the sound of contented birdsong and a few blokes like me, thirtyish or older and totally harmless looking and looking forward, for whatever reason, to an afternoon at the football.

The away supporters entrance, conspicuous by the absence of football supporters in its immediate vicinity, I found shortly afterwards. If 4500 fans constitutes a crowd at a professional football match, then that was the size of it that day. In retrospect things were quite busy along Stevenage Road, Fulham FC's main drag at about twenty to three. This was the first game of Jimmy Hill's coming to rescue this ailing mini-dinosaur of the Football League and an extra thousand or so had turned up hoping to spot the man himself to see if the man's chin really did resemble a hairy Olympic downhill ski-run.

I have at this point to make this confession: I felt hugely pleased with myself for making this trip. I actually thought I was rather clever. Across the country right now men my age were queuing up in Sainsbury's or they were hanging about with lost, hangdog expressions outside women's changing rooms in Marks and Spencer's. They'd be dutifully washing the car or they'd be up some ladder painting, because their wife (or partner, to be fair) had been wanting the hallway doing for a couple of years and they'd finally admitted defeat and resignedly rescued some turps and an old brush from a back cupboard. At best they'd be sat at home in front of Grandstand. But not I. I had intrepidly negotiated two kinds of rail transport to get to the totally foreign, unexplored territory of a football ground I had only ever seen on the telly and was now about to re-connect myself with one hundred years of football history. And as an away supporter. God, but that felt good.

It's a cliche of football writing in the sixties that football grounds were the new cathedrals, but to me they were all world landmarks. On family holidays when I was a child, if we went through a town we would, almost without fail find the ground. Then we would just mooch around outside it for five minutes looking wistful and happy. I was always helplessly excited every time, awed even. Once on a family holiday we stopped across the road from Doncaster Rovers' ground. Even now I can hear my father's voice telling me 'Now Alick Jeffery plays for them: great centre forward....'

The sight of floodlight pylons in the sky anywhere from Torquay to Aberdeen (usually via places like Swindon, Arbroath and Stranraer) was to me the most incredibly exciting event. I can't explain it really: that feeling was always there when I was young. It was a very long time indeed before I realised that a building like Chatsworth House or the Louvre was possibly of greater significance. In fact I'm sure looking back I had to somehow teach myself that, and later made myself accept it only because a university education made me aware that the wider world, which I was now aspiring to be a member of, said it was so.

But even at 30 years old, I was chuffed to little mint balls that I'd arrived at Craven Cottage and I walked up some steps of concrete and chippings towards the away terrace feeling like a prince in my own world.

We lost 3-1 but it didn't much matter, we were going nowhere in the league and we weren't going down. I was there not so much for the result but just to be there. And I was desperate to rub shoulders with our away supporters, to see how many there were, find out what they sang and chanted, see what club accoutrements and insignia they wore. Perhaps I'd get talking to some. Well I wasn't a kid any more so of course I got talking to some: Derbyshire people, man for man, are as friendly as they come and will make idle chat with anyone, including, it happily transpired, me.

There were only around a hundred fans from Chesterfield on a wide and open terrace of about fifty or sixty steps, if that. There were some noisy, younger ones right behind the goal in a cluster of around a dozen and the rest were scattered around the rest of the available space as if they weren't sure whether they wanted to be associated with the rest of the tribe. This was odd, in that they'd all come for the same purpose and many would have travelled on the same coach together. In theory it's a great opportunity for people with the same interest or obsession to get in touch with each other, make new friends and so on. But this is the British we're talking about, and we like our own personal buffer zone around us, our own air castle walls. So I had to bust through some and did.

Near the back of this great expanse of concrete steps, were a group of about four very ordinary blokes, a mix of ages from a twenty-something to two forties and a sixty something and all wearing clothes you wouldn't want to be wearing unless you'd been born before the word 'fashion' was invented or you lived in a land of blind people. But I could have hugged all of them that afternoon because they let me talk to them about Chesterfield football. I was desperate for knowledge: details concerning the players, what position they played and who they used to play for. I needed stats like how many games they'd played for Chesterfield, how many goals they'd scored and when they'd made their debut. And I needed basic up to date stuff like who was good and who wasn't, who was up and coming and who was on the way out.

I drew the line at their chosen pre-match meal unless it was something like deep-fried monkey brains with chocolate sauce (though every football programme I read over the next ten years was going to tell me and almost every time it was chicken and beans). The dormant train spotter not far from the surface of my personality was now not so much waking up as putting on its open-toed sandals and asking about breakfast.

Whole new fields and villages of investigation and data to take in were now coming in to focus, spread out before me like a vista of the Derbyshire limestone plateau or like a well-paid prostitute. Itching, I was, at the prospect of unearthing juicy nuggets of facts, putting them in buckets and hauling off to the storage space in my brain where the treasure goes.

So I started in with a polite 'excuse me, but, how's the team been playing lately, I haven't been able to see them in the last few months?' hoping to pass as an exiled London supporter who'd unfortunately got stuck with the local accent and made inroads from there. More important than anything about Tony Reid's knee or how well new prospect Darren Wood was developing, was making contact with fans, any fans. These fellows were interesting to me as well as the team. How often did they go to away games? Every one. Every one? How do you get there? On the Supporters Club coach. Oh, Supporters Club, interesting, so they have one of those; I used to be in the Manchester United one when I was still in short trousers. And what's it like going to every game, do you get fed up? The one who was responding most articulately, Clive, one of the forty-somethings wearing bad shoes and a 50s style sports coat, threw his head back and laughed at this one. And this beautiful sound, rich with irony and the wisdom of the football ages told me that following the team was a long, hard road to travel, full of more pitfalls, pot holes and pratfalls than good times and glory. There was no Wembley for you, or big semi-finals at Villa Park or Hillsborough, no watching the highlights on Match Of The Day, no long articles about million pound transfers or match reports in the big papers to pore over on a lazy Sunday morning. There were long, boring rides on clapped out coaches without drinks or toilets to forgotten or ignored outposts of the game like Port Vale, Doncaster and Wrexham to reach a match to see no stars with no devastating skills, guided by no tracksuited tactically refined managers, playing a brand of football that belonged at the bottom of a tub of discounted jumpers in Littlewoods. Count me in right away, I thought. This'll do me.

The last dregs of a totally forgettable season for Chesterfield Football Club which I watched being poured away up at Saltergate later that April of 1987 formed a valuable lesson in terms of what awaited me in the near future at least. I went to two games, the visitors Brentford, then Chester, on my own, wanting to absorb everything about the experience into my blood. I had always been a weak, total slave to football grounds and now I was going to inhabit my own, one I had chosen for myself, one I could go to as a place of worship. I went and I felt like I was free.

It was just a shame that just as I was finding a way to nurture the full flowering of a seed that had been planted deep inside me when I went to White Hart Lane twenty-four years before, the team and the club were on the verge of falling apart. On the pitch the team were like a car on its last ride to the breakers yard. The only player who looked remotely capable of scoring goals with a regularity that would keep a team from being relegated before October, never mind the traditional Christmas, was Dave Caldwell, now very much a Town player and a lower league Denis Law lookalike: bright white hair, flaming temper and Scots. He was out injured for the Brentford game. His replacement, eighteen year old star in waiting Jamie Hewitt was normally right back, and amazingly he scored the opening goal. However, any sign that this may have been an example of a deep, tactical acumen that would win a game against the odds on the part of the manager was only a mirage: the Bees came back and won 2-1, and with ease. Chesterfield hardly produced a shot on goal after they'd scored early in the game, and that had come as a bolt of lightning from a blue sky.

A week later, as I squeezed my frame through the turnstile as all fans bar stick men and children always do, I heard a voice up ahead calling down to his mate who was still at the bottom of the steps that led up to the top of the home end, the Kop, 'Caldwell's playin'!' with the excitement of a small child seeing the postman coming up the path on his birthday. Thank God for that, I thought. Perhaps some goals and points today then.

Some hope. For the second time in a week I paid the pound that would transfer me from the terracing up to the wing stand where I could get a great view of the game thanks to the necessary perspective that only a position of height can give you. For the second time in a week the team were hopeless. Caldwell looked out of sorts, still injured probably. And get this: the manager had done a very stupid thing. The team had a midfield player who had some skill to go with some experience, both of which allowed him to play with a hopeful degree of confidence. He was the team's leader and prompter going forward. Only he was capable of using any degree of control he and the rest of the midfielders might win in their part of the field (which was most of it, between the two penalty areas). His name was Mick Henderson and he played the whole game at right back. The manager was still John Duncan and I was now in the process of discovering with the help of the fans around me that he had a reputation not just for producing dull, mechanical teams but for producing dull, mechanical teams whilst employing eccentric ideas in terms of player position on the side. Putting Henderson in defence was like getting an estate agent in to tarmac your drive: he might have picked up a few DIY tips along life's highway, but he'd be a lot better off back at the office making phone calls. It was madness and the longer the game went on we looked less and less like scoring.

Chester were only three points better off in the league, and they were a pretty nondescript bunch, but they had a goalscorer called Rimmer who duly did what these specialists do: score. He did it only once but it was enough to bag the points. We were again dismal, as infertile (I'll be dealing with the goal as substitute penile explosion later, so look out) as a horse with no nuts, but the most worrying thing to me was the fact that nobody was there to watch it. Just over two thousand people showed up against Brentford, which is awful enough, but on the lovely bright sunny day of the Chester match, barely more than a thousand turned up and paid. This would have been bad enough if we were in the fourth division and we were Halifax Town or somebody, but we were in the third and we were Chesterfield. Not so long ago, as my programme told me, not so long ago they or from now on as far as I was concerned, 'we' had won the Anglo-Scottish Cup knocking out Glasgow Rangers no less in the process. This thousand-and-a-bit paying customers is a wonderful number if you're B & Q and it's a Sunday, but for a professional football club it's an utter disaster. The place was empty and there was almost no atmosphere whatsoever. You could not only pick your spot in what was by any standards a small main stand, but you could hear pidgeons conversing just above you about the prospects for quality leavings from half time sandwiches and discussing who the best fan was to drop a subsequent payload on top of later on. A choice of seat is quite nice, but then again you don't go to football to experience the pastoral.

Typical, I thought. Here I am ready to make a long term commitment to this institution and now it looks, after a long and noble century or so (I didn't know how long the club had been in existence at that point*) to have about the same remaining life expectancy as the Indian Tiger. Supposedly knowledgeable people in and around the game had been predicting the demise of a swathes of unprofitable clubs in the lower two divisions for years now, organisations operating and playing in a state of permanent technical bankruptcy, and whoopee-do, here I was in on the ground of the most spectacular structural change in the history of the sport: a load of it was about to collapse like a ton weight on a cardboard box.

Instead of cheering goals scored by new heroes among happy throngs of like minded people, I'd soon be popping along to Saltergate to rake over the corpse of a once proud football club liberating souvenirs like a chunk of terrace or a wooden tip-up seat from the stand** as bulldozers get ready to tear the old Recreation Ground down like some old, unwanted cinema.+

I quickly buried the thought though. It wouldn't happen. It couldn't happen. I had to believe that. I'd only just got here, for Christ's sake. If all this collapsed, what on earth was I going to do with the rest of my life? The thought made me shudder.

Back at the positive, despite a haul of no points out of six on these two visits, I was very happy about being at Saltergate. It was still wonderful. And I have to tell you, my feelings went deeper than this.

---

* It was founded in 1867 and remains the fourth oldest of the existing Football League and Premiership clubs in the country.
+Though normally called Saltergate by people in general and Town fans on 99.99% of all available occasions, the official address and name of the place where Chesterfield FC have played all their home games since 1884, is Recreation Ground. When it is ever referred to by this name, it is as 'the Rec.' spelled exactly thus, and not as 'The Wreck' as some ironic comment on the state of the place.

**When Spurs, under Irving Scholar destroyed their west stand, a magnificent edifice designed by the best known of football architects, the Scot Archibald Leitch, which opened in September in 1909, my friend Mr Glasser did exactly this kind of trophy hunting and came away with a board painted in white which hung inside the referee's changing room. This excellent wheeze occurred to the said Glasser when working the ticket office one early August. A way in to the stadium being spotted, and sussing that the workmen who were in the process of paving the way for the destroying of a sizeable lump of Spurs' history had knocked off for lunch, he sneaked further and further into the under-workings of White Hart Lane to have a look see. Any serious football fan will tell you that this is the equivalent of a young priest from way out beyond The Pale accidentally finding his way into the Pope's inner chambers at Rome.

He told me he then found his way into the dressing rooms where he made a beeline for the plunge bath, more or less as good as a font in the Sistine Chapel to our callow young left-footer of the Mother Church. Here Mr G. looked down at this sacred monument, scene of many a trophy celebration down the years, and recalled moments spent spellbound gazing at photos in the football annuals of Christmas, showing the likes of Blanchflower, Greaves, Bobby Smith and Bill Brown foamed, wet and laughing in the big bath . Now, I'm no Spurs fan, but he's relating this tale and drool is dripping from my gob like saliva from a T-Rex.

'...and every fifth tile is white, but with a cockerel in the middle.' (this is the Tottenham Hotspur emblem, for the uninitiated.

'Then what did you do?' says I in wonder. He's Spurs, but, God, he's doing this for all the football fans ever born, everywhere on the planet.

'Then I walked up the corridor where I saw the steps up to the pitch and walked up them: Craig, can you imagine? Where all the greats trod? Then I went back and the last room before the way out was the ref's room so I went in there and propped up against the wall was this sign, so obviously....'

'You nicked it...'

'Liberated it: of course!'

'And you just walked out with it tucked under your arm?' It's a big chunk of wood, about two feet by two. 'I bet you were shitting yourself.'

'Of course,' says Frank, giggling. 42 and he's giggling like a girl. 'I was trying to whistle innocently and waiting to hear an 'Oy!' any second, but nothing.'

Imagine our priest nipping back on to the streets of Rome with a lump of Michelangelo ceiling under his arm.

'But Frank,' I said aghast, a sudden thought occurring, 'the tiles, didn't you get one of the tiles?'

'No. I couldn't prise one off.'

The blue paint on the white background says thus: 'Referee: Please Press Bell Push For Five Or Six Seconds As You're Going Out Before The Match And Again At Half Time.' It now hangs in his bathroom, so when a guest of Mr G. one can pause during one's ablutions and gaze upon this fine thing. It's a lovely thought that when I used to stand at the front there at the Park Lane end at five to three waiting for the teams to arrive at last, refs would be obeying the sign, and the greats of that football age would hear the bell and come out on to the pitch to do their work.

I sat up there in the wing stand on my allotted portion of wooden bench, I thought about how deeply I already felt about the place how much I wanted to belong to it and more, to be involved in it in some way. I knew that this meant that I desperately wanted to get myself on the inside of things. I wanted to know the players and the manager and to be able to walk around the club from the other side, not be forever on the outside. Being able to watch some games now was fantastic. Really. But in reality not enough. How I would get to the other side I hadn't a clue. What would I do, work for the club? As what? The club would be run on a shoe string budget so would employ a tiny full time staff and anyway I was a teacher and I lived 160 miles away. And I had a wife and two children now who relied upon me totally, for the time being at least, for their economic welfare. What was I to do, turn to Louise one night in bed as she lay there about to fall into weary sleep, exhausted after looking after our tiny twins all day and say, 'Darling this is what we're going to do: we're going to sell up and buy a house in Chesterfield and I'm going to offer my services to the club, unpaid, doing whatever it is they want me to do.'?

'So, (yawn) we starve, do we?'

'No, we learn how to cope with life on the benefit system with half the rest of the country.' The other half were dogging it up on the proceeds of the Lawson Boom at the time, but if you've ever known a teacher, you'll know that all they ever do is moan.

'Oh, great. That's cheered me up no end.'

'No, honestly, it'll be fine, you'll see....'

'Zzzzzzzzzzzzz.'

What else was there, put a lemon bib on and become a steward? I couldn't see myself doing that, I had too much ego: it had to be something grander than trying to stop pitch invasions. I'd have been hopeless at that anyway: a child of three would get past me if they bit me on the leg hard enough.

So there I was, seemingly marooned in a sunny end of season day-dream. Was I aware of how self-indulgent I was being, and how childish? Nah. I'm a bloke, when all is said and done and if there's one thing we're great at, it's not facing up to our responsibilities. Everybody knows that these days. I'd started to walk along my own little yellow brick road, to trot off into the future of endless harmless escape. I'd made up my mind and I couldn't see anything that was going to stop me. The Eagle had now definitely landed and with one hell of an angry beak.

8

The Priestfield Millenium

'It only takes a second to score a goal.'

Brian Clough

Time, here at the western world, is measured in seconds, hours, days, weeks, months and years, give or take a decade, century or if you have to make me cringe in embarrassment, millennium. You use that system essentially, but we don't have years, we find it natural and comfortable to think in seasons. Say '1964' and it doesn't spark off more than say, two immediate associations: A Hard Days Night and a sublime, golden summer holiday in Stranraer at my great-aunt Mary and uncle Jimmy's. That's all I can muster. Alter that to '1964-1965' and it sets off an explosion of memory: my first game at Chelsea, with Richard Attenborough and Lance Percival sitting just in front of me; my cousin Ian's wedding.

I can date Ian's wedding precisely in the same way; because Spurs were at home to Liverpool and a brief reference check in a Tottenham programme from that season will give me the precise day-number of the month in a jiffy. And I've always known which programme to fetch because this deeply memorable event is still lodged snugly in the '64-5 folder in my head. I have a crystal sharp image in my mind from that day that almost scares me: we're standing outside the church in Tottenham and suddenly we hear an 'oooooh' from possibly seventy per cent of the White Hart Lane crowd. A crowd of around 55 000 gives us about 40 000 people instinctively pushing their lips out into the shape of a windsock in a gale who together can send that 'oooooh' traveling a heck of a distance. We heard it easily and we must have been a good three-quarters of a mile away. Alan Gilzean had probably just gone very close with a header.

Ian's wedding itself sends a shower of home movies across my white screen, almost entirely concerning that man Uncle Len again, who that night gave a unique performance as an entertainer fuelled by a couple of buckets full of pale ale and scotch. It's not so much the magnificent rendering of Brook Benton's Blueberry Hill I mentioned earlier, though that memory is one I will take with me to eternity. It's more seeing him shortly before we left the reception. This nocturnal celebration was held upstairs at a local pub, but I remember Len saying something to my Dad about a little jazz band playing in one of the bars downstairs. Len's enthusiasm for little ideas and plans was wonderfully, cutely boyish and infectious. Cut to around eleven PM and there was Len sat on a wooden chair four feet from the sax player who was, as they might say in the States, blowin' his ass off:' it seemed pretty loud to me. This didn't seem to be affecting Len much. His head had flopped onto his chest as if someone had snapped his neck like a stick of celery: he looked like he was dead alright, which just shows you how much fun he'd been having. What always, but always, makes a huge smile inside me about this is the fact that there was a sizeable dance space in front of the band but no-one was dancing (this was the sixties after all, not the forties). There was just Len, on his own, away into his own dreamland. The boyish enthusiasm, the stuff that never left him when I knew him had tired him out, bless him.

The years 1987 and 1988 then are really 1987-88 and though professionally I have to interpret 1-9-8-7 as the year of the third Thatcher election win, in my mind's personal reality it is simply part of the season where I fell into the volcano cone. My first thought now when I awoke was often where Town were in the league, or where the next game was and could I somehow get there. I now had my own home shirt (way before the wearing of football shirts became de rigeur for the fan, I might add). My last thoughts were the same only more so, because I had more time on my hands. Time to consider the team's weaknesses and strengths, the possibility of transfers in and out, to dream of a time when Louise and I might move ourselves and the twins north, so I could go to every home game and more away.

I was certain now that what I wanted most to do with my life was to be a Chesterfield Football Club supporter in the fullest possible sense. And this meant going to every match. I daren't confess this to my friends or colleagues at work, they thought that I was mad enough already. Back then, to admit you liked football enough to want to attend a match was little short of owning up to exposing yourself to strange women in the park. Football fans are supposed to attach themselves to their local team and usually did. For a devoted follower exiled through work to travel fifty or a hundred miles back home to get to a game was in those days unheard of, not least because no-one in the media was interested in writing about real fans. So you didn't know it was happening.

When in reply to the innocent question of friends in the late summer-early autumn of 1987-8, 'What did you do at the weekend?' or 'What have you been up to lately?'

I replied, casually, 'Oh, I went Tuesday night to see Chesterfield play at Aldershot' I heard blank spaces of incomprehension down the other end of the telephone from Colchester, Sunderland, Paris, Kentish Town, Welwyn Garden City, the places where my dispersed marras resided. People at work looked at me 'gone out', as they say in north-east Derbyshire: they didn't know quite what to say, apart from a small, 'oh' and already they'd be thinking about something else or be trying to figure out what the fuck I was up to.

Frankly, and this is perhaps the key sign of addiction, I didn't give a tuppenny toss for anyone's opinion about rushing down to Brighton and back for the evening. I was in love, I was happy and that was it. I was happy at home, too. I adored Louise like I always had and now had a baby boy and baby girl to complete a little, or should I say, large, i.e. hugely significant, circle: fatherhood a big step and all that.

Perhaps a life of domestic bliss in a one-bedroom shoebox in Orpington, (I know what you're thinking: you can have domestic bliss in Orpington?) actually left me free to throw myself upon my new obsession, free to expend my time, energy and spare cash on a new toy. Unhappy in love I might have deprived myself of this pure and unalloyed pleasure, decided I was too inadequate to deserve it: a place where the stresses and strains of work were completely and utterly forgotten. Where you could completely lose yourself and be yourself and no-one would care or be there to watch as you shout, swear, sing, dance, jump up and down, whatever you like. Some even swung punches or threw things at other people in as free a form of self-expression as you are going to find anywhere, though it wasn't quite my cup of tea. If it was frowned upon at work to open the emotional floodgates thus...

'Roberts you hopeless little wanker! How many fucking times have I told you not to write 'I think' in an A level History essay?: 'I think that James I was ultimately a disastrous role model for a son who went on to lead his country into the miseries of civil war.' What the Pope's arse do you think an A level examiner is going to think of that?'

...it wasn't at the match, where, if you had a mind, you could lighten your heavy load with a.....

'Fook off and die, 'Yewitt, you useless twATT!!!' or slightly more sophisticated

'You fooking useless bAAstard, linesman! Who's shagging your missus while you're doin' a fookin' pathetic job 'ere, then?'

Such examples of verbal release were often accompanied by extravagant facial gestures and body movements. Faces were screwed tight in Hitlerian frenzy as a definitive analysis of the team's centre-forward was delivered by an outraged supporter. At times of particular enthusiasm for the task, the speaker would rush down a dozen or so terrace steps to increase his chances of the advice reaching the ears of the guilty, pointing a fearsomely aggressive straight arm for emphasis. People really would shake their fists at officials like you saw in the Benny Hill show or the old silent movies of Hollywood.

I used to marvel at the fact that often an outstandingly violent accuser and shouter was normally the most mild-mannered of men, who you'd see laughing and smiling at people on the way into the ground or even at half time, five minutes after haranguing a tense, packed Reichstag on the perils of not crushing Communism under the implacable jackboot. No doubt such men went home to wives who, when asking their man how the game went, would receive the reply, 'Oh, not so good, dear, we lost two-one,' with the gentleness of a kindly churchman.

I may exaggerate the numbers of such people, but not the example. There were women there too, of course, who could have given lectures in advanced football fan demagoguery. They profaned less, but were otherwise fine exemplars of the art of the terrace frenzy.

The Shouters and Declaimers who made the biggest impression on me were those whose specialism was to abuse the referee and to a lesser extent the linesmen. And it never ceased to astound me how, to a fan, utterly predictable in the practice of their art they were. At exactly the same point of the match (i.e. from the first tackle or throw in after the kick off) they would make exactly the same gestures, raucously ejaculate exactly the same insults and complaints to exactly the same people and receive exactly the same response: be completely and utterly ignored. And this they would do game in, game out, as if it were merely the playing out of a precise, sacred ritual of an ancient tribe. What they were doing was so utterly futile, you had to laugh. Sometimes I just felt sorry for them. The monotony and predictability of their habits spoke of the workings of a mind I didn't want to inhabit.

Not that I felt I was above telling a referee what I thought of him not giving Chesterfield a penalty when it would have saved the day, and with a pretty expletive lobbed into the sentence for good measure. I was there to forget myself too, after all. But I was a new boy still that 87-88 season, and feeling my way. As a southerner, an outsider, I felt I needed to act with a certain amount of restraint and certainly not draw attention to myself, less someone think, 'who does he think he is, pushing his way in where he doesn't belong. Bloody southerner'. When we played a London team, the chant of 'we 'ate cockneys and we 'ate cockneys...' would usually go up at some point or other and I used to wince. I was on their side, supporting their team but I knew they meant me.

Added to this, I was a new boy, a junior fan, so I had no real claim upon the rights other fans had to rant, rave and chant: I was not yet the real thing. I had squatter's rights but not a real residency permit, no bona fide passport, so for the time being I needed to know my place, bide my time and ease my way in gently and respectfully.

If ever there were a reason to shout at the team and call them, in one form of the fan lingua franca, 'all the bastards under the sun', it was at my first game of the season at Gillingham on September the fifth. Memory escapes me as to why - despite the season beginning in the middle of my long six week holiday - we hadn't nipped up to Tupton so I could see one at least of the opening home games. Perhaps Louise's parents had been on holiday. Whatever, the fourth Saturday of the season saw me fully able to present myself at Priestfield Stadium and with ease. After all, this was the one Town game I could watch in my present county of residence. Louise thought it might be a good idea to make it a family outing: she could take the wee bairns to the park and mooch around a shop or two while I went to the match.* Excellent.

Practically terminally exciting, in fact. There is nothing quite like the first game you go to each season: you've been lying idle for months as the summer drifts slowly, slowly by, in a form of hibernation, and come August you're salivating at the prospect of returning yourself to normality. This was me for the first time now, itching with eczema to get back to where I left off the previous May. This was my first full season as a Chesterfield fan. When I tell you I had a lot of catching up to do, I mean twenty-five years worth. Most little boys go to their first game and immediately attach themselves to the club Dad's taken them to watch. It's normally the start of a relationship that can only be severed by death (and only then after their ashes have been scattered over the pitch for some devotees). But I started at Tottenham and hated them practically on sight, as you already know. I had never regularly watched the team I supported, so I'd missed out on the experience of 99.99% of football fans. I had never gone regularly to see my team, and as I was about to discover, this meant that I had never been what I would call a proper football supporter. So I had a 25 year old reservoir of enthusiasm and emotional energy pent up inside me waiting to flood itself upon the world. Every game I could go to now was to release some of this massive, primal sea.

So it was with a bit of heart-thumping excitement here and sweaty nervous tension there, that Louise stopped by the ground to let me out of

---

*She was later to claim that Gillingham was the most boring town in Britain, a verdict she has yet to rescind.

the car. I practically threw myself out through the windscreen on to the pavement next to the away turnstiles because I was late! They'd kicked off! This is always a disaster for a deeply committed fan especially for me: I'm the lost twin brother of Woody Allen's character in Annie Hall who refuses to go in to see a film when the ticket attendant informs him that he's missed the opening thirty seconds. If these days we're late for a film and Louise somehow outwits me and persuades me to go in I sit there in a deep sulk and only come out of it if the movie happens to be particularly good.

However, on this occasion I was so thrilled to be seeing the lads play I contained my natural instincts and ran up the steps to the terrace like the kid rushing downstairs on Christmas morning to see if Santa's left the presents. Immediately you get into sight of the pitch in this situation your senses get instantly mugged as you rush to take in what's happening: The ground was awash with bright sunshine so the pitch was fabulously green; the players' kits were making wild, expressionistic stabs on my eyesight and now inside the bowl of the ground, the noise of the fans in roars, cheers, songs and individual shouts and the sight of the concrete terracing and gaily painted crush barriers made me giddy for a few seconds. You think you only want to know the score so you know you haven't missed anything vital and that your team aren't behind, but this is a fast-action event you've just walked into so it's like trying to jump on to a moving train for the first thirty seconds or so.

I quickly found the fan nearest to me and breathlessly asked the obvious question whilst still looking at the pitch to try to get a grasp of where I was:

'Wassa score?'

'One-nil,' came the reply from a man who looked straight ahead of him not taking his eye off the play for a second. He had a face that looked like he'd accidentally found a cockroach in a cheese sandwich so I knew it wasn't us that'd scored, but hope springs....

'Who to?'

'Them.'

Bugger. This is awful at the best of times. You always, no matter where you are in the league, think today is the day when you're going to win. 'Pull off a win' if you're away and the home side is above you, 'pull off a shock win' if you're down at the bottom. At worst, wherever you are, whoever you play, you always watch the match in hope of a 0-0 draw. To be a goal down in two minutes is rotten. Away from home, that fills you with foreboding. Against a team who'd demolished Southend 8-0 at home the previous week as Gillingham had, its to have a wall wheeled across in front of you with big writing on it.

So. I hadn't been wrong then when one of my few sophisticated sense mechanisms had picked up a somewhat Romanesque aroma to the noise of the local crowd when I rushed in. They were used to watching destruction and already on this beautiful late summer's afternoon, they'd tasted blood. They soon tasted more. 2-0. The crowd erupted and the sound of celebration swirled round the tight bowl of the ground in insult. We hadn't got out of our half since we arrived. This was beginning to look very, very serious indeed.

However, we quickly rallied. Dave Waller, our new £3000 striker from Shrewsbury Town had a great chance, but blew it. Still, it had its effect in giving the lads, in quite scrummy new away kit of white shirts with thin green pinstripe and black shorts today I noticed, instead of the usual blue, a dash of much required confidence. And why not? We were top of the league after all! O yes. Much to the surprise of all those who took any notice of the Football League division Three, which in those days was about a quarter of a million passive and active fans of the twenty four clubs and no-one in the national media, we had played four, won three, drawn one and had ten proud points. We hadn't even conceded a goal yet! Last season's gaffer John Duncan had gone off to better things with Ipswich Town and new man Kevin Randall, previously Duncan's assistant had stepped off the team coach no doubt having contemplated on the journey down the fact that a decent result against the rampant Gills might well cement him the August Manager Of The Month award for the division. This was the first game of the new month, but if the vote was close, continuing the good run would help. If he did allow himself this little daydream, he'd be hoping the judges hadn't noticed Town's ignominious exit from the league cup at the hands of fourth division Peterborough.

For twenty minutes it was even-stevens, attacks traded equally and the game began to resemble a meeting of two sides riding high and looking forward to the rest of the long season ahead with huge optimism. If we could only stick one in their net, we could really start striding about with a serious sense of purpose and they would start doubting their ability to win the game. That's how it is with football; a 2-0 lead is sometimes a weaker hand than 1—0. One goal behind, a team away from home still plays within itself, hoping that if they don't concede another and they keep plodding away, a goal will turn up like an extra bus. That makes them an easy team to defend against. But a team two-down knows that it has to score to get back in the game and throws itself forward abandoning its goal-inhibiting caution. The home team themselves have often by this time eased up, thinking the points are pretty safe so long as they don't concede one. So they begin to be less adventurous. Midfielders drop deeper to protect their back four while full backs conservatively stay back so they don't leave space behind for opposing forwards and wingers to exploit. Thus initiative is conceded to the team that's behind. I've seen it happen many times, and even Manchester United fall foul of this universally found problem for teams with a two-goal buffer zone.

And the thing is, if the game does go 2-1 like this, it's almost impossible for the erstwhile two-nil-uppers to regain their old advantage. The fans who were singing joyously only a quarter of an hour ago in full expectation of three points and a slaughter into the bargain are now getting anxious and the more thoughtless among them will be shouting angry remarks at the same men who were just now unassailable heroes. Meantime, the 80 or so intrepid away supporters in their lonely pen who were resembling a group of funeral mourners from the year 1931 at 3.12 are now, at 4.30 defiantly roaring their eleven on and though only forming 2% of the crowd they are now inexplicably the loudest thing to be heard in the ground.

If you're a fan of the team that's led 2-0 and the match goes 2-1 you better hope it was a lucky breakaway. If not, the team that stole the initiative from you is going to come at you like a train and before you know it it's 2-2 and you are one angry person. The impossible, a 2-3 home defeat is the next thing you're dreading and you can hardly stand to watch the rest of the game.

All we need is one goal and at 3.29 we get our opportunity. Again it's Waller, the ball breaks to him in the box with a clear sight of goal in front of him and he puts the chance over the bar. Sheeyit, goes half the away end. Then the next thing you know, pandemonium has broken out.

We're still pressing for that crucial breakthrough straight after the Waller chance, then a three-pass breakaway and wham! it's three nil, hope shattered, afternoon over. The home end are up and singing as before and everyone on the away end is looking disgusted, as if someone just put cigarette ash in the custard. I might not have got my Spireite wings yet but it doesn't stop me feeling crushed like everyone else. I look down at the concrete around my feet as is my wont at such moments and suddenly there's a huge roar: four-nil. Defenders in the new white shirts are standing round in the immediate aftermath of the impregnation of the goal looking like car crash victims. Dazed, as if unable to comprehend what's just occurred. I was to witness Town defenders looking like this many, many times over the next nine years, and though the faces and the shirt designs changed, the body language was always the same.

The Gills are really swarming all over us making mesmerizing patterns all over the pitch. We're now looking like a non-league side putting up token resistance against a big club. And it just looks ridiculous. The known system of normal emotions no longer applies, like football has laws like physics and suddenly and inexplicably they've caved in. You're trying to construct new ones so you can cope with the situation but everything is just swimming in front of you. Another attack, another shot and it flies in past our keeper who will later claim to be handicapped by a hamstring injury*. Five-nil. The scoreline in a game sometimes remains the same for a whole ninety minutes. More usually fans are accustomed to making gradual changes to the expectations they start out with. Usually, the gap between your team and the opposition never goes beyond two goals. In a bad season it will happen maybe five times in forty six games. In a reasonable one once, in a good season, perhaps never. Supporting a team unbeaten in the league coming into the match, you think at worst two-nil or three-one. You're mentally attuned to this before you even get to the ground. Three-down before half time shakes you up completely. Your essential raison d'etre for your attendance is already comprehensively routed before the whole thing is even half over. This scrambles your internal mechanism for dealing with this completely. But five-nil. Five-nil? At half time?

I got myself a drink from the tea bar and sat at the top of the terrace facing away from the crowd. Fortunately the top step fell away to a grassy bank, so I plonked my shattered self down and sipped, disconsolately. This was completely humiliating. Unfortunately I didn't yet know any Chesterfield fans so I had no-one to talk this through with. Not that anyone said very much, even those in pairs or in groups. In fan terms this was already a bereavement. For the new season, for a start. This isn't a team that's going to win anything, you can be certain of that. What the second half did to these feelings I've still to work out.

The teams come out, we've made a substitution and maybe, surely, things will calm down. It's a very common phenomenon indeed in football for potential landslide scorelines in the first half, three-nil, four-nil, to somehow solidify at half time. This could happen to us. It must. We have

---

*Our goalie was ex-Scottish international Jim Brown, as honest and decent a man as you'd wish to find anywhere. So if he said he played most of the game with a hamstring injury, then he played most of the game with a hamstring injury. Which still begs the question why wasn't he substituted by the manager? I've twice seen heroic performances by substitute goalkeepers, one of them in 1995 by defender Jamie Hewitt. And who was playing in defence that day eight years earlier? Yes, indeedie: Jamie Hewitt, or 'Jamie Lad' when he was playing well ('good tackle, Jamie lad,' the old timers would say).

to get better at the back. They have to go off the boil. But the play restarts and I'm thinking '8-0, 8-0, they won last week 8-0,' and if I'm honest with myself, the second half was written in the faces of our players as they trooped off at the end of the first forty five minutes. They should have said 'fury' which would have suggested a determination to put things right in the second half, but they just said 'we want to go home.'

Humiliation turned to complete obliteration. More goals came like a rainstorm and they were all at one end. By half past four the score was ten-nil to Gillingham and a score of thirteen or fourteen-nothing was well on the cards. Luckily they eased up. Their players may have felt that enough was enough at ten, though they all looked as pleased as anything when it went double figures, I can tell you. I felt sorry for our lot. I think all the Town fans did. I later saw us draw games one-one and watched the players get a verbal m.llering like you wouldn't believe. Home fans en masse can misjudge football completely, usually their intelligence level being directly proportional to the number of hard-core fans present. So in good times you see and hear wholly ignorant reactions to events. In bad times, more sagacious judgement. To be among an away crowd a long way from home in 1987 was to be generally among Solomons. How could we verbally insult the players? You think they didn't know how crap they were, how gutless on the day? One or two shouted things, but only those who had no other way of coping with this disaster. The rest of us stood and watched the final scenes being played out with as much dignity as we could muster and I for one fretted about the effect this was going to have on the team, whose morale and self-belief must have stood on the verge of complete annihilation. How many games would we now go before we won again, or even got a point? And where would we be in the league when we did?

A few Town fans left early which I found silly, completely childish. It later became my policy never to leave a game early whatever the score but I could just about understand why at four-nil or something someone might want to call it a day and head for home. But here was history being made. Scorelines come along like this one every ten or twenty years among all the ninety two league clubs.*

We would never lose like this in what was left of our entire lifetimes, or ever win like it, so we might as well see every second in case we miss a detail we might want to tell our grandchildren about.

---

*Funnily enough, the next one occured only two months later when Manchester City beat Huddesrsfield Town 10-1 at Maine Road. No team has posted a double figures score since.

'Tell me what it was like when at Gillingham scored another four in the last five minutes to make it 16-0 granddad.'

You don't even want to be making something up to answer that sort of question. You want to be able to confidently tell them,

'Well, lad, it was like this: about five yards down the terracing, a bloke ran at the fencing, leapt up in the air like a salmon on drugs and impaled himself to death on a clump of top spikes. Blood everywhere. It wasn't a pretty sight, I can assure you.'

Or what about, 'What was it like when Dave Waller scored a hat-trick in the last two minutes of the famous 10-3 game, granddad.'

You don't want to admit that you were sulking like a four year old who had to go to bed early and missed an overhead kick from thirty yards plus an eight man dribble.

So this is why I always stayed to the end through thick and thin: I hated the thought that I might miss a brilliant Chesterfield goal. I thought the knowledge might torment me for ever.

I had agreed to meet Louise outside the station. She already knew the score but wondered whether the Gillingham fan was mucking around.

'No,' I said, as she stood there behind a double-buggy full of twins, the little darlin's gurgling and kicking their legs in the sun all the while, oblivious to their father's distress.

'We lost ten-nil.'

She laughed.

If she'd asked me how I felt right then - she didn't, she knew better - I wouldn't have known what to say. On the one hand I was devastated. I had this competitive nature and I was already taking Chesterfield results personally. They were my team now after all. On the other hand, it couldn't be denied that I'd just been privileged to witness an extraordinary event. I'd been supporting this club for five minutes and I'd already stumbled into history. And I'd now seen something that 99% of Town fans had missed, which as far as I could see put me into some elite group. Suddenly I was feeling like a proper supporter, the real authentic thing. I may just have seen a game that bordered on the traumatic - no, was traumatic, but a part of me knew I had entered the realm of the true fan partly because only a select band of Town fans saw this unmistakably historic event and I was one of them. I now had an authentic bullet wound I could wear with pride.

If Louise had asked me how I really felt about the game that afternoon in Gillingham on September 5th 1987 - she didn't because she knew the look on my face all too well - I'd have ignored her or worse.

But fourteen years away from the heat of the battle, I know that really, I should have looked at her and replied, with perhaps a crooked smile on my face, 'It was perfect.'

9

'Is this one of them 'fan-zynes', then?'

'*Some men become what they were born for.*'
Sheenagh Pugh

It was indeed a long time before the team could go out and play away from home without browning their underpants in fear of another clobbering. They lost the next seven away games straight before mounting a sensational comeback in an FA Cup first round tie at Meadow Lane, residency of Notts County, drawing 3-3 after being three-down. Sadly, I wasn't there to see it. I did see sixteen games though that season after Gillingham, and living 160 miles away from Saltergate and not being able to drive, I felt dead proud of myself. Going off to Hampshire on a Tuesday night seemed to me to be as exotic as camping in the foothills of the Andes. To me this was adventure! And, as the most dangerous thing I'd done in my life to this point was to wear a somewhat outspoken purple paisley patterned shirt at Cuffley Youth Club one night, I suppose it was bound to feel like that, thinking about it. Thirty years of age and my primary motivation in life apart from to keep breathing as long as possible was to see Chesterfield Football Club play as often in the season as I could. And then? Do the same again. Not exactly the stuff that put the Great in Great Britain.

I never could get my head around real ambition. When I was eleven and about to go off to Grammar school, rich, successful Uncle Victor turned up at the house one Sunday afternoon in his big Rover and bald head. We hadn't seen him for years so it was like a royal visit. He bought my mum a huge bunch of flowers, a trick I'd never seen Dad pull out of nowhere for her. Just before he left a couple of hours later he sat me on his knee and said, 'Now I want you to promise your Uncle Victor something: promise me you'll go to university one day when you're old enough.'

I don't remember saying anything to him: I just sat there perched over a mountain top of tears. I've no idea why. It was just one of the worst feelings of my life and perhaps the scar from the explicable emotional upheaval made me happy with mediocrity as I wended my meandering way through school life.

I never wanted to be rich, I never wanted to travel, I never had a dream smouldering inside of me to make the most of the talents nature or God had endowed me with. I never asked out gorgeous women because I assumed, rightly, that I hadn't a prayer. I was offered a chance to join the Lord's Ground Staff when I was eighteen, the cricketing equivalent of being asked by Alex Ferguson to sign on for Manchester United, but I was too scared of facing really fast bowling. I didn't organize the trial, either, someone else did it for me without telling me. And I went into teaching for reasons which defy rational thinking.

When I first heard of something called global warming in 1980 a spray of shit almost exploded from my rectum out of a feeling of vast, primal fear. Six years later I heard about the hole in the ozone layer at school just as I was about to teach a class and minutes later I was nearly fainting from shock: we, or more to the point, I, was doomed. I remember distinctly while a pupil was giving a talk about Lenin's plans for post-revolutionary Russia a few minutes later, thinking that what I wanted to do was just lie down on the floor right there in the classroom - it was a Friday afternoon so I was knackered anyway - and let oblivion take me. Not that I had the courage to get anywhere close to a suicide attempt. The knowledge that there was no escape from the world made me feel worse.

Having virtually no psychic defences against the trials and tribulations of the modern world, escaping into football was the obvious solution. I hadn't been smart enough to do it for this reason, though. I wasn't organized enough to have thought a solution like that through. I was just lucky enough to have an addictive personality, just as an astrology book about Pisceans had once told me. It also said that being a March 14th baby I was a dreamer, a worrier, I was untidy and disorganised. I was likely to be creative but I almost certain to have no drive, no ambition. I liked all-embracing solutions to the wider problems of the world so I would probably be a socialist. Stuck in the eighth of nineteen years of Tory rule I obviously wasn't down for much luck either.

Small wonder then that I was using all my powers of persuasion to get Louise to think weekend and school holiday visits to Tupton were just what she needed.

'You're tired out looking after Lyall and Tasha, Louise, your mum'll look after you, pamper you.'

'I don't remember you being this concerned about me before you became obsessed with bloody football.'

Louise though, as I just told you, did not give me a hard time about my new found lover, friend and companion. I have to admit here to exploiting the pact, of sorts, that we made when we decided, against all the odds when my earlier romantic history is taken into account, to get married.

'I'll never tell you what to do or stop you doing what you want to do,' she said back in 1982 just before the big day.

'Oh, really?' I teased, raising an eyebrow at her suggestively.

'Within reason. If you ever go with another woman you'll find your bollocks on the sheet lying beside you next morning.'

And if you knew Louise you'd know she meant she'd start with removing those with a rusty knife and move on from there. At least you know where you stand with someone like that.

So we drove up to Tupton on a fairly regular basis to home games that same season, 1987-88, and I managed to make good headway with my project. Up at Saltergate I was practically a talisman for the team: I saw nine games there and we won seven of them. And in that time I found a new hero: Dave Waller. In those games we scored sixteen goals and he bagged ten of them. Never mind missed chances on the 10-0 day he was brilliant, a natural goalscorer every fan dreams about their club possessing and somehow, Duncan, as a parting shot had persuaded some complete fool at Shrewsbury Town to give him away so he could come to us. For a measly three thousand quid! Against Rotherham in October we lost two early goals but he put things straight with a hat-trick, thank you and goodnight. The first goal said it all about him. Edge of the box, neat little dribble past a defender and smash! the ball screamed into the roof of the net in true Roy Of The Rovers fashion.

He didn't exactly look like a great footballer tends more and more to look these days. He wouldn't have married a Spice Girl, had such a ghastly specimen existed back then: a member of Bananarama wouldn't have looked at him twice. He had a pudd'n basin haircut, an extremely dubious moustache and was far too thick set and hunched at the shoulders to skip elegantly across the grass a la Beckham. Neither was he fast: I suppose if he had have been it would have been like seeing a gnu outpacing a cheetah on the Serengeti plains - can you imagine this? Neither can I. Mind, if he had been able to outpace one of the larger cats (spotted), he sure as hell wouldn't have been playing for us. So it was all just as well. His limitations were our reasons for smiling.

I loved having heroes, it was one of my real weaknesses, and I was overwhelmed with pride that I could watch this low grade genius in action. He was simply one of those footballers who, as is said over and over about such people, players like Gary Lineker and Kevin Phillips, know exactly where the goal is and if you give them a sniff they'll have the ball heading for one of the corners or looping over the keeper's head unless you can find a way of stopping him.

Away from home he always seemed to be injured, or he got no service when he did play, which are two major reasons why we kept losing: we had no-one else who could score, no striker who would have been any better than Dolly Parton would have done if we'd somehow managed to stuff her into a blue shirt. Except at Fulham where I returned again one wonderfully gloomy December afternoon to see a 3-1 win with Waller bagging two. Only a week or so later he was giving me a happy Christmas as we beat the later-promoted Walsall 2-1 and the local enemy Mansfield 3-1, Dave scoring in both. We were going rather nicely at that stage, four wins out of five over the holiday period. Then Waller got injured and we dropped down the table like a broken lift.

Never mind. Over Christmas Louise and I finally decided to make a big decision. The shoebox wasn't getting any bigger, but the twins were. We were getting more and more fed up with the south-east where in the hallucinogenic bubble of an economic boom-time, the people around us were getting more and more gimme-gimme and I'll have it now, and the kids I taught - comprehensive kids, I'll have you know - were treating my colleagues and me more and more like slaves - 'how can you be clever when you're a teacher: you've got no money!?' We'd never wanted to live there in the first place (only somebody with Reddy-Brek for brains or brought up there would actually choose to live in south-east outer London*) but clever-trousers here couldn't get a job anywhere else when he left college, or didn't have the gumption or patience or move to a nice part of the country and work it out from there.

We had one big thing going for us: we had a mortgage, and property prices in the south-east had taken off like Apollo XII. If we could get away before the bubble burst, we could cash in our chips for a decent sized house. It wasn't fair, but as we'd been stuck with the Knickerbocker Glories for the best part of a decade, we decided we deserved a break and to hell with our socialist values for five minutes. Perhaps there was something contagious about the zeitgeist - it's more than possible. If ever I felt guilty about getting my hands on some silly property money I thought of the children and rehearsed my arguments for my Red friends should any of them look at me askance for grabbing at the ill-gotten gains the capitalist system occasionally affords one.

'Well, Barry, it's like this: if it was just me and Louise we wouldn't do it, but when it's ya kids it's a different story. You can't inflict ya politics on

---

*Cue rock bottom sales for 'Losing My Religion in south London from Croydon to Deptford.

ya kids. You've got to look after their interests and we can't stand to watch 'em grow up in a rabbit hutch just 'cause it's got a fitted kitchen on the side.'

And nor could we. We were all sleeping in one bedroom, and cosy as that was, I didn't want to still be waking up two feet from Lyall the day he got his first leather jacket or Tasha taken to be fitted for her first bra. The logic was irresistible: we had to go.

'I'll go anywhere, I don't care.'

This wasn't me trying to be magnanimous, this was The Boss not bossing.

'Okay....how about moving to Derbyshire? The countryside's beautiful, great place to bring up the twins, and you'd be near your Mum and Dad....'

'Look, if you want to move to Derbyshire so you can go to football, say so. It's fine by me.'

'Oh, right, okay then, good.'

Mabel Snr, who in the two years since my Dad died had been very, very difficult to deal with, would never forgive me, would practically have a stroke through jealousy, with Louise's parents being close to the children, but anything was bearable so long as I could get to the football.

That's how it was.

So by February I'd found a teaching job advertised in the paper in Derby and, having decided I was going to take the first job in the ancient shire of the ram I could throw a piece of chalk at, I applied. It was temporary, it was a crap school and the only people interviewed alongside me were misfits, oddballs and me. Now: I know what you're thinking, that one or other of the former epithets/descriptions applied to me, but sat there in a staff room with the other candidates waiting for the head to come in with the panel's verdict - that's how they did it in those days, no humane killer used on the failed applicants, just the Miss World or Oscars system every time - I was the only normal, genuine member of the human race in the room. I had to get the job. I did.

The interview worked out perfectly. We were at home to Bristol City that night so my trip north got me to a game. I can hardly tell you how great it was to stand on the Compton Street that night like a normal, ordinary North-East Derbyshire bloke, knowing I was soon going to have a Derbyshire address and be breathing Derbyshire air every day, watching us get outclassed and stuffed 4-1. I was now moving close to being able to think of myself as a real Town fan. If anyone asked, I could now proudly inform them that I'd moved home just to be near Saltergate so I could watch the Spireites. I may have been a Londoner by birth and upbringing, but look at me, I've changed my job and sold my property for the love of

Chesterfield football club and that has to count for a lot, your honour. I plead honorary supporter status also by virtue of my wife being as Chesterfield as the Crooked Spire itself and furthermore, her father, in his day was Birdholme's champion fighter. And finally, I'd ask the jury to take into account that I'm only a southerner on my mother's side, my father having been born in a tenement in Glasgow, and the fact that I wore a club tie at my interview.

Me lud, I rest my case.

It was indeed a momentous evening. On a freezing night barely 1500 people turned out, which is a doomladen figure for a club heading to the relegation zone of the third division with no money to spend on players and, well, no money to spend on anything. There was nothing grand about the facilities for the fans. No frills, no gimmicks, no special offers and no obvious fundraising. You couldn't sponsor a game or a match ball. You couldn't even sponsor a player's kit, a ruse all the other lower league clubs used to raise the cash to buy the club's washing powder for the season or for the electric light in the bog for the next few years. In other clubs' programme all the players had a little photo in the club programme and the sock or shirt sponsor got to see their name sitting proudly in a semi-public place for all to see. I asked about it at the Commercial Office, a prefab hut on the club car park run by Town's goalie Jim Brown, but was told the club had stopped it because the amount of gaps next to the players' pictures was proving an embarrassment.

The club was run just as it had for the past seventy or eighty years. There was little investment anywhere apart from nice licks of paint on advertising hoardings and terrace crush barriers. There was no pride on display from the chairman and directors, a new lot who had just come in, and the programme itself was, after a row with the previous editor over financial cutbacks, of non-league standard. The catering for fans was abysmal in its lack of imagination and basic quality, all weak coffee and chewing gum. On match days officials and fans turned up and did what they'd always done. Tea bar ladies put on earns, local women made sandwiches and sausage rolls for the boardroom at half time and the crowd paid the gatemen who'd been there since Lloyd-George were a lad, paid and shuffled into their usual places to watch a bad team unless Waller was in the mood and tonight he was still injured.

At half time you could go for a piss in the open air, if you were stood on the terraces (how could I possibly put this more delicately?). These were two toilets you could use if you stood on the Kop or the Compton, built out of brick and with no roof. This, you understand, was not because the ceilings had collapsed or because vandals had nicked the slates for a laugh: they'd never had one in the first place and that place had been somewhat before the second world war was fought if I was any judge of twentieth century architecture.

If you wanted to buy good club souvenirs, you couldn't. There was a club shop, a prefab on the tiny car park for officials in front of the main stand, and in it you could buy old programmes, which I'm not knocking for a second, by the way, scarves of bog standard quality and a comb and key ring on a good day. A few years later on the Danny Baker Saturday morning show, a lad rang in from Scotland to tell the world that the Arbroath Football Club Shop was a bloke near the terracing with a suitcase. Ours was bigger, but probably had less merchandise.

I tried not to let the ramshackle, not to say 'couldn't be bothered if it all ends up in the knackers yard' nature of Chesterfield Football Club make a dent in my joie de vivre: my life had recently taken on a new and vital purpose through this institution, after all. I tried to concentrate on the romantic quality of what I found when I went to Saltergate. There was certainly a historical charm about the matchday experience, but this was a less careful, loving preservation of a way of life which could still offer timeless pleasure to its devotees than the almost pitiful decay of a part of the country's culture worth cherishing for as long as possible.

However, I think I could have put these worries that gnawed at the outer edges of my comfort blanket for a long time, were it not for my collision that night with the future: the future for many football fans, including me. In the club shop that night on a back shelf I saw a small, insignificant looking little magazine with blue and black writing on the front cover and a small black and white photo. This little stick of dynamite was to change my life. Put pretentiously, it was to be my glory and my nemesis and, whether I like the fact or not, it filled most of my free waking thoughts for the next nine years. It had a name, artistically displayed in vertical style from the bottom up in the shape of a local church. It was The Crooked Spireite.

A football fanzine.

10

The Roar Of The Crooked Spireites

**'They remind me of children, With a faith so simple,
With a faith so gigantic.'**

Brian Patten

To say that an 'independent fans magazine' was something I was looking out for is to say that British prisoners in Jap camps in World War Two would have been mildly interested in the appearance of Yankee Stadium loads of GIs on the far horizon. One thing holding back my attempt at becoming a satisfied, as well as proven Chesterfield football supporter was a chronic lack of information about the team's performances and all the peripheral gossip and rumour surrounding it, especially while I was still living in the south.

To try to make good the deficit, I was 'sad' enough to try to empty a baffled barman at the social club of the Chesterfield supporters' organisation of all he knew about the current state of the team as often as I could without wearing out his fund of goodwill.

I was in such a bug-eyed frenzy to get my head filled with knowledge that it didn't cross my mind for a second that anyone remotely connected to the club could be any less besotted with the team and its attempts to stave off relegation than I was.

I thought once I'd established that the bar-keep was a) a fan and b) not run off his feet serving customers, we'd have an engrossing conversation up and running in seconds about the difficulty of playing centre halves in midfield, Lee Rogers' in-growing toenail and the chances of getting at least a point at Grimsby. And I would be one happy chappy for, say, an hour afterwards until I started worrying about whether anyone was going to come in for Dave Waller on transfer deadline day, thus stealing our passport to third division survival.

Ian, the name of said barman, was not ready for an exchange of verbal inconsequencialities at that stage of his life (often a Monday lunchtime, so you can hardly blame him), with a bloke from London claiming to be a Town fan who he no doubt thought was a plain idiot. My needs were simple: an obsessive local who saw fifty Chesterfield games a season with verbal diarrhoea and a degree in Football Analysis. A cross between Arsene Wenger, Bill Shankly and Stephen Fry would have been just about perfect.

I was to feel frustrated and short-changed. Ian fitted the fifty game a season description but saw football, and I daresay life, in simple terms and was as tight lipped a talker as a cabinet minister with three teenage mistresses and a part time job as a drag act. As the weeks of that fateful season slid by I brooded and moped all week and waited for the Saturday results for all the world as if they were exam results in August. Until I saw the Crooked Spireite sitting there in the club shop like a book of answers to the mysteries of life that is.

The birth of what might reasonably be called 'the fanzine movement' can be attributed to the crisis the game went through in the mid-80s. The Heysel Stadium Disaster, the Bradford Fire, the widespread hooligan problem, the attempt made by Margaret Thatcher to force fans to carry ID cards, the catastrophic fall in attendances and the vast contempt in which the game was held by most so-called opinion formers caused a suffocating miasma of pessimism to surround football. This grievous situation produced a reaction from a certain kind of fan that was inevitable, in retrospect. Sooner or later, fans who cared desperately for their clubs and this football way of life, whose spirits weren't crushed, who possessed some initiative and who knew which way up to put a typewriter, were bound to fight back.

The punk music phenomenon of the 1976-78 period was hugely catalytic, not only in encouraging the nation's youth of that era to work up a healthy 'bollocks to the establishment' attitude, but also in practically inventing this thing called a 'fanzine,' an instant, energetic, roar of home made passion and enthusiasm in writing (and pictures). These were small stars of fiery energy which burned themselves out quickly, but the impression they made and the example of their existence was pricelessly not forgotten by the blokes who founded the first football fanzines, like Mike Ticher's avowedly national When Saturday Comes, which poked its head above football's muddy surface in March 1986.

There is possibly no better voice to listen to than Ticher's if you need to understand precisely from what wellspring of thought and emotion the first fanzines were born:

'You could say that When Saturday Comes was created to provide a crusading voice for previously unheard football supporters at a time of momentous change. But you'd be lying. It really began as a form of catharsis. Clearly the game in Britain was in a terrible state, yet the football authorities seemed complacent and out of touch, and the football press let them get away with it.

Not only were there few places where serious issues, such as ground con-
ditions and racism, were properly addressed, nor was there any acknowledge-
ment of football's life away from the spotlight - not just on the terraces, but also
in the lower divisions of the league.'

He also vividly describes early fanzines' primordial production methods:

'Articles were typed with little or no regard for column widths, headlines
were Letrasetted or worse, and photos plundered from books, with everything
undergoing several reductions on the photocopier to make it fit, after a fash-
ion. It wasn't deliberately amateurish, just amateur.'

Which is just how I liked the first manifestations of the genre I saw:
magnificent in their raw, bedroom produced glory.

'An independent supporters' magazine' is like calling Marilyn
Monroe's chest a pair of child milk-providers. It was a football fanzine (I
hesitate here to give you an adequate description of Marilyn's bust), a
place where fans could say exactly what they liked about footballers,
directors, other clubs and other clubs' fans. If they wanted to call the
team's number one striker a useless donkey with the skill of a dead moose
they could. If they thought that all Mansfield fans were the product of
incestuous relationships and that it was axiomatic that Wrexham fans,
being Welsh all fucked sheep on their time off, they could, and of course,
often did.

If you wanted to be somewhat more political about your football,
rather than just do it for the fun involved in taking the satire out of things
and key individuals, you could rail against the prison camp fences that
had been put up everywhere now to keep fans off pitches or exorbitant
ticket prices and be more of a campaigning outfit. At York City, a bunch
of fans were getting together to start a mag that would help them campaign to raise cash for a roof over their heads, for example. Or you could
do both.

One of the best things about fanzines were their names. 'Brian Moore's
Head (looks uncannily like the London Planetarium)' is undeniably the
most quotable and quoted - even if it was a straight nick from a song by a
band of crazed loons from Birkenhead called Half-Man, Half Biscuit - but
it wasn't the best. I preferred Dumbarton's The Gibbering Clairvoyant,
Kettering's Poppies At The Gates Of Dawn and Dover Athletic's Rhodes
Boyson - Oo's Ee Play For?, though there were many other fine and funny
examples of the type. Call me biased, but Basson's own combination of
local identifying landmark and team nickname was, I have always
thought, a peach.*

To open up a fanzine was to be released from the tedium of football coverage on the BBC where, on the radio and the telly, every referee was fair and competent, all the players nice young men you could take home to mum and Liverpool fans knew everything about football and could all keep a crowd the size of Trafalgar Square on VE night rolling in the aisles til dawn with laughter. ITV was the same only tacky looking and with adverts. It was also to be released from the insufferable boredom of club programmes where the life of every league club was given a Disney gloss of unreality, where most manager's notes (every programme had a manager's column and they were all, bar one, utterly dreadful**) were ghost written and all the players were the happiest they'd ever been at any club and success was just around the corner if only the current injury crisis would go away.

The Cold War was still supposed to be rattling along in its usual jolly way, but in terms of the football media in England (and Scotland from what I found out from Scottish fanzines) we might as well have been stuck on the other side of the iron curtain too reading the Pravda sports section and watching Soviet Match Of The Day. The fanzines now exploding upon the British football scene proved that a whole other world existed out there on the terraces. Corrupt club chairmen were out-ed or were pilloried for being mean or dictatorial with their fans. Players performing lazily or ineptly were held up to public ridicule, especially those from the past considered to be particularly dreadful, who might turn up in a series called 'They Disgraced The Hoops'. Managers were treated with more respect than players but it was a marginal thing. Those who deserved none got none and of those there were many.

A good fanzine back then was a little freedom of information act all by itself. You could pick one up of another club and if it was well written one edition of twenty-four pages could make you feel you'd been watching

---

*Half-Man Half-Biscuit were a neo-punk genius-comedy band who, though I never heard their music won a place in my heart for refusing to play the seminal 80s TV music programme The Tube which only went out live because it clashed with a normal Tranmere Rovers Friday night league game. No greater love for his football team can a man or woman have, in my opinion, when an appearance in front of a national audience for the first time would have doubtless furthered their career no end and made them a bob or two. How can you argue with a band which calls a song 'Fucking Hell! It's Fred Titmus!' either.

** The exception was Colin Murphy of Lincoln City whose notes were like trying to sprint through a three feet depth of porridge: sentences weren't so much mangled as choked to death with cake mix. E.G. from 17.3.90: 'Everything is taking shape, but the shape is a big shape. By normal precedent shape of the league table at this stage of the season is indicative to a small portion of Clubs being in the race for honours.' It's best if we stop right there.

them all season. To me the people who wrote these things were as cool as Keith or Lou or David and the editors as near as dammit the men who were piloting the universe to a better and safer place.

More to the point, they formed an actual movement, for goodness sake, that - and I think this was clearly apparent at the time - was steadily re-shaping the mind-set of millions of fans. How far this effect would change, or moreover, preserve all that the fan saw as best in the game remained to be seen.

When I got my first Crooked Spireite back home and settled down to start filling up the gently floating gargantuan spaces in my CFC education, it didn't matter that it wasn't a burn the palace down and hang the board of directors by their dangly sections half way up the twisted steeple* sort of fanzine. It was an 'erudite club programme meets mischievous working class kid writing a university underground DIY mag' sort of publication. Its editor and certainly ex-working class kid was Stuart Basson, a quiet, curly haired, overweight genius (overweight, but he'd enjoyed almost every drop of beer that put him there) with a restrained sense of outrage about the places where the doings and sayings of those who ran the club crossed the interests of the fans. His helpers consisted entirely of, indeed, those who had a year before produced an award-winning club programme but whose editor had fallen out with the club because of a row over production values: the writers had some.

The editor-founder's reason for breathing life into his particular baby, unlike Ticher's was based squarely and absolutely upon events at his club, rather out of a despair for the game in general, though the two are connected in a Siamese way. As he was to write in a fanzine compilation a few years later:

' 'So we'll have it ready for the Mansfield game', says I. At that moment a brick came through the window of the pub where we had met to finalise the publishing of The Crooked Spireite. 'Who wants to do the bit about crowd trouble?'

We had first talked of setting up a Chesterfield fanzine a few months before it hit the streets on January 1st 1988. We were appalled at the way the club was going down hill so quickly, with seemingly no-one prepared to (or aware how to) pull on the brakes. Our board consisted of a solicitor, a builder, and tax exile; they would be our first targets.'

As it turned out, the board resigned twixt drawing board and printer pick-up, but it didn't stop issue 1 from appearing. Inside, an outlay of 30p got you an editorial, articles on club crests, the need for a new national

---

* Did I tell you that there's a saying in Chesterfield that goes, 'the spire will untwist itself the next time a virgin gets married in the church?

stadium in the midlands, the first in a strip-cartoon series (called Bryan of The Boro), a cut out whistle, a page of moaning at Sunderland fans, fanzine reviews, the editor's resolutions for the year ahead, away fan details for up-coming games including pub recommendations and a report on a Chesterfield game from a local paper in 1892 which worked as a critique of the local Derbyshire rags as well as being quite wonderful in itself. And if that wasn't enough, the middle four pages gave you the first installment of a season by season club history, beginning with Chesterfield Town's first league foray in 1891-2.

If his first love was history, Stuart's genius lay in his Private Eye-style photo-bubble covers, many of which were magnificent examples of instant visual-cerebral wit. The cover of the first edition, from two months previous, saw a picture of local rivals Derby County's manager of the time, Arthur Cox, plastered in scarves on the day his team were promoted to the first division. Stu had subverted this by putting a mock-headline above him announcing, 'Cox In New Derby Job Shocker' and shoving a bubble in his gob with the words, 'buy as scarf, pal?' inside it.

My proudly owned copy of issue 2 saw Clark Kent pulling aside his shirt to reveal his Superman undervest with the banner 'Newport's New Manager!' emblazoned above his head in large lettering. Newport County were on the way to crashing out of the football league with a bang heard in space at that moment in time, and, as it turned out, not even a grand coalition of Superheroes had a chance of saving them.

Now. To you, those two examples of the Basson Art might not even have pulled the dustcover off your smallest chuckle-muscle, but in the context of the world of football in 1988, I promise you, it was like having the cast of Monty Python, The Young Ones or The Marx Brothers performing in your living room and staying for tea afterwards. The sudden availability of such satire was so risqué, discovering that a sub-culture of glorious entertainment was emerging in one's midst was a hugely exciting thing: apart from a prototype fanzine of legendary proportions, Foul! in the mid-seventies, if you wanted to follow football in the media it was the patronising outpouring of the party machine or nothing.

It is extraordinary when you stop and think about it, that the audience television football was aimed at was presumed to be not so much unsophisticated as educationally sub-normal. The broad mass of fans were assumed to be Neanderthal terraced chanters and street brawlers, middle or old aged men with whippets (north of the Trent), middle or old aged men too busy washing their car on a Saturday to watch the football preview (south of the Trent) and children who just wanted to watch the goals.

I'd watched every morsel of what little televised football there was on

the box since I was a kid and I suppose like everyone else I'd been worn
down by the grey wall of patronising propaganda over the years. Until I
came face to face with The Crooked Spireite I had never imagined a world
where the football media could give me laughter and intellectual stimulation all in the same package. With the coming of the fanzine, football
crossed over a rubicon and joined the part of my head where P.G.
Wodehouse and Stephen Bochco sang songs by The Blue Nile in the setting sun before retiring to watch mid-period Woody Allen films. Football
had previously been removed since childhood to a cupboard under the
stairs with a sign saying 'My Childhood - Irrelevant.' I celebrated this
event unconsciously for months and months, perhaps even years. Like
minded people all over the UK did the same, without doubt. One of the
reasons that early fanzines were so good is that the first editors and writers, who quickly shared their work among themselves, could hardly
believe that the huge stack of knowledge of the game they possessed could
now be used, sprung on to a waiting fan base who gobbled it up in handfuls. The first Crooked Spireite sold out in about twenty minutes without
any advanced advertising.

The fact that a network of supporters who all agreed that pictures of
footballers' haircuts from the year 1970 were unconditionally funny existed then. released a surge of energy and excitement which fuelled the pio-
neers for the three or four years at least, before routine set in and it began
to feel like work.

And thanks to Stuart Basson, Chesterfield fans were now connected to
the zeitgeist, while the editor of The Crooked Spireite busied himself with
typewriter, paper, paste and scissors having already helped to create it.

As the CS quickly moved through editions three and four that late
winter and early Spring of 1988, the team began to slide towards the oblivion of the fourth division of the football league. Between the cuffing
Bristol City gave us and a trip to mighty Sunderland a month later, our
ragged collection of old never-made-its and young never-woulds had won
one game out of six - against the rock bottom club York - and lost four.
The other point had only been nicked off another band of relegation fighters, Grimsby. We stood, or rather lay, semi-prostrate, third bottom of the
table, three points behind the next club Aldershot. Above them were
another three clubs only one point better off than the Shots, so there were
teams as bad as us out there. This was a comfort: the problem was, we had
to pull back a four point deficit on at least two fellow strugglers in six
games because we had the worst goal difference. On the last day of the season, that 10-0 day of September murder could sink us.

The next game up was one we had to win at all costs. Thankfully it

was against a team who were to football what Dame Judy Dench is to baseball that season: Aldershot. If we couldn't knock them over we deserved
to go down. A few days before, I'd made it up to Sunderland in the Easter
holidays. After watching games among sleepy crowds in tiny grounds,
Roker Park, Sunderland was like a child's trip to the London lights: twenty thousand fans, big stands with nice flecks of red paint splashed here and
there, and really bright floodlights, as if we lower league clubs could only
afford rows of miners' lamps for illumination. The evening was warm and
spring-like in the gathering dusk and all in all, this was as atmospheric as
football can ever get. This is what I felt about the occasion when I eventually got there, anyway.

Unfortunately, the supporters club coaches had had one of their typical disasters on the A1 with Bilshaw's Coaches, Chesterfield's cheapest and
scraggiest, and we arrived at five to eight, nearly half an hour late. This is
crap enough when a game only lasts for ninety minutes, but Roker Park
was the big trip of the season. Even worse, I'd missed Waller score twice
in ten minutes to put Town 2-1 up. I didn't know whether to shout in triumph or bite myself. As we paid to get in, we heard a roar above us, but
couldn't be sure who'd scored. It seemed loud enough to be Sunderland,
but it had been our second. We were stupefied upon receiving this news:
we couldn't possibly win at Sunderland.

Despite being a league game, where we stood in the ground the atmosphere was like a cup tie. Though nominally fallen on the criminally hard
times of division three - a tremendous ignominy for one of the games
supposedly giants, though it was all becoming a bit of an historical thing
- they were as good as promoted back to two already. So visiting the home
of the virtual champions in their grand surroundings from the relegation
zone we felt like non-league underdogs who'd made it to the third round*.
And here we were ahead: not the natural order of things. 'The travelling
Spireites were pinching themselves at that stage, hardly daring to believe
the 2-1 scoreline,' as the match report in a later club programme recorded.

We were laughing manically on our spot on the Roker End, the usual
fenced off parcel of terrace for the away fans. There's something about
being ahead in a game you're supposed to lose and lose easily, a feeling of
naughtiness that puts you back in the classroom again giggling, nervous

---

* Third Round of the FA Cup. It is considered an enormous achievement for a
non-league club to reach this stage of a competition most of them begin in August,
the first of five qualifying rounds. In round 3 the Premiership and First Division
clubs enter the proceedings, the surviving non-leaguers having met up with the
second and third division clubs for rounds 1 and 2.

that teacher will find out that you've glued Fatty Harrison's skirt to her chair. I'd fallen in again with a bloke I'd met on the train going back into London from the Southend game a few weeks previously. He closely resembled Terry Collier from The Return Of The Likely Lads: he'd just come out of the army, had got divorced and wore a permanent sense of outrage at the Fates who spun the world on its axis every day just so's he could be miserable. But he loved his football, loved Chesterfield and had a useful sense of humour. Every time the Sunderland fans in the paddock just across the way made a noise he'd shout, 'Why don't you fook off back to your whippets, ya Mackems.'

I hadn't the faintest idea why he called them 'Mackems' - probably some choice piece of army slang picked up on service in Africa or somewhere that means 'camel-shagger,' I assumed, though why not have whippet-shagged and have done with it? - but he had the natural timing of the good comic, so that even when he said things like, 'it'll be half time in a minute' your face was on the verge of breaking out into a loud snort of mirth. Mind, the Mackem stuff wore a bit thin second half, as the game got more tense: 2-2 with twenty-five minutes to go, twenty, fifteen, fourteen, thirteen...my army companion screamed more and more hysterically at their fans, at all of them now, as if even the vast sea of faces at the Fulwell End a hundred and twenty yards away could all hear him, 'You fookin' bastard Mackems, fook off back 'ome to shag ya moothers, ya dirty fookin' Mackem bastard, fookin' Mackems*!' he screamed as the red and white shirts attacked our goal at their home end with increasing intensity and confidence.

'Aah, fook it,' said Army in resigned disgust, his sails now fully bereft of wind, as their third goal was coolly slotted in with twelve minutes to go. I'd seen enough football in the last year now, twenty matches, to know when a team had lost and we had. We'd not mounted an attack since half time and after thirty minutes of constant defending you can't get a rhythm going again just like that: not while they're at the top and we're at the bottom. It was over.

At what seemed like three in the morning our bus hobbled into a motorway services in the bleary eyed dark, probably somewhere near Carlisle knowing Bilshaw's sense of direction. As we queued up for a drink

---

* A Mackem is a person from Sunderland, so called because the working people of the town (now city) used not to say make as in bake, as in 'if you don't shut up you sheep-shagger (fans of the two Derbyshire professional clubs are occasionally referred to thus), I'll come over there and make you.' Rather they say 'mack' as in tin-tack as in 'bligh-me, me former Giyils are macking mescratch me-sell lack ah've got a flea sorchus practussn oop me trowsers, man'.

of hot chemicals and a chronically overpriced bun, there was Jim Brown, our goalie (who also doubled as the club's commercial director: that's how modern an outfit we were), paying for his cuppa.

"Ey-oop, Jim, bad look, t'naight,' said a respectful voice, 'boot wee still in't shit aren't we.'

'Och, don't worry, lads,' replied our one ex-international player - 1 cap, Scotland v Rumania, 1974 (every home should have one) - without making eye-contact. For the first time, and certainly not the last, I noticed with surprise how afraid footballers are of their fans. Jim had been worried less someone in the colours had said, 'Huh! Brahn! Ya yooseless setta bastards, we've lost again. Weeas good as relegated; thanks ya scotch prat!'

Jim of all people could've relaxed: he was the most liked of all the players, loved almost and as likely to hear this sort of thing as he was likely to hear the words,

'And the winner of the best actor award is...Jim Brown!' at the Oscars. He'd played a lot of games for us in two spells (210 and scored one goal) and was the nicest, but the nicest and most honourable of men you could ever wish to meet.

His optimism was a weapon against the wounds fans could inflict upon a player's ego, but I hadn't sussed this at the time. As I sat on the coach again I took him on face value and wondered how on earth he could be so cheerful and unaffected by another defeat. We were on the cusp of disaster and his body language said 'it's alright fellas, the championship trophy will be ours by Saturday tea-time, all we have to do against Sheffield Primary School For Blind Girls is get a draw: I think we can swing that, ha-ha.'

Saturday against Aldershot we needed three points or it's doom and at almost a quarter to five we were level and we hadn't scored in eighty-seven minutes of honest but fretted trying. We were cramped up with tension on the Compton terracing, ill with suppressed emotion. Tick-tock, tick-tock, look at the watch, look up at the game and will the lads forward, we have to score. But we haven't and people have gathered on the top step of the terrace in a big group for a quick getaway as they always do and the ref surely is going to blow any second and we're as good as gone to the land of the hopeless, stinking, alcoholic vagrant that is the Fourth Division.

Then a cross from the left and Sir David Waller is at the far post in front of the Kop and he dives low to head in his 21st goal of the season. 1-0. The fans around me are throwing themselves about in an outpouring of pure amphetamine emotion that would not have disgraced a Who gig circa 1966 or have run up to the fence at the front, climbed up and are now screaming and yelling like wildmen. 'Army' has run off roaring like the jungle fighter he thankfully never had to be, somewhere into his own private ecstasy. I am yelling too and laughing like a fool and wondering at the same moment how I could possibly not have spent the last fifteen years of my life not watching football.

A red shirt kicks off again and we calm down and worry for a bit then one long peep on J. Rushdon's Acme Thunderer and there's as big a roar as a crowd of 1800 Town fans can make and we're still in there, still fighting.

The rest as they say....we had to wait ten days to play again but when we did we beat Brentford at home in another completely and utterly vital game. At 9.40 that night after not being able to concentrate on anything for three hours I rang the club.

Brrrring, brrrring. Click.

'Hello, Chesterfield Football Club,' said a gruff northern accent.

'Um, hello, could you tell me the score tonight please?'

'2-1.'

'Who to?'

'Chesterfield.'

'Really?' I couldn't believe this. We couldn't possibly win again. Not my team. Not when we need to with the desperation of drowning sailors in a freezing ocean.

'Yes. 2-1 to Chesterfield.'

I composed myself to notice something steely and authoritative in the voice down the other end of the line.

'Who am I speaking to, please?'

'Kevin Randall, the manager.'

'Oh, er, erm, um...oh, right, well: brilliant, well done. Fantastic! G'night.' And I put the phone down shaking with excitement. I had spoken to a real, live English football club manager for the first time in my life. This for me was a conversation with royalty. I could now see how someone face to face with the Queen of England could lose their tongue. I'd just crumpled up words in my mouth and dribbled them out like a moron. Amazing. I rushed to find Louise, as far as you can rush anywhere in a shoebox: turn a two second rush into three and you collide with something and fall over.

'Louise! That was Kevin Randall, the manager! I just spoke to Chesterfield's manager!'

'Well done, dear,' she replied, patting me on the head like a schoolboy. She always did know the best way to deal with me in this kind of state.

The miniature fairy story went on for another three weeks. We inexplicably won at Wigan who were virtually in the play offs straight after

Brentford, but drew 0-0 with Chester at Saltergate. I didn't make it to either of those but travelled to Blackpool who we climbed all over but lost to by one goal. We made great chances on a day where a win would have made us safe with just one game to go, but why give fans a chance to celebrate early and watch the last game of a long, curving, disintegrating highway of a season in peace?............ (The loss made me gloomy, but I still thought, 'Blackpool..to see Town..This is very, very groovy. This is what real fans do. I still couldn't get over it.)......better to set up a Hollywood v Art Movie ending where you turn up like twelve stones of nervous wreckage not knowing whether death or glory awaits you at the end of the afternoon.

As it turned out, the afternoon of Chesterfield v Fulham was a little anti-climactic. Waller, of course, scored in the early minutes of frantic excitement, Fulham soon had a man sent off, then another in the second half, then the manager, then his assistant, and we held on quite easily. At kick off five teams were competing for the last relegation place: we could win and still go down, but it was hardly likely that six motley collections of badly paid, just about professional footballers would all win amid such fraught anxiety. We stayed up, don't worry.

At the end, we were ready to run on and cuddle the players like long lost relatives. At least, I was. But there was just one wild roar of pleasure mixed with relief, and the players, far from rushing to the crowd to accept our joy and gratitude, just embraced one another quickly, looked sheepish, clapped a bit, and walked off. Just like that. It wasn't enough and it never is. The blue backs disappear down under the stand out of sight and you don't even know whether they'll still be there again next season, though you know you will.

What should happen is this. Tables full of food and drink should be brought out onto the pitch, those in the crowd who want to should come onto the grass (or what's left of it by May) and start in on the comestibles, followed by the players and officials, who then mingle with the fans chatting amiably and earnestly - with the odd joke or two of course, 'remember that penalty you gave away at Northampton, Nobby, hah-hah!' - and we can all reflect on what has been nine whole months of our lives: watching, thinking, talking and breathing 'Town.' Then we can all say our goodbyes, first passing on our inadequate thanks to Dave Waller for his goalscoring prowess, and go our separate ways for the summer, helping out with the washing up first before we take our leave on the finest place on earth, our home ground.

Top idea though this is, what happens is we all go home to own little anti-climax, hanging up the scarf for three months and wonder what the friggin' hell we're going to do with all that time and all that wide open space in our heads where all our football thinking used to be but which is now a static-humming void. The players wonder about transfers to better (or worse) clubs and think about two weeks in Marbella. The board of directors drink their last glass of whisky with their counterparts in the boardroom and think about the golf course, the villa in the West Indies and their private business affairs that have no pauses during the financial year. The good ones worry about the team for next season and finalise their thinking about making good the shortfall from the deals they make to get the five new players the club needs to stay up again, out of their own pockets.

The bad ones think, 'this club's not getting another penny out of me,' enjoy the kudos of being a member of an elite national club of only 92 and pour another drop of Scotch into the glass. No-one inside the portals of the football club that afternoon gives a thought to the fans, without whom there is no wage packet and no shares, and who will still be turning up at Saltergate whatever is offered at whatever price, long after the chairman has sold out for a profit or is six feet under in his box.

11

To Build Me A Cooker

'Show me a hero and I will write you a tragedy'
F. Scott Fitzgerald

By the time the next long march through a football season began I had arrived in the promised land. In August 1988 I became C.W.Thomas, resident of Derbyshire, northern England. Ppfff if some people called it the Midlands. Midlands, indeed. Birmingham was the Midlands. Northampton, Stoke. Chesterfield was twelve miles from Sheffield, once the steel and grime capital of the north. Are you telling me that anywhere a dozen miles from that lot is the Midlands? Say that to my wife and she'll do a country dance on your head in her pit boots.

So there I was, ensconced in the Promised Land of easy football. A bus ride from Saltergate. The Eternal Siren of Football, plump with her motherlode of fifty games a season beckoned me like Helena Bonham-Carter in a blue scarf carrying the 'Spire Review'. She is not someone you turn down.

Next season 'The Woll' again gave me an excuse for reverence. Eventually, when he recovered from a late Summer injury he was brilliant, and I mean that. He equalled the club record for goals scored in consecutive games, eight, and ended the season with a tally of 18 league goals from 36 games including 16 in the last 22, when he really found his form. And he nearly got me into a fight.

We were fighting relegation again, it was March 25th 1989 and we were at home to hated, loathed rivals from twelve miles up the road, Sheffield Urinals (United to most people). I was up in the Saltergate main stand when just before kick off four lads in their early twenties came swaggering in and sat down in the row in front of me, five seats to my right. They began taking the piss out of the ragged surroundings they were forced to endure to watch their red and white heroes and one stood up to join in a song from the terrace to our right.

At this, a woman immediately behind the Urinal youth told him to sit down, and she received this warm, generous reply:

'Fook off, you silly cow,' and this far-sighted genius of the age sneered derisively at the lady who was well into her sixties.

Now, you already know that by the time I was thirty I'd won the International Coward Of The Year award so many times they'd given me the trophy and told me not to come back because it wasn't fair on the others. But there is a limit, even for supreme champions. My hackles were raised. I almost said something, but thought better of it. The issue rumbled on for half an hour like an appendix, before full blown peritonitis exploded in the thirty-fifth minute: we scored: Dave Waller.

Like most Town fans I was very fired up for and by the occasion. Though a soft southerner I had heard enough about the long standing rivalry between the two clubs over the previous weeks and months to feel pumped up with adrenalin as I'd never been before. I'd also had a taste of what it meant for the Spireites to beat Sheff' United because we'd been to Bramhall Lane in January and against all the odds beat them 3-1 (we were bottom of the table at the time, they were on their way to promotion). After each goal and at the end, more Town fans than the entire crowd for that Aldershot game I was telling you about, went into frenzies of celebration, and that day I truly learned what it meant when football fandom was described as a tribal phenomenon.

So when the first Waller goal went in - oh yes: there were two and the second one was the winner - I stood up, waved the large trilby I was wearing in the air and whooped like a caricature red Indian as loudly as I possibly could to wind these prats up like a clock: not difficult in the circumstances. The adrenal gland was pumping the stuff out of my brain and it was now surging round my system like you wouldn't believe. I looked to my right-front and two of the four were looking very sharp daggers straight at me and one said,

'You're fookin' dead, you,' while the other joined in,

'We'll see you outside, afterwards.'

I - and this just isn't me, this is football - laughed in their faces.

Now, before you get the wrong idea, I had rapidly worked out the dynamics of the situation over the previous half hour. They were far enough away not to be able to try to hit me without having a couple of quite large obstacles in their way, i.e. men, who were Town supporters. And if they tried to climb into my row to start something I calculated that I could squeeze past other fans' legs at least as quickly as them and reach safety. I also had the supreme advantage of being among friends, they being among enemies. If there was a chase across the stand there was a fair chance that one or two likely lads up there would do something to, shall we say, impede their progress.

Because here's the thing: they weren't that hard. You can spot the ones who really mean business because you can see it in their eyes, a coldness that says 'I hit people.' This bunch had 'Mum, can you take my library books back' in theirs. Leastways, they weren't the real thing. They were too noisy, too brash. They'd come into our main stand and had a quick look at all the sensible folk around them and thought, 'we can do what we like 'ere.' Only they couldn't. The woman who'd been jeered at, and a few others nearby had summoned a steward to complain when the 'ard boys kept standing up each time United attacked. A yellow bib had duly shown up and told the boys to behave and they had. So, I thought it unlikely they'd really be the type to beat me to a pulp at the end of the match. It was funny, I felt very secure surrounded by even mostly the well-to-do end of the Chesterfield support. Most comforting, it was. Anyway, if things reached a bit of an awkward climax at ten-to-five, I knew the exits far better than they did and the ones at the front of the stand led straight to the main body of Town fans on the terraces where any number of locals, fathers included, would have been most happy to stick a boot up the arses of four spoiled, overgrown only children from up the road.

It was true though, the occasion got to me, and I lost a lot of my fear of combat. Here were these people insulting the flag, and I was overcome by the need to stand up and be counted. When the Urinals equalised they gesticulated at me and I looked straight back, poked my tongue out at them and made a face which just said, 'Bollocks.'

When Waller put in the decisive goal with only eight minutes to go I just stood up, looked at the pitch where a mass of blue shirts had gone into a huddle and clapped my hands so hard they hurt. I ignored our four visiting friends for the time being. For the final minutes they just sat and sulked and at the whistle disappeared from whence they came.*

So that's what football heroes can do to you, nearly get you into big trouble. I should tell you however, that the cause of events that day wasn't so much Mr Waller, but the man who was, I think, inspiring him to great things at the time, manager Paul Hart. He became, I'm afraid to say, my Chesterfield hero number two.

Kevin Randall had gone the day Preston North End became the latest in a long line of clubs to humiliate us at Saltergate. Wolves were the first, then Blackpool, then Bury, then Preston. Away from home we

---

* Just for the record, the result that day kept in tact an unbeaten home record against the Urinals which had lasted for 38 years. It now stands at the time of writing at 50, perhaps principally because we haven't been in the same division since and haven't met each other in the cup.

were easy meat for Bristol City (0-4), Northampton (0-3), Port Vale (0-5) and Notts County (0-4) in consecutive games. The week before Randall was sacked we somehow got an away win at where else but Gillingham. This was the perversity and unpredictability of the game at work plus the fact that the players were prepared to give everything to avenge the savage humiliation of the previous year. Additionally, this wasn't the same Gills of twelve months before. Can you believe this: of the managers involved in Gillingham 10 Chesterfield 0, the gaffer of the former club, not the latter, had been the first one to get the pink slip? What possessed the Kent blues, in many respects a southern mirror image of CFC, to rid themselves of the seemingly excellent Keith Peacock heaven only knows, but they had.

Kevin Randall had been understandably tormented by the memory of the Mullering ever since, and had sported a black armband at the club on the anniversary, to the bafflement and dismay of the players still at Saltergate: the last thing they needed was a reminder of the event. Obviously, some know how to motivate and others don't.

Which brings us to Paul Hart. His appointment to the job of manager was the result of an interview process where he shone. And how could he have done anything else with his pedigree? He had been an excellent centre-half at Leeds United, Nottingham Forest and Sheffield Wednesday principally, though not quite outstanding: he won no England caps. He was a central defender in the classic mould: tall, powerful,* terrific in the air and as tough as an Aeroflot rissole. He was the sort of player that if an opposing forward had ever got mad with him for being dominated all game, lost it, bit off the whole of his nose and spat it onto the floor, Hartie would have just picked it up, wiped it on his shirt, slapped it back on his face and got on with the game. Might carefully chin said forward behind the ref's back at the next opportunity, but essentially, as I said, get on with the game.

He also came with a junior partner, one Chris McMenemy whose father was the famous Lawrie**, and if I know anything about small

* For this read: 'built like a brick shit house.'
** Lawrie McMenemy was one of the most famous managers of the seventies and early eighties, achieving much success with Southampton where he won an FA Cup and promotion. He went on to Sunderland where he suffered a conspicuous lack of glory, and turned up later as assistant to Graham Taylor in his England days. He can be seen on 'that' video, making himself as scarce as possible, doubtless embarrassed by many of Taylor's utterances (such as the wonderful, 'demand it Les........well.....yes, well you tell 'em, Les, you tell 'em!') or possibly by the presence of Taylor's parrot, Phil Neal (Taylor: 'this is a test.' Neal: 'yeah, a test.' repeat to fade).

town businessmen, this brush with a national celebrity would have been enough to clinch the deal.

Despite allowing themselves to make total nit-wits posing for the local papers holding up a Town scarf aloft between them+, an idea that was already a creative stretch for the first sports editor who wanted such a picture, I think I knew they were going to make a difference on the night of their first working day, a reserve match at Saltergate, which I hereby confess to having attended. One of our players, a very, very average defender called Paddy McGeeney, went down and stayed down. After thirty seconds or so, a couple of blokes in the long, padded coats of football-type people walked on to the sodden grass to see if they'd just lost a centre back for Saturday. The scenario announced this to those of us chewing the cud in the stand with nothing else to do on a rainy Tuesday night in November: professional. Here, obviously was a manager who was going to be totally serious, totally hands-on.

He was a hands-on-throat sort of motivator too. Even though the team lost the first game three-nothing at home, and didn't win for seven, it was quickly clear that the team were improving and this didn't happen because Paul Hart was a nice bloke. The players stopped conceding so many goals - they went back to Bolton in the cup and drew 0-0 a fortnight after getting thrashed there 5-0 in the league . In the replay we led 2-0 until a freakish back passed own goal demolished the fragile self-confidence being built by the new men. We went down in the end 3-2. That was one bad, bitter night down on the terraces. We then got a draw at Reading and led at Chester until again fading in the second half.

In the local media it emerged that players under the old regime had been getting things rather cushy. The injured, it was hinted, being kept company in the treatment room by lead-swingers, eating crisps and chocolate and reading the paper instead of working. That sounded like the Chesterfield I'd been supporting so far: it was a nice and cosy scene for everyone, but all in all a Mickey Mouse operation staffed by well-meaning non-specialists on low pay going nowhere. Obviously things were going to change from now on.

Eventually the tide turned after a terrible home defeat against Mansfield after which, rumour had it, many cups were thrown and worse. However. We drew in a lower league cup match at Notts County where Waller scored an outrageously good goal, dribbling round two defenders at speed, then the goalie before netting, then

+ Something the author was later to do himself, but that's quite another story.

beat The Shags* in the same competition at our place, Hart's first win. Christmas saw a draw with Huddersfield, before the big breakthrough against Fulham. This time we faced a top 8 club and we turned them right over 4-1. Finally it looked as though we could now go out and compete with good teams; so, although we were still bottom of the league with a paltry store of three wins from nineteen games, we had a chance of making up for lost time, a poor manager and a miserly board.

Hart improved the club in many ways. One of them was to drill a hole through the seemingly impregnable skulls of chairman Barrie Hubbard and deputy Norton Lea, and try to communicate the fact that it is impossible to run anything but a hopeless, failing football club on a shoestring budget. Most of the fans knew this, but football directors are slower than your below average Fred Blenkinsop in the street and have to be led to the punchline carefully and slowly. Once you're there, you come to the hardest part: getting them to part with some of their cash. It's a known fact the more brass we have the more we want to protect it, and if it's hard for the likes of us on our meagre salaries, imagine what it must be like when you have a few million tucked away. Tough going, I'm sure you'll agree. And of course one pities these multi-millionaires greatly.

Mr J. Norton Lea, at the time an unknown power behind the Hubbard throne was a few years later thought by one player to have been worth somewhere between twenty or thirty million and apparently could be heard at the club openly boasting that he could lay his hands on a million fish within the hour. Which rather has one worrying for the poor man where he'd mislaid the other twenty-nine.

Anyhow, after spending nothing in the close season, also because apart from Waller there was no-one to sell that we'd have got more than a polystyrene carton of chips and gravy for, Paul Hart managed to get the

---

* A disparaging tag for our rival fans across the border in Nottinghamshire, Mansfield Town, whose nickname was The Stags, after a county emblem. Rivalry between the two sets of fans was intensified in 1985 during the miners' strike when Nottinghamshire miners formed a breakaway union, defecting from Arthur Scargill's National Union of Mineworkers. The new union did a deal with Margaret Thatcher, she promising to guarantee the future of Nottinghamshire pits in return for a no-strike agreement. Inevitably, after the Conservatives closed the majority of the pits in Lanarkshire, Durham, Yorkshire, South Wales, Kent, Leicestershire and Derbyshire, soon after the striking miners returned to work in the spring of '85, Thatcher's successor John Major wiped the Notts pits from the map of industrial Britain also. Town fans still nurse a grievance against Mansfield fans - the home of the new union was in the town - however unfairly, and still remind them of the fact during derby matches.

moth spray onto one or other of the two wallets to get £90 000 for a new centre-half. He was Tony Brien, as quick over the ground as a champion greyhound and hungry for action. Hart also persuaded an excellent keeper, Steve Cherry, who was desperate for a move somewhere in the midlands or a little further north, to come to us on loan. He did and he was top class.*

So, game on. The second half of the season began on the back of three more great wins, including the totally memorable win at the Urinals. We won a string of games at home in the new year, seven out of the next ten, and no defeats. This wasn't so much dream team stuff as totally ridiculous compared with the miserable failure of the team back in the late summer/early autumn. Eight of the players were part of that mess, yet here they were able to go twelve games unbeaten at Saltergate in the league.

The trouble was, we just couldn't find the same formula away from home. Defeat followed defeat, six of them**, then a draw at last, then a fantastic win at Blackpool with Waller this time looking fully like a half a million pounds worth of class striker and scoring two great goals. Trouble was, the home form began to collapse in on itself despite Waller being now deep into his record equalling run of eight in eight games. Port Vale, about to be promoted, were too strong; against Chester anxiety caused the loss of two killer goals through a little fat man called Eamon O'Keefe, a one time big time player running rings round us in midfield.

With four games to go, we were fifth bottom. As it turned out, the other bottom of the heap battlers ended strongly: three wins from these games were needed to save us, but even Paul Hart couldn't turn cheap coal into gold. We were nowhere near our target. We lost three. We were down. It had been one hell of a ride after Hart arrived: if only it could have been sooner. If only he hadn't had to make third division footballers out of men who belonged in lower divisions. Of the total playing staff that season, only one player was sold to a club in a higher division - Bob Bloomer to Bristol Rovers, and he went down to non-league Cheltenham Town after a season or two after having played above himself for Hart. He'd inspired effectiveness out of people playing on the outer rim of their ability. However, you can only play on determination and guts for so long. Sooner

---

*Before the season started, goalkeeper Jim Brown wanted to concentrate on the club's commercial activities and persuaded Randall to let him come out of nets. His replacement, Mick Astbury was either one of the worst goalies of all time or one who'd had the biggest loss of nerve of all time. Said Dave Waller the following season, 'we were a bit worried when he started training and everything was going past him: everything!'

** Astbury came back for one game: we lost 6-0 at Preston.

or later, absence of talent will do you. If Mr Chairman had shoved some loot into the transfer fund to purchase a couple of decent performers we'd have hung on: they'd have got a lot of it back in gate receipts before the season had ended: around a thousand more fans were turning up for a home game than under Randall. Asking Paul Hart to have kept us up that year, in the final analysis, was like asking Jamie Oliver to make another series of Naked Chef but telling him he had to build his own cooker.

I was still a small distance from inconsolable at the outcome. I'd walked away from the penultimate game at Mansfield knowing we were down unless Mother Mary herself came along wearing a Chesterfield enamel lapel badge, and felt very, very sorry for myself indeed. I'd been to twenty of the away games and all the home games when I wasn't ill and I was becoming known to the diehards who were regulars on the support-ers' club coach. You couldn't help but get to know people, there were so few of us going to some of the far flung places like Swansea and Southend.

My condition had deteriorated - or progressed - to confirmed addict, fast hurtling to the point where too much was simply nowhere near enough. The man I spoke to in the fresh Thames-side air at Craven Cottage two years earlier told me he'd been to every single Town game since 1981. He missed one that year because some concerned friends dragged him into hospital because he collapsed at work. It turned out to be just a virus and he was back for the next match. I wasn't like this bloke Clive, I told myself. I wasn't that bad.

Town were down but as far as was possible under the circs., I was happy. I was comforted by the knowledge that next season I would be travelling to the real heartlands of romance of the game: Halifax, Rochdale, Hartlepool. One half of me was hurting like Bambi. The other half was spilling drool down my coat.

12

Free To Legends: The Great Dave Waller.

'Micky Mills is Micky Mills and has been since the year dot.'
Bobby Robson

I started to write for The Crooked Spireite around the time Randall was sacked. I guessed from the tone of Stuart's editorials that he was keen, if not desperate for material and here was a chance to step one foot closer to Chesterfield football's inner pulse and to the sort of people who were changing the game for fans. The wider media world and the government still hated everything about the game with a passion bordering on spite: everything about it epitomised to them what was wrong with Britain: the lobotomised fans, the squalor of grounds, the seemingly moronic mono-syllabic players, the managers in stupid coats and fat egos leaving a slug's trail of cliche behind them. Every paper still had its football writers, some gamely trying to swim against an infected tide of shallow, effete, vacuous opinion formers. Out here in the wild, I tried to have as much fun as I could before it was too late.

To get in on the action I had to write something at least vaguely interesting about the club or the team: the revenge for the September Massacre seemed ideal, so I sat one afternoon at my mother-in-law's dining table and scratched myself into immortality. Or so it seemed to me at the time.

> 'Yesterday saw the laying of a ghost. Gillingham 0 Chesterfield 1. I was lucky to be one of about 25 Tahn fans there to see it. [25? Is that all we took that day? I don't remember that.] Thirteen months ago I was also present when a little piece of modern history was made - and lucky to be there too!

Oh dear, was that the best I could do? It reads now like tenth place in the Cuffley Junior School 'What I Did On My Holidays' essay competition. Despite lacking most of what made a really good piece of writing, Stuart published the feeble little blighter, thus adding to the rapidly growing body of soccer literature. The kindly soul was obviously more in need of space filler than I thought, because my bound edition of the nappy years of this esteemed organ tells me that in the next issue, no. 9, December 1988, I was responsible for an article concerning misprints of players' names in club programmes. Did I say cutting edge? Make that bandit-warrior of the terrace fan fightback!

After I'd progressed, or rather regressed even further in issue ten, polluting the environment with a 'change your anorak, not the world' piece of irrelevance about the quality of third division club programmes (zzzzzzzzz), I actually from somewhere, dragged a half-way decent idea out of my head. Player interviews. A bit obvious perhaps, but it was to be my good fortune that none of The Crooked Spireite's honest scribblers had got on to this particular pony and carved out a nice little niche for themselves. Here was the chance to get myself on the inside. It was nineteen months since I'd sat up on my little wooden seat and watched this poor little club strive pathetically to contribute something/anything useful to this dying sport, and wished myself a part of its world. And now here I was, one letter and phone call away from the door.

Where better to start than the legend himself. I wrote to Dave Waller asking for an interview in December '89 and saying give me a call if you feel you want to do it. Sure enough there was 'connection.' A few days later the phone went. Louise picked it up and turned round to look at me and said, 'Dave Waller.'

My heart stopped dead for a millisecond while my stomach froze and heated up at the same moment, realising its owner was about to come face to face - well, alright then, voice to voice - with a real, live professional footballer. Somewhere inside my consciousness, images of Spurs and Ipswich players standing still in their pitch positions observing a minute's silence for Winston Churchill and of being in tears at my uncle Len's flat because I couldn't go with the men to see the Tottenham team riding on an open-top bus with the European Cup winners cup, swam behind my surface reality in a single speck of time. This was completion. This was destiny.

The sound of a clipped Mancunian voice down the other end of the line stirred the spoon round a gurgling stomach and I tried to concentrate on sounding sober and business-like despite feeling like I was ten and speaking to George Best. I may as well have been. My nervousness shocked me. I was older than Dave Waller. Yet I had gone up to him after training one day and asked him for that autograph; deliberately walked up to the ground from the town centre, calibrating carefully my timing so as to arrive before he came out of the changing rooms to get into his car to drive home; whipped out a programme which contained a ripe photo of him scoring one of his eventual sixty-two goals for Town. There I was, one rung down on the ladder from those who chug off to Blackpool car parks on Bank Holidays collecting coach registration numbers.*

Not feeling guilty about being dry mouthed and itchy with suppressed excitement about meeting a footballer - and a lower division one on a crap wage at that - was a mighty difficult trick to pull off. I was supposed to be educated. I was supposed to have graduated beyond the need to indulge myself in such pointless exercises.

But it came to pass that I went round to Dave Waller's neat modern semi on the outskirts of town and we talked about his football career for the best part of a Sunday afternoon, which was great, let me tell you. Not only was I in the presence of a hero, but fact is, I have always been what is known technically as a nosy bastard. I wanted to be on the inside of things, not so I could show off to the three people who might have been dull enough to care that Town's left back knew who I was. Not so I could ingratiate myself in the wettest possible way in the players' lounge after a game. I wanted to do this because I wanted to understand what I was watching on a Saturday afternoon. I wanted to get an exact grasp of how matches were won and lost, what, when you were actually out on the pitch, actually turned a game. Beyond that, all I wanted to know was everything.

There was a practical purpose to this: watching a bad result and dealing with it afterwards was always pure torture. Now that I'd been to enough games for the sheer thrill and beauty of being there to have finally worn off, 0-0 home draws tormented me: why couldn't we score? who wasn't doing their job properly? should one of the centre backs come up for corners? Round and round I went, my mind circling like an aeroplane with no airport to land in. One-nil defeats away from home I could just about cope with: it was supposed to be hard to play in front of someone else's crowd. One-nil home defeats tormented me all weekend. I replayed the conceded goal in my mind night and day and tried to work out how we should have dealt with it. If Darren Wood had just been a little tighter on his marker. If Jamie had just fouled the winger instead of just letting him go past and get in a cross. To deal with such angst and ward off the inevitable depression, I needed expert information and for that, I needed to meet the people who played the game and of course, who controlled things from behind the curtain, the manager. Maybe they could tell me what I desperately wanted to hear: that Chesterfield could win every match they played. Or maybe he could slap me round the face and tell me,

---

*This is not a joke: in August 1995 I actually saw men, I hesitate to say grown, doing this, in very low quality short zip-up jackets.

'Look, son, we have to face losing football matches - you have to face it too. We don't like it any more than you do, but it's time to face up to the fact that you have to start taking it like a man.'

I didn't feel man enough to deal with Paul Hart yet, but perhaps 'the Woll' could start my healing process.

What he felt about being the centre of attention like this for once I can only imagine. If he wondered quite why an amateur hack who looked old enough to know better was spending a good Sunday rooting around the dustbins of dead matches and new training routines, he didn't let on. In fact he seemed to enjoy telling me about his early days at then eternal strugglers Crewe Alexandra, about how his fortunes rose and fell with each passing manager, how he was inexplicably frozen out two divisions higher at Shrewsbury Town and how he landed like a big Christmas present on our doorstep.

Eventually we got on to CFC, the 10-0 defeat, old managers, the new man Paul Hart, the this and the thats of the then current situation: would we stay up, would we go down? He told me many interesting things - mind, it goes completely without saying that every single thing including 'would you like a cup of coffee?' was interesting - among them this: when I asked him what the manager who snaffled him for us at Saltergate, John Duncan was like, he said, 'Very odd: some days he'd walk by you first thing in the morning and say 'hello' and everything, but others he'd just cut you dead, completely ignore you.'

Interesting.

I knew now that this was what I most wanted to do in the world: give myself up to all this knowledge of the world of football and footballers. It felt so right. This was what I was brought up on. This is where I came from. And I'd be a complete an utter liar if I didn't admit that sitting there with Dave Waller made me feel dead important. I was the only Chesterfield fan doing this, wasn't I?

I escaped much later in the afternoon with self-respect I think, intact. Not only did I not let the anorak under my jumper show itself too much or talk in the awed, grovelling manner I feared I might, I didn't spill my coffee over his nice living room carpet and didn't accidentally knock over any furniture. So, I was on the expected high when I was shown out into the gathering January darkness. My watch told me two hours and more had disappeared in the service of accruing a greater knowledge and under-standing of the great game. It must have gone well. I felt a bit odd though on the way home so I couldn't really tell.

What happened next was fortunate for my nearest and dearest. Having come through my self-appointed assignment having achieved a lifetime ambition, I would have been impossible to live with for a couple of weeks. However, that afternoon my internal organs sank into the pit of hell nestling an extremely unpleasant type of food poisoning called campilobacter. This little feller I would only wish upon my most fearsome enemy and only then coming at me with a loaded gun. If this particular case of the shits attacked them as they were on the verge of pulling the trigger, they would have to stop mid-squeeze and say, 'excuse me, I can't blow your brains out until I've found the smallest room in the house'. 'It's just upstairs', I would say. The time it would have taken them to empty their entire intestinal tract, then the contents of their stomach, which would be simultaneously flying out the other end, would enable me to make good my escape. By the time they'd then slept off the worst of the other symptoms - about four days - I could have been in another continent and already immersed in another source of gainful employment.

In my time of triumph and fulfillment, the shits. Typical. At the end of the day is that football?

I was off work for two months. I even had to miss two home matches. Somehow during this time my Waller article made it to press and my first decent contribution to the world of the fanzine reached the readership of around a thousand people. When I recovered I set about interviewing other players, and made the acquaintance of striker Andy Morris and local boy-made-footballer-made-scapegoat, Jamie Hewitt. I indulged myself hugely, uncovering more team trivia, sometimes something more substantial about the game, such as how thin the dividing line was between these people and a very ordinary job indeed. Bruno, our black, six feet five heavyweight TV star lookalike told me he wanted to get an HGV license when he quit.

The Big Catch, though, in this world of pauper journalism was of course Mr Hart himself. The timing was sticky, though. As he lifted our U-Boat from the ocean floor, there was still the long, long run in to the end of the season. With all to play for and the outcome unresolved as February became March became April, we thought we'd let the man get on with the job and not push our luck. Eventually though, we landed him. He agreed to an interview at the club. Stuart didn't fancy going mano-a-mano with such a forbidding looking man, fearing that an awkward question would have Hartie out of his seat to bust him one. So it was up to me. Fine. I really could not wait for this, and if I had any doubts, the thought of the flood of information that would, with any luck fall into my lap and the article to follow hardened my resolve. I was a big boy now anyway, for pity's sake.

So, I had a two o'clock appointment in my pocket shortly before the launch of the first post-relegation season at the football club, I knocked on the tiny office window at the main entrance to the club* on a warm, bright August day wild with trepidation and expectation. This was supposed to be an educational experience of a lifetime: an occasion which would turn my recently earned GCSE in The Game into a fast track A level. It turned out to be the start of a training course which made me into the best sixth form teacher of History on the planet.

---

*It had a sliding frosted glass panel which could be pulled up and let down, like something from a Dickens novel. There was always something very Victorian about the way the administration dealt with you. The tiny sash window said 'who are you, what d'you want? Why don't you bugger off. Sometimes the staff were like this, if they were male, that is: the women had manners. This rudeness was always at its worse when Chairman-in-waiting Norton Lea spoke to you. I always thought, 'with that big company to run, why haven't you got any work to do.' He seemed to confirm the theory that rich men became football chairmen because they were bored or needed a new set of people to push around.

13

The Man With Seven Broken Noses

'People will endure their tyrants for years, but they tear their deliverers to pieces if a millennium is not created immediately'.

Woodrow Wilson.

I have Ronald Reagan and the Russians to thank for becoming a teacher. And my own idiocy, naturally. A life of getting up in the afternoons for two and a half years, the latter part of my university 'career,' isn't a preparation for life in any way, shape or form. I eventually fulfilled Uncle Victor's aspirations for me by getting a couple of goodish grades in English and History at A level (not 'English Football' and 'the History of Football' unfortunately) which somehow persuaded Leeds University's department of the latter subject that I wouldn't be a complete waste of their time and effort if they took me on.

Being the first on either side of my family to enter the portals of such an exalted educational institution (to somewhat overstate the case, but this is what I hoped I'd just wormed my way into), I worked like an eager little terrier for nine months and got told that rather than being on the verge of being sent back to where people from my class usually belonged, I'd done very well. 'Right, I thought: I've arrived, I've made it!' I took a look around me and saw there were no exams for another two years and tried to become the most idle, wastefully subsidised long haired git I could. Only Mabel Jnr said she wouldn't let me in the house with long hair, so that last bit didn't happen.

Though my older self winces regretfully at the memory of this now, it was all rather wonderful. It was like that joke of George Best's: 'at university I stayed up til three o'clock every night playing records, playing cards, playing with girls or drinking pints: the rest I wasted.'

If you were a tax payer during the years 1976 to 1979 I apologise deeply for wasting your money. Granted I did write a few essays and eventually, rather than fail my finals, did read a small shed load of history books. And if you need to know anything about international relations between the wars (1919-39), Nazi Germany (particular propaganda meth-

ods) and the reigns of James and Charles the firsts (1603-25; 1625-49),
I'm your man. If you have a son or a daughter even now struggling with
the stuff at school, get in touch and I'll gladly lend a hand. It's the least I
can do to pay back the country for my lost two and a half years.

It was at Leeds that I met Louise. I was going out with someone else
at the time, but having the manners and self-respect of the weedy last
Viking to get to the rape and pillage, I didn't let such a trifle get in the way
of a possibly satisfying romantic liason. University students were, and still
are a wanky bunch, and quite what Louise, well, you know the modest
drivel I'm about to dump on you, so I won't continue. But it's a frightening thought that young blokes - they're certainly not men - who do things
such as smoke pipes in their first year because they suddenly think they're
an intellectual (me), drink their age in pints (this was engineers, not historians), wear boiler suits when they appear to be fashionable (this was
me again) and say ludicrous things to young afro-carribean girls like, 'I
didn't realise til I saw you what they meant when they said black was
beautiful,' (me again - oh dear, oh dear, oh dear) actually get girlfriends.'

Eventually. You'll be pleased to know I did a lot of moping around and
being professionally miserable in these years too: your money wasn't completely pissed up against a wall. It was the least I deserved for going away
in the first place with a girlfriend at home who I thought was worth
perservering with. We didn't even like each other much back in sunny
Herts, though we pretended to. Yet somehow we were sufficiently brain-
less to bravely try to keep the fakir up the rope if we could and did so,
expending much wasted time and effort in the process until gravity inter-
vened about four terms later. We learned so little from the affair, apart
from realising that it was impossible to have sex standing up (almost losing the proclivity to procreate in the process), that's what depresses. I only
hope Juliet was two-timing me on the sly all the while: I hate the idea of
all those golden droplets of youth being poured down the lavatory bowl of
time so senselessly. I know that's what happened to a lot of mine. I didn't
do the dirty on Juliet, though it wasn't for the want of trying.

After a very long time - a time which included nightmares like getting
invited to Brussels to stay with a Sheila, losing my luggage on the way then
getting there only to be unceremoniously dumped - a girl from the north-
east picked up my ruins which got me some desperately needed confidence back. Through her I met Louise, who, suffering brain disease,
thought this loud Londoner with a nasty moustache was the way to
improve her life. The rest is a complicated history of the twists and turns
that befall many a relationship. It came to some sort of crunch the day I
placed a letter in a pidgeon hole of a house in Barrow Lane, Cheshunt at

the Waltham Cross Sorting Office at 5.55 one May morning after I had finally left the old Yorkshire wool city for good.

An unfortunate hiatus in our coupling was ended by a flash in my head that told me that Louise was the girl from the Bounty adverts and Julie Andrews all rolled into one; I ran out of the building, ran all the way to Heathrow airport like Dustin Hoffman in Marathon Man, Kramer versus Kramer, The Graduate and every other film he was in before he hit fifty, caught a plane to Germany, where she was completing a spell abroad as part of a language degree, found her, swept her up in my arms and carried her to a bed where I made sensational Olympic gold medal love to her and we were married by a one-eyed Lutheran pastor with bad breath the very next day.

Of course, I may have been exaggerating one or two elements in the narrative, but the essentials are correct: I did have a blinding flash of enlightenment in the sorting office, I rang her up in Germany and pleaded with her to take me back and we did, in the end, get spliced.

Being straightened out by a Simpson (Louise's maiden name) - it was true in those days that young men did need taking in hand, and still is - was a process that was more or less completed in time. In the early days her attentions weren't sufficiently calming to stop me being a bit of a worrier. It may well have been the oceans of time that weigh heavily and flatulently upon a History student with a weak mind, but in 1980 when the Soviet tanks rolled across the borders of Afghanistan, I rather got it into my mind that Thatcher was going to bring back conscription to build up our armed forces, and that with my nuts being twenty-two years young and ripe for the shooting off, I was directly in the firing line.

There was one way out, it seemed to me: stall her by doing teacher training for a year. Maybe after that, teaching would be a reserved occupation or something, or they'd need me to teach the new recruits how the Rome-Berlin axis was sundered by Mussolini's invasion of Abyssinia in 1936. Well surely that was possible. Whatever, the idea of buying a year's extra time to think up an excuse to stop Adolf Maggie's call up papers arriving through the letterbox seemed as ripe as a soft mango to me. So I went down the local recruiting office and signed the necessary papers to have me shipped off to training college in Canterbury to be put through my paces in a few Kentish classrooms.

My teaching practices would not have won the approval of the successive Education Secretaries of the right wing backlash. Neither would Mr Blair have liked my style. At Robert Napier Secondary Modern School in Gillingham (there's just no escaping the place at the moment) where the mob was held in check by the whiplash willow rod of fearsome deputy head Mr Masters (he scared the living shit out of me and I was on his side!). I tried to look the part of a sensible young member of the establishment by donning an old suit of my father's a size too big, but the beard I tried to grow to make myself look at least two years older than the lower fifth, that I might deal with the strugglers in the third, didn't really get going. According to my mentor Lorraine, my face looked like that of someone disguised as a teacher who slept in the park at night: she told me to shave it off and take my medicine like a man.

I passed my first T.P. despite getting so wound up by some cocky cropped haired gonads in 3C one day that I found myself picking on a girl in the class who had a leg in plaster. All she was doing was understandably laughing at one of the tough eggs throwing some poor kid's exercise out of the window (which shouldn't even have been open) while I was trying to calm the general mayhem, when I rounded on her, shouting, 'What are you laughing at, you cripple?'

Cue an immediate flow of tears down her face. Her friend cuddled her whilst shooting me the filthiest look you've ever seen this side of a mud swamp in Alabama, while I rolled my eyes at the ceiling at my utter brainlessness and tried, nobly I thought, to explain why Louis XVI got separated from his head in 1792 while trying to avoid the thought that I myself deserved a similar fate.

'Please don't tell your mum what I said,' pleaded me to our distraught be-plastered one.

'I'm going to the hospital this afternoon and they're going (sob) to tell me whether I'll be able to walk without a limp for the rest of my life (wail).'

Oh, God, what have I done, I thought. Will I ever learn to keep my big mouth shut?

There was no complaint from the parents of the poor girl but the angst I so richly deserved arrived at my second stop on the Education Express at a sixth form college in Ramsgate. Although I was spared having to put the crash helmet on every day to face thirty cases of exploding hormones, the methodist husband and wife team under whose wings I was thrust took one look at my earring and ran for the telephone to complain to the college.

The timetabler's warped sense of humour - some form of educational terrorist or something - had created the world of the two hour lesson (two hour lessons! you could drive to Leicester between taking the register and setting homework!). Actually I was more in my element in this establishment. Even in John Lennon glasses and red shoes, following on from Mr and Mrs Boring, I couldn't lose in the popularity stakes: for the students I was the equivalant of a rock concert and a night out at the boozer even when I was lecturing them on the erosion of monarchical powers by the early eighteenth century Whigs. Strangely this didn't prevent me from being on the receiving end of a real, perfumed love letter from a not unpleasant looking member of my A level class to deal with after I left. I'd be lying through my teeth if I tried to claim that this gave teaching sufficient allure for me to chase a full time job. The sad reality of my world was this: what else was a 24 year old with zero ambition and a severe indolence problem going to do? The thought of doing something actually enjoyable and fulfilling to earn some corn terrified me: where was I going to get the energy from? And what if I failed at it? What then?

So I stumbled all the way into teaching like many a drowned ex-university rat before me. So I chased a job. I'd have gone anywhere in he country outside the inner cities: I wasn't cut out for heroism or masochism, but then again, I did end up In Orpington. I was desperate - but not so desperate that I didn't have the sense to turn down the opportunity of teaching in Romford; I mean, I'd have had to live there, were they kidding? - by the time Ramsden School For Boys, themselves sweating on an end of summer appointment, rang me to ask me to come to interview. What they saw in an application that nearly a hundred other schools had happily ignored I can't say and didn't stop to ask at the time.

At the interview with members of the humanities department I replied to a not unexpected question about my weaknesses.

'I don't have any,' I replied. I think they were too stunned not to give me the job. Well: be confident when you go to interview, they said at college.

It wasn't a bad school. The staff were wonderfully friendly, and bright and funny. The facilities were good and class sizes very reasonable indeed. The trouble was, it was full of boys. And in silly black ties, black blazers, black socks and black shoes. Like a bus, every school staff has it's loony. Ours was John Teulon, head of upper school. I went to see him about something or other in my first term and as I entered his domain he was busy bawling out a fifth year lad. It quickly emerged that, brimful of insolence and subordination, he had tried to pull down the whole ethos of order at the institution by flagrantly wearing a pair of light grey Daks with the rest of his immaculate regulation attire. When John had worn himself out and the wounded, deflated boy had exited, he turned to me and with a weary shake of his ageing napper he said, 'Do you know, Craig: if you let them come in today with grey trousers, tomorrow it'll be blue hair.'

Thank goodness that nice Mrs Thatcher had been elected last time to stop the rot. She'd obviously inspired Mr Teulon.

The only time you could get to teach girls was if you taught A level History. The sixth form was mixed and was made up of the elder element of the two single sexed schools which served the Ramsden housing estate and which were only separated by a huge expanse of hockey and rugby pitches. Sixth form teaching offered the promise of lessons without giving lines, giving detentions and giving up. However, we were all hopeless at it. We'd all been taught in the same dreadful style at our own schools, writing down dictated notes from the same robotic History teachers, whether growing up in Winchester, Wallasea or Wimbledon. So all five of us intermittently involved in the more academic end of the trade inflicted the same interminable boredom on our own youngsters each week, now we were on the other side of the fence.

And if there was one splinter of idealism in my reason for going into teaching, ironically it was so I could get my revenge for the dreary afternoons I had to face for two years by doing the job properly with new generations of hopefully eager scholars. How I was going to do this apart from throwing in allusions and analogies from the world of rock music and football as liberally as I could, in an effort to keep people awake as we waded through the parched deserts of Castlereagh, Canning and Palmerston, I hadn't a clue. And over the next three years, boy, did it show.

The thing bottomed out one year when out of the class of twelve students I shared with an equally gormless individual from the girls' school, only one passed. That summer three staff left the department and I was left temporarily in charge for a year. That's it, I thought. I can't sink any lower than this. It was time to tear up all the plans and start again from scratch. I junked nineteenth century England for a syllabus with a special paper on Nazi Germany and threw the lecturing style into the skip.

By luck I met a guy in the trade who switched me on to something called 'child centred learning', something the Mail and the Telegraph have been saying for the past twenty years has been destroying the country as we know it - in short, it means not boring the kids to death with lectures.

So the following year instead of doing that again I'd send the students away in twos to research each fragment of the course and they came in to deliver presentations to the rest of the class who could take notes from that if they wanted to. The youngsters were simply heroic. They found pictures and quotes from all over the place and photocopied them for everyone. What they didn't find out and didn't know I filled in, and tied each part of the course into a coherent whole.

It was a raging success. That year, 1986-7, I had my best lesson ever with this upper sixth class. It was the day I wasn't there. I was unexpectedly off sick with the trots and when I came in on the Monday Mick Banns from the English department told me he'd witnessed a strange event while I'd been away. He'd gone into my classroom looking for me only to find a class of A level historians teaching themselves. I was so proud Mick said it would have been a pleasure to have pushed a heavy duty stapler into the back of my throat.*

That August the results came in. Every student passed in one group of ten, and all bar two in the other where my new style hadn't taken so effectively. We had success stories like Judith Berryman who, when I gave her back an essay at the start of the year, which was only worth using to line the bottom of a birdcage, got up and left the room in tears. Six months later when we'd swung past the consolidation of the dictatorship, propaganda and the dismantling of the Treaty of Versailles, the first shoots of confidence were appearing in her, as she would now answer a question with telling accuracy where before there was struggle and befuddlement. When one day Judith explained to the class why the Nazi salute was a vital weapon in suppressing opposition to the regime, I knew we at last were on to something.

We also had the first 'A' grade the schools had seen in History since Sherpa Tenzing went for a long walk up a hill in 1953. At long bloody last: six years in teaching and I'd actually achieved something. Hoo-flipping-ray.

It was me who moved on this time, northwards. After a year working in what is euphemistically called an 'inner city school,' but which folks in the trade call 'a school you'd only work in if you were penniless, a Christian missionary with a fear of travel, or if no-one else would have you' I was scrabbling around for any old kind of teaching job in Derbyshire and outlying districts. I'd had some tremendously encouraging advice on my first working day in my new beloved adopted county from the head master:

'Start applying for another job, there won't be one for you here at the end of the year,' and he'd been right. Ten months down the line I was out on my ear and was so exhausted that when I got interviews for new positions I came out with answers to questions which didn't exactly do me any favours.

'So, Mr Thomas, tell us why you think you'd be an asset to this

---

*Mick was often an inspirational figure for me at Ramsden. I remember being especially star-struck when, telling him one summer how down I was getting because of all the exam marking I had on my plate, he said, 'Just do what I do when it gets too much: chuck the papers in the bin and make up the marks.' 'You mean you...?' 'Yeah, of course: I'm not going to waste my time marking exam papers', and he looked at me as if only a madman would disagree.

school?'

'I'm a really good teacher.' Nothing wrong with a bit of confidence, surely. Why are people across the table suddenly frowning at me?

'Would you like to give us some evidence to support that, shall we say, rather bold assertion, Mr Thomas?'

'You've got my bloody references in front of you, why don't you read them? Do you think they're all a pack of lies?'

No, I didn't piss on my chips to quite that extent, but I thought that and proceeded to come out with a long stream of vain, self-glorifying arse-wind which sounded completely awful even from where I was. I dread to imagine how embarrassing it must have been to have been on the receiving end of it. I stank the place out wherever I went and faced the summer holidays with nothing.

For the unwanted and outcast in this sort of teaching game there is always 'supply,' which means filling in for sick teachers and blow outs wherever there were holes. One thing I'd gained from a year teaching in the educational equivalent of the wild west was the ability to keep the unruly end of the Jesse James gang sat in their chairs and giving their pens at least a gentle run out (most of which I had to supply myself each lesson) . If I could get into comprehensives where they'd heard of competent management and taking exams at sixteen on supply, I should at least be on for a bit of paid rest.

It was indeed soon 'ker-ching' for two terms: no marking, no lesson prep, just baby-minding. I gave out the materials and instructions passed to me by heads of department relevant to the absent teacher, and made sure they were silent while I wrote articles for The Crooked Spireite. The year in Dodge City was the relegation season I've already told you about, and football kept my head above the water line: somehow my kids, my wife and my 100 year old stone cottage weren't enough. Come Saturday, wherever we were playing, I bussed it into Chesterfield and got on the supporters' coach to wherever the Blues were scrabbling around for three points that day (how and why did Louise put up with me?)

By the time I got my free transfer from the concrete classroom to the easy street of supply teaching, the need to go everywhere to see the Town was too deeply embedded in my guts for me to change tack. My attachment to the fanzine grew ever stronger too. I wrote more and more. And got to interview players. Which gave me the confidence to take on Paul Hart.

I really did think this man was going to take the club to a glory never seen in its history hitherto. This might not have been saying much, as the highest Town had ever finished in the football league was fourth in the old

Division 2 in 1947, but he still had a way to go from Division 4 to match it and I thought he was going to if he got reasonable backing from the board.

The first sentence of the first interview article I wrote went, 'We wanted this interview really badly.' Meaning I did. This was my passport to the inner lining of the garment. This man controlled my team, held its in the palm of his hand. Which meant he held mine too. To talk to him meant everything to me, in a footballing sense: for the fanzine writer, this was Wembley.

From the first of many interviews as it turned out, it was clear that Paul Hart was a formidable individual, overflowing with charisma. I haven't met many famous people, but if there are 'stars' out there with much more than this man possessed, then droves of people must pile up on the carpet in dead faints when they appear. He made uncle Len look like a tax inspector with a small moustache.

I was not just in awe of the man, I was frightened. To walk to his office door (after the first couple of appointments, Nicola in the office would say 'go through, you know where it is, when I tapped on the window) was to feel like a scruffy urchin caught wagging it from school being sent to see the Headmaster. He was indeed a considerable human being. P.G. Wodehouse said of one of Bertie Wooster's aunts that she was so fierce her eye could open an oyster at fifty paces. This was Hart exactly. When he looked at you quizzically after you'd asked a question he didn't quite like, you felt as though you were stuck to the plastic chair with sweat and wouldn't be able to unstick yourself. If I ever really asked or said something that upset him, I would have simply no choice but to leg it, leaving the tape recorder and notes behind if necessary. On the inside of his door there was a fist sized hole at about chest height. I always wanted to ask him if he made it, and why, but a moment where I felt sufficiently confident never arose.

His eyes were set deep in the upper part of his face and said power, dominance, control. There was undoubtedly something threatening about him, however it wasn't really physical: it was more psychological and while it made you uncomfortable, it made you excited at the same time. You didn't meet people like this every ten years, never mind week. I was not only in awe of him because of the people at the very top of the game he'd played for: Brian Clough and Howard Wilkinson for example, and played on the same park with: the cream of the English game from 1976 to 1985, I was in awe of the personality inside his huge frame.

The first time I was allowed into the inner sanctum at Saltergate, the manager's office - yes, Mission Unlikely achieved - we talked for two and a quarter hours, 'a marathon' as he later described it, and I felt I got a really clear sense of the man. He was the most intelligent British football man I've ever come across in the flesh or on the box, with the possible exception of Steve Coppell (but then he does possess a degree from Liverpool University in Economics), and deadly serious about his work. His high level of articulacy made my job easy and each meeting a boxing match I had to be wide awake for or I might get a verbal smack in the teeth. He spoke quietly and thoughtfully, which gave what he said immense authority.

Football people are suspicious of outsiders and find it hard to talk to them because they think they know nothing about the game. Though there is a huge amount of truth in this, it is at the same time grossly unfair. Without letting others in on the game's secret codes, its eternal mysteries, we on the outside will forever be left trying to complete a Rubic Cube wearing a blindfold and therefore unable to spread the word as so much light into the darkness of the ignorance of the fan. So Paul would easily get impatient with me if I didn't ask questions which at least demonstrated some evidence of actually having watched a lot of football.

This was especially so near the end of his two seasons at the club, a ridiculously short amount of time given his capabilities, when his patience and his spirit was worn down to red raw nerve endings. During our last ever meeting, I asked him in an idle moment why defender Lee Rogers' nickname was Nobby, thinking that there might be some obscure or interesting reason driving the issue. Hart kept his eyes fixed on the patch of wooden desk they'd been lasering a hole in for the previous ninety seconds and replied, 'You don't half ask some fucking stupid questions.'

Oh, right. Lee is extravagantly gifted in the manhood department, I see.

If he'd looked up at me and laughed it would have been a happy, light-hearted moment where his humorous riposte would have been a recognition of his acceptance and approval of me. The fact that his facial muscles refused to relax for even a flickering, transient moment told me he clearly wanted to pose this rhetorical question to all four us in the room:

'Do I have to sit and waste my time talking to this cretin?'

Much as I practically revered the man, there comes a point at which sanity prevails. His team were struggling desperately to win games and were not far away now from a losing streak that would send them to the ignominy of standing just one off the bottom of the football league: 91st of 92. He was disillusioned and all but completely defeated in trying to carry through a job he'd started brilliantly. But it didn't mean he had the right to treat me with such disrespect. He hadn't been forced to invite me in: it was his choice. I got out of there as quickly as I reasonably could and clacked out an article on Stuart's old typewriter the same. I just wanted rid of the miserable little experience and to get on with something else.

It didn't stop me being outraged at Halifax in December of that year, 1990, when the 'Hart Out' chants began among our away fans. I was so disgusted I felt almost physically sick. The previous season, the one immediately following the relegation, Hart and his team made it to the promotion play offs where they made short work of Stockport County in the semi-finals. At Wembley, a Chesterfield side seeing and feeling its famous turf for the first time, lost by a single Dion Dublin goal to Cambridge United. Forty nine 'league' games after it began, to vast optimism among fans - 'we'll be up by Christmas' we all said - the season ended in ruins. We stayed down. After the dramatic impact Paul had made on a club rotting away from the inside out, this felt like another relegation. It didn't in the end matter that later the victor's assistant manager rang Hart to tell him the best team on the day lost and that in a way he was sorry. It was true, though: only some bad, nervous finishing (and injury to Dave Waller) cost him his place among fans as a managerial Town legend. He never played for the first team again).

As Hart himself had told me at our first meeting, 'Matt Busby was once asked 'if you were looking to employing a manager, what would you ask him?' And he replied, 'is he lucky?'

Not only did luck desert him at Wembley, it deserted Hart at board level. Here was one whose conception of the job did not involve suffering fools and all football chairmen are fools of one sort or another. He would not kow-tow to Barrie Hubbard and Norton Lea and he paid the price. In the close season period after Wembley, and despite the highest gates for years the season before at Saltergate, they sent a miserably small amount of money down the corridor from the boardroom to the manager's office. When we were underway again there were injuries and an early season flu crisis to battle against as well as a psychologically damaged squad.

The circumstantial evidence has it that the board wanted Hart to fail so they could rid themselves of someone who wouldn't be treated like a serf. It's happened over and over again in the game, at every club over the game's century and more of history. On January 1st 1991, after an unrelieved spell of eight winless and sorry league games he was sacked, to be replaced by his assistant McMenemy, who some said had been circling around his number one like a shark around an injured swimmer.

However, the memory of Paul Hart which has wrapped itself around a vault in my memory bank like wet toilet paper around a shoe, is of watching him play for the reserves towards the end of his time as the manager. He couldn't let go of playing so turned out for every game, no doubt with the full intention of bringing on the youngsters. He played in the centre of midfield, the position of supremos, and tried to run the game like Puskas. Paul and the Hungarian maestroissimo didn't really have much in common, except perhaps for a paunchiness around the middle. Our new kit design was unfortunate here, I reluctantly noted from my place in the centre stand one half term afternoon, in that the shorts were white with a broad blue vertical stripe down each side, making Maestro look like an ageing Muhammed Ali.

If the game went badly, the end was tragi-comic. I watched in horror throughout actually, as my hero struggled in a way he could never have done as a centre half. He harangued the referee whenever there was a decision he didn't approve of, which was almost the whole time. This was terribly embarrassing as, sat in an almost deserted main stand you could hear every word and the exact inflection placed upon them. He droned on and on, a performance that almost rivalled Kenny Dalglish at his best. This was a manager who fined his players for dissent: how could he not see that he was being hypocritcal?

We were ahead late in the game and the referee's performance wilted like discarded dressed lettuce under the pressure of Hart's running commentary. From a cross, a Northampton forward punched in an equaliser. Everyone saw it apart from the linesman and the ref.. Paul was beside himself. Then in the dying afternoon - the game was in midweek and kicked off in daylight to save floodlight money - an opponent took on Paul in the penalty area, and rather than risk a penalty, he stood to attention to let the young tearaway go by to be left to the attentions of another Chesterfield defender. The forward fell over anyway. Peep! The inexperienced official, whose nerves must have been in shreds from having our manager in his ear for nearly a full hour and thirty minutes, had blown, possibly by accident because you never saw a clearer dive on a football pitch in your life. But there was no doubt at all that the referee's whistle had indeed squirted a short blast, causing all the Northampton players to shout 'Hooray! penalty!', which they duly scored from, causing us to lose 1-2.

It was like an SAS assault on a creche. 'You cheat. You fucking cheat.' The words could be heard across the other side of the town. I was bright vermillion in shame and embarrassment as the verbal assault continued as the assembled trooped back to the centre circle .

As PH copped the most feeble of bookings I didn't know who to feel most sorry for: one miserable referee, one fallen idol or me. So this was the man I had been in awe of all this time. There were fallen scales everywhere. It just wasn't fair. Football was supposed to be football. Just that, no more. A simple form of escape from everyday life. But that day I felt the whole weight of reality standing on my foot right, a place it was not supposed to be.

14

. ....Makes A Genius Of A Teacher

'A teacher affects eternity; no-one can tell when his influence stops'

Henry Adams

Such repressive measures as the The Nacht Und Nebel laws of the later 1930s were hardly necessary in cementing the Nazi Party's complete control of a country where the forces of socialism were desperately retreating into what was becoming a rapidly shrinking and increasingly redundant workerist laager. The fact that the Fuhrer possessed only one gonad may have been a factor in his desire to wreak a vicious revenge on society, but.....oh, sorry. Am I boring you? I was just indulging in a spot of nostalgia, there.

When I finally landed a job, it was at Louise's old school where I'd already got my shoes under the table on supply. I was expected to teach an A level course straight away, but instead of the home territory of nineteenth and twentieth century English history, I had to deliver the teaching of The Reformation in Sixteenth Century Europe, stuff I'd never been near before. At the start I knew more about the one-way system around the centre of Swindon than I did about Martin Luther and the downfall of Catholicism through all those monks and priests living lives of wild debauchery.

This was something I could mend with a lot of reading. Fine. Problematical was the fact that the model for success I'd worked out down south wasn't going to work here. For one, there weren't the number of books around that the students needed for research, neither at the school nor in local libraries. Unfortunately, the history of religion didn't quite have the sex appeal of Nazi Germany, so shelves weren't crammed with the texts we needed. The youngsters all had one standard text book and it was useless.

Secondly, the use of our four lessons a week was strange: two lectures, one on the European side of the course, one on the English, and two seminars. My timetable had me down for two seminar-style lessons with two different groups. I'd have the pupils for ten weeks at a time. We couldn't possibly cover the material using the pairs projects in eleven and a half hours. Back to the drawing board.

When I'd taken a look around, I found that the results in the department were quite good, but only according to the staff who worked in it. To me, they were dreadfully mediocre and something would have to be done. I'd now seen with my own eyes what you could do with young scholars if you gave them some responsibility for their learning . The pressure the child-centred approach had taken from me, in terms of lesson planning and preparation, had given me the energy and time to assess the students' individually much more effectively. Better still, in the classroom, because I wasn't droning on all the time I could see far more clearly what the class learned each time and could fill in the spaces easily. But now it seemed as though it would all fall back on me once more, and with potentially boring material to deal with, disaster loomed upon the horizon like a plague of locusts getting set for din-dins.

I decided I wasn't going to go back to those days though. I may have had no ambition for myself but I was as competitive as Billy Bremner when in the mood and watching your football team a century of times and being desperate for them to win on each occasion with a fervour that was practically a mental disorder rubs off. And then a weird thing happened. The lower sixth did their annual history exam the first week I was there and I marked my part of the syllabus: my predecessor had been working on it for two terms. The essays were worse than terrible. They didn't understand the first thing about the conflict surrounding the formation of a broad new protestant church and even less about how to put together a piece of writing. Suddenly, I could see the job I had to do as clearly as sometimes images in a dream are focussed for us: an intense clarity we almost never encounter in our day to day existence.

PH: I think I talk simply to the players and ask them to do simple things. There are simple criteria to follow; everything beyond that is a bonus.

Analyse Liverpool's play. If they lose it, they get it back as quickly as they can. When they've got it they try to keep it as long as they can. When the ball's put in the box they've still got to head it, like any other team.

The beliefs I have now will go with me wherever I go. The same basic training, the basic way we talk will go with me. I learned that from Brian Clough. He's got great players, right? But all he says is, 'head the ball, win your tackles, do the right things at the right time.

CT: Is that his secret then, simplicity?

PH: Yes. I couldn't believe it. I came from Leeds where if I passed the ball more than ten yards they wanted to know why. I went to Forest and all he said was 'head it, and boot it; anything else is a bonus.' Well, I'd been a centre half for many years but that's all he said to me and I used that from being 30 to being 35, 36. If I was struggling, I knew, 'whoof!' (makes an imaginary header that goes forty yards up the pitch). Or 'whoof!' (an imaginary thump sixty yards up the field), and I'm doing my job. Through that my confidence has grown, and I'm back to doing that (makes imaginary sweet pass out to full back). If I'd have played under Brian Clough earlier in my career I'd have played for England. I'm certain of that.

CT: And the way Clough went about motivating players, what's the mystery?

PH: No mystery, it's simple really: you give 100%: if you don't, you feel his tongue. He has a lot of players around him of the same calibre - good lads, no stars, who all want to do well and who know that if they don't give a hundred per cent, that's it.

This was part of my transcript from the first interview I did in Paul Hart's office.

Even as the conversation unfolded at the time it must have made a deep impression on me, because right here was the answer to the problem of having twenty-four seventeen year olds struggling through a clarty field of thick mud called 'Reformation Europe' on my hands. The rest of the course must have been a nightmare for them too, judging from the lessons I had with the upper sixth who were about to leave and begin taking their exams. Going in with them was like a dressing room after a sixth successive home defeat. They had no confidence and no fight in them by the look of it either. The one book they had they didn't understand, and I tried to cheer them up by telling them that I wouldn't have used the pages of Geoffrey Elton's 'Reformation Europe' to wipe my arse on, let alone give it house room in an attempt to pass vital exams. I told them straight, 'If you don't understand it, it's not your fault, it's Elton's for writing the most boring, pompous pile of crap I've ever clapped eyes on in my life.'

You weren't supposed to talk like that to your innocent young charges but I used to be well behaved in the first few years at Ramsden and look where that got me. Did Brian Clough give not one but two desperately mediocre football clubs three league championships and two European Cups between them by behaving like the Queen's vicar? By never offending people and making no enemies? Did Paul Hart transform the team in his first season then get us to Wembley by being ever so well brought up and asking the team nicely if they felt they could perhaps go out onto the pitch and try ever so hard? By God, no.

Slagging off Elton and opening up the possibility to them that they weren't stupid just because they didn't understand a badly written text book by a supposed expert made them look up suddenly. This sort of talk they were not used to. Well something had to be done; For pity's sake, it was like trying to teach a set of professional losers. I saw a glimmer of hope in at least two sets of eyes around the table. Maybe the two out of that lot who actually went on to get a decent grade. Maybe not.

Unfortunately I only had four lessons with them to try out the Paul Hart Method. So the results in August 1990 were cat piss. Yet at the first department meeting of the new school year, the team sat around congratulating themselves on a job well done. Hardly anyone failed, but big deal: you only needed 38% over two papers to pass and only 59% that year to get an 'A'. These stats told me that if I could get things moving, we could absolutely clean up. If.

My first problem was dealing with a little consumer resistance. Back in the summer term, two weeks after my appointment there had been a lower sixth parents evening, and my head of department, who couldn't motivate a drowning man to swim, told me next morning he'd had some complaints about my teaching.

'I'll see you later about it, I'm going off to teach.' Thanks a lot. I may have come into the school a bit of a brash, know-it-all, I called it 'knowing where I was going,' but underneath it all I was the over-sensitive, delicate flower I'd always been. I was all Earth's crust on the surface, but soft squidgy magma underneath. I'd always had a tendency to worry myself into misery about insignificant things, and not be bothered in the slightest about the things I should have paid considerable attention to. No-one likes criticism. Everyone hates it. I've always reacted to it in two ways: terror if it's justified and deep, brooding resentment if it isn't. And when someone says, 'Oh, Craig, I've got some slagging off to pass on to, it could be a sexual molestation charge, it could be the head wants to suspend you for using a four letter word with your sixth formers: I'll tell you in a couple of hours,' the suspense sees my whole nervous system packing up within minutes.

I managed to force the man into a book cupboard and have it out with me there and then. Making me feel worse was the awkward fact that I liked to please people and I did not want my new boss to have a low opinion of me, without a very good reason anyway, and right now I couldn't think of one.

'Two or three parents don't like your approach. They think you're too, um, confrontational. You're changing things and they don't feel so sure of themselves all of a sudden.'

Oh, really. We'll see about that, I thought, working up a temper I could light a bunch of wet logs with. I'll give them bloody confrontational.

I was upset, but like the total luvvie-tortured-artist I was, I would have been upset if someone told me I had a shoelace undone. I'd calmed down quite quickly and was relieved the criticism wasn't more potentially damaging. Blimey. I'd only had them for two lessons, what did I say? Let me think. That the standard of work they'd produced in the exams wasn't good enough and would have to improve. I'm sure I said it nicely, though. That I'd be teaching them a completely new method of essay writing from front to back, inside to out. It had been the classic 'things are going to have to change around here' speech and it had terrified some of them, obviously. Girls. The complainers were all girls. Typical. The one thing I loved about the school from the first day, apart from the fact that I'd never seen such happy and contented children, was that at last I had a proper job in a mixed comprehensive. There were girls everywhere: it was lovely! At last, a proper community just as nature intended. And now they'd given me a kick in the teeth.

I gritted the ones they hadn't kicked out and got on with the mission. 'What we say is, a sensible way of working,' I kept hearing Paul Hart say in my head, 'sensible and simple.'

Sensible. work hard: get your essays in on time; be at every lesson, no excuses. Organise yourself properly. Don't write essays with headphones or the stereo on. Always sit quietly and do it. Don't go out in the week clubbing and drinking 'til all hours, get proper sleep.

Simple. Rule one: follow the rules. Rule two. Take the advice you're given every time, no excuses. Three. Ask questions in class when you need to, don't bottle out. Four. Come and see me outside lessons when you're stuck or need advice. Five. Get up each day and work as hard as you can. Then get up the next day and do the same.

I taught them how to write a really effective essay, step by step. One. Always plan it. Break the title down into sub-questions and after the introductory paragraph answer each one in turn. Try to save one for your conclusion. Introductory paragraph: answer the question briefly. That's it. Simple. Sensible.

The main problem I had was that their other history teachers were familiar and loved. Here was I tearing up what they'd been taught and starting again with things they'd never heard before and hadn't thought of themselves. I was new. I was indeed, confrontational, and occasionally banged a fist on the table.

One lesson a seminar class told me that they'd been told to revise a topic for the exam and their teacher hadn't had time to teach it to them. They were given a thick booklet of notes and told to learn them.

'YOU CAN-NOT STUDY A TOPIC PROPERLY FROM A SET OF NOTES!' I thundered. This sort of thing undermined everything I had set out to do with these people. I told them to throw the notes in the bin. We didn't need the extra topic.

That was another one of my hobby horses: notes. I had studied for three A levels and a degree and got them all and had never revised from notes. I was a hopeless note-taker, and thankfully, notes were a waste of time. I just read and read, and let my memory do the rest. We all have wonderful memories, I told my students. Let's use them.

Cue complete and utter freak out, the first time I told each of the three seminar groups. Come to think of it, perhaps I'd told them this the week of that parents' evening. Ah.

All these exam hopefuls had been educated since before the age of eleven to believe that everything that was worth knowing at school had to be written down in a little object called an exercise book. All this did to them was strangle their ability to think about what they were supposed to be studying. As far as I was concerned, if you weren't thinking, you weren't learning. Girls, being industrious and organised and conscientious wrote and wrote with hands that were sore by the end of the lesson. It's a gender thing. I've been to meetings of history teachers where at the start of the session a course leader has informed, helpfully,

'Coffee break will be at 10.45 in Room 23 which is down the corridor to the right, fourth, no, fifth door along,' and seen just in front of me teachers scribbling frantically: 'Coffee. 10.45. Rm. 23. Corridor - right, 4th. Crossing out. 5th door along.' It's a disease. Refrain from reading me wrong: I really do believe that the world would be a much better and happier place if left to be run by the female sex, but fortunately for us men, they're not perfect.

This was one of the problems I had to face, then, notes. 'If you don't want to write anything in lessons, don't.' The first time I said this there was a slap!: the sound of five jaws crashing against the desk tops. The four which remained in close contact with the rest of their faces belonged to boys. Who were sitting there smirking. 'We're going to be thinking about history in here: thinking, understanding, then writing.'

I knew I was beginning to get through when I was sent to answer knocks on the staff room door.

'Can you help me with this essay?'

The callers began as an odd one or two, like cats waiting to be let in from the cold outside. Then it was a trickle, then I was working every lunchtime with them either individually, which was better, or in twos and threes, which was still good. Little by little the essay scores went higher, though some who couldn't jump on the bus straight away made sudden jumps forward later. Lessons which at first saw me doing most of the talking, though I tried the odd presentation (they didn't go well and I calculated we didn't have the time to persevere), graduated to a to-ing and fro-ing of discussion, the contributions to which became more and more confident and well informed as the weeks ticked by. By Easter, I knew all the students individually and any residual frost had long since thawed, with the exception of Miss Millington who held on determinedly in her underground bunker to the view that I was not so much a History Teacher as the Creature From The Black Lagoon. No matter: in every other respect, we were all moving onwards and upwards.

If there was one key word that tied this together it was a Hart word. Though it's been used by whole long football-coat loads of managers down the years in interviews, and makes me yawn with unwakeable boredom when I hear it, it sums up exactly what I was doing and I was doing it consciously too:

Organisation.

Hugely ironical this was, because I could never find anything and left things behind me in classrooms with the regularity of a cathedral clock. However, the key to teaching, I was discovering, was organising other people. Organising them collectively was important, but organising each individual the factor that made the difference, making sure everyone knew exactly what they needed to do to kill the cow and bring it home for tea, and perhaps even more importantly, when the cow couldn't be found, or the weapon not sharp enough, or you couldn't get it together to get out there and kill, making it clear what they had to do to turn the situation around. All I did really was tell them 'whoof!' then 'whoof!' and anything more was a bonus.

The exams came. I remember going down to the gym during the exam to see what questions had turned up on the paper, reading it, grunting thoughtfully at it, then walking back towards the exit: then turning to look at The Tapland 24. Marguerite Wright caught my eye ten feet away. I clenched my fist like a footballer at her as if to say, 'come on!' And she smiled, almost laughing, and carried on.

The family went on a long holiday in France that summer. I sat in my friend Hugh's car in a village in Provence with a bottle of Pschhtt! in my hands listening to the BBC World Service for the first results of the new season. But much as my stomach churned in nervous anticipation of a home defeat, I was already dealing with the inner turmoil produced by the knowledge that within a few days a letter would be arriving full of other results. Soon enough, the first piece of news came through:

   Chesterfield beat Maidstone United 3-0 to open the first full season without the man who had been cast aside by the club like a pile of cold chips. The second would tell me whether I'd been correct in placing all my faith in The Method he'd left behind.

15

Results Day

*'On the blackboard of sorrows
he draws a face of joy.'*

Jacques Prevert

If you roll up early enough in your car at your local secondary school on the third Thursday in August, you'll see little copses of students, almost in huddles standing round. Like the women at a pit head waiting for news of a disaster below, there is little talk, just waiting, thinking and worrying. But this, of all days, is when you're on your own. No-one, whatever they say, cares about what anyone else has got: it's just you, in your own little world, against the world. Sure you'll sympathise with your friends who didn't make their grades, even throw your arms around them in consolation and actually cry tears, but it's ersatz emotion. Today is about your future, and no-one else's.

If you hang around in the car park you'll see a door open and the youngsters will troop in at a steady rate with only a few at the front, and they'll be girls, unable to hold on to their composure any longer disappearing into school at speed. At some stage over the next hour you'll see, three or four times probably, a student emerge, being led away in tears. They needed two 'B's and a 'C': it was all 'C's. Or worse. They think it's all over for them, as if there was a note attached to the slip of paper breaking the news:

'No University in this country wants you. Ever. Now go.'

Though a soap would write girls who got in, screaming with joy like, well, girls. I've never heard this myself. A little laughter sometimes, of course; dozens of genuinely shocked 'I can't believe it!' faces, yes. Young females shrieking and screaming together with semi-disbelieving delight, never. There's too much awareness of the grief of others for anyone to make a big show. If such histrionics occur on results days, it goes on in bedrooms and back gardens, when the successful meet and share their triumph while proud parents beam, open the Champagne and think 'buggering Ada, it's all been worth it: who'd have thought.'

And boys? The successes smile quietly and think about going down the pub, while the failures look rueful, occasionally deadly serious, and think about going down the pub.

Now I've stayed in teaching because I like young people and enjoy their company in classrooms. Believe me. But one year I had a pupil I really didn't like: an over-confident medical student-in-waiting who missed the required grades by a mile. I saw her in the front seat of a car on one of these mornings sobbing her heart out, and inside I was in fits of laughter: 'good,' I thought, mentally swigging bubbly from a bottle; serves you bloody right for making my job so difficult for two years.' I'm that kind of guy sometimes, I'm afraid.

Anyhow, This Year In Question I was literally a thousand miles from the emotional scenes of a results day. Whatever went on that particular Thursday I was not privileged to know, but my thoughts were there alright. Four days later I was sipping a second cup of french coffee on what was still a fresh morning. The slamming heat of another Provencal August day was gathering itself together in some anti-chamber in readiness for another grand entrance around midday, and I was trying to make the most of the time I had left. Mediterranean sun wasn't my thing at all, but we were here to see my mate Hugh who'd married a local girl ten years earlier and had now ditched Bexleyheath for the south of France. I can't think why.

Mid-swallow, Hugh rolled into view clutching a brown envelope. This must be it: my slip of paper containing my...I exaggerate if I say 'destiny', but it was true, my personal sense of self-worth depended upon the grades penned against the names inside that envelope as well as professional. I opened it in a predictable flurry of slapstick comedy: took me eight times longer to get inside than it should have done and by the time I did there were scraps of cheap buff on the floor and the envelope looked like the dog had tried to eat it.

I say letter. I had hand written a list of twenty-four names on a sheet of lined A4 on the last day of term, whacked a stamp and an address on the outside and handed it to my friend Chris who'd be in school on the day, to send on to me. Immediately.

Unfolding it, there was my scruffy handwriting in blue with the list of what were more than names: symbols of my success or failure, surnames I might one day raise statues to in my mental Hall Of Fame or spend years desperately trying to forget: Lord, Cresswell, Millington, Varney, Peet. Nineteen others. Letters had been scrawled alongside each of them in Chris's weird hand. I scanned down fast, too fast. It was just a blur of 'A's and 'B's and the occasional 'C' and was there a 'D' in there? I looked and looked, but each time my eyes flicked up and down, up and down, all I could see were grades I could hardly believe. This is a tarted up version, but this is roughly the sort of thing they were struggling to grasp:

Cresswell, Linda	A
Millington, Ruth	A
Varney, Pauline	B
Wright, Marguerite	A

Cresswell, Linda. Her parents were among those who had complained about me when I took over the class. Millington, Ruth. Her mother had lined up to have a go too, a vicar's wife I soon learned, which at the time threw me into a fit of rage. What sort of Christian went behind a man's back? Where was compassion when I was getting a slagging off before I had been given a chance to prove myself? You hated me and I got your daughter an 'A'. Chew on that, I thought, while trying to understand exactly what had happened.

Sixteen 'A's and 'B's and no fails was what had happened, miles and miles above any national averages anyone could pull out of any book or document. It suddenly looked like our school was the centre of excellence for the teaching of A level History.

'If you hadn't come, I don't know what we would have done,' said Linda Cresswell when I ran into her six months later. Phew. Relief. You can think you've done a good job, but you need to hear it from those on the receiving end before you truly know. This was manna: this was the proof I needed that The Method worked; now I knew beyond all possible doubt that it did.

A year later things weren't going so well and my boss one day said, 'what's the matter with you, you've lost your usual spark?' I shrugged as if I didn't know what he was talking about, but I did.

I found that I couldn't keep up the intensity I'd worked with that first year. Like a fire, it seemed to burn out on me. I had better students this time, it seemed to me, and they had the advantage of being taught the basis of The Method from the start. I didn't think they needed me clapping my hands and urging them on from the sidelines all the time. I got complacent. The results weren't so hot. They were still good but they weren't great, and that's the way it stayed, basically. One August we had eleven 'A's out of thirty-three students, a jackpot; twelve months later we had only three and I scratched my head and tried to figure out why. Now, to be honest, I couldn't be bothered to work out the answer.

There was only one time where I got back the form of old, when I took over a big class from a bloke who said he knew his seventeenth century history but, it turned out, thought James the First was an olympic runner and The Interregum a pub on the Brampton Mile. With a classroom full of dropped heads and despondency I could make the place a dressing room at half time again and inspire the team to turn a three-nil defecit into a six-three stroll in the park. Which I did. Meanwhile, the class I'd taught from the off alongside this one I got too cosy with and couldn't lift them or myself above mediocrity.

Like true football people I take my defeats hard, but treasure the times I had something to put in the trophy cabinet for ever. The Paul Hart Method worked brilliantly. However, teaching history cannot always be death or glory; it can't always be like football. The best on the planet? Although I felt like it at the time, to be a genius, like Adolf Hitler I needed a crisis, a Wall Street Crash. Even then, I needed to pretend I was a football manager, which at the end of the day, has to be cheating.

16

Mabel Snr

'Nothing is so soothing to our self-esteem as to find our bad traits in our forbears. It seems to absolve us.'
Van Wyck Brooks

I don't remember why, but I was in a good mood that afternoon. Or maybe it was just me being pleased to see Louise appearing through the staff room door out of the blue.

'He-llo? What are you doing here?'

'Don't smile at me,' she said, negotiating her way around a circle of easy chairs to reach me sat in the corner. It registered straight away. No fuss. I was already feeling strangely elated. Moments of high drama always did this to me.

'Is it my mum? Has she died?'

Louise had reached me now and enclosed me with her arms.

'Uh-huh. Keith rang me about half an hour ago.'

I pulled away and tried to organise my thinking. The world seemed to be turning on its axis all of a sudden, while I stood still. Dizziness.

'Um, what do I need. I should tell..'

'I've already done it. Come on, let's go. There's a train from Derby at five to four.'

It was a Thursday.

The room shuddered continuously as I tried to compose myself. She was gone. She was gone. It was almost terrible news. But she was gone. It hit me: I was free. Alone in the world now for the first time, but free. This was an enormous moment, I knew that - I felt that the instant the look on my wife's face told me the news.

But nothing I could do or think could cover over my instant reaction: a part of me was pleased.

Mabel and I had been getting on very badly indeed. The last reaction I ever saw in my Dad's face was when Mabel leaned over him sitting upright in a chair in the day room in the hospital.

'Wilf. Louise is going to have twins. Isn't that wonderful? They're going to have twins!' and she said it loudly as if the Alzheimer's had taken his hearing. Well it might have done. How would you know?

There was a flicker, not just of a smile on my father's face, but of a big one. And a film of liquid spread across his already watery eyes. To me, through all that sickness, he was still beautiful. And he knew. If he could still formulate thoughts in that impenetrable dark room of his, he would die knowing that his second son was heading for fatherhood. Like father, like son.

This is the only moment of light I can connect to my mother in perhaps the last ten years of her life. After Wilfred died she was continually and totally inconsolable. That's what I have in my memory. But the birth of our children did bring her round to a position of near normality for a time, at least outwardly, and this pleased me very much. I couldn't cope with the same misery Keith and I had faced for six years every time we went home. She just had to find a way to face the rest of her life from some sort of advantageous bargaining position, or we would be dragged under with her.

Mabel Snr had only just bit the dust at the age of 98 and I had every reason to believe Mabel Jnr would last at least as long. She would do it to spite me, I reckoned in my darker moments.

When she visited in the early days, she could be bright and cheerful. She wouldn't be seeing sixty-five again but people thought she was much younger than this, despite everything always fast on her feet, sprightly somehow. She and Tasha formed a bond, even when the little one was tiny. It was uncanny, but it was there. There was no mistaking that. But there was still an oppressiveness in the air whenever we met. She would still want us to visit her every holiday and for longer than we could possibly manage.

Her presence was immensely helpful though, I'll give her that. She would look after both babies while we sped up to London to see friends. The first summer of the twins' lives, an exhausted Louise and a pre-Town me spent a week in the Beaujolais while both mothers-in-law - who'd always got on like a pair of burning houses by the way - played parents chez Mabel. We had a predictably excellent time: we had no money, but we had sunny weather, countryside you could write poetry about if you were of a mind, good food and each other. We had no car and there were no buses between the villages so we walked everywhere and it was an arse-load of simple pleasure. My mum had played an essential role in all of this and we were very grateful. And she seemed to have a wonderful time with the brats: she loved and adored them, no question. And they loved her.

Then when Lyall and Tasha were past two and we'd been in Derbyshire for a time - and oh how she hated us moving up there near

Louise's parents: nothing would convince her there wasn't a conspiracy going on behind her back - she began complaining regularly about indigestion. She'd been to her doctor who always seemed to be sending her for something called a berium meal. This sounded revolting, but would reveal to the medics whether she had an ulcer. Most likely this was the problem.

Then the next time she got the train up to see us she was in pain most of the time and wasn't sleeping at all well. She kept asking for more pillows, and short of actually going out to buy her some more, we did all we could and gave her what we had. Indigestion though, she thought it was and how bad could that be? Then the day before she was going home a school rang Louise asking her to go in on supply. We needed the cash and Louise desperately needed the mental stimulation.

'We'll take you lot over to Betty's and you can all have a fine time together,' I said.

'No, I can still look after them myself: I'm not that ill, you know,' she said.

'Well, if you're sure,' Louise said.

'I'm sure,' she said.

Soon after she got home the phone rang. Keith. We hadn't been looking after Mabel properly. What were we thinking of? Pillows, she needed pillows, and you couldn't get any for her. And you've been using her. Making her look after the twins while Louise is out all day.

That was it. The frozen bloody limit. I could stand up to her. Finally. Or she would make the rest of her life miserable for me, and that would affect my wife. No way. No. Fucking. Way. Ever since I can remember you've tried to push me around, tell me what I should be doing with my life. You didn't want me to get married, you always wanted me to be respectable and settle down to a boring job, wear a suit and tie and have children. And look at me, I practically did all that, worked hard at school (well, some of the time), got the qualifications you wanted, went to university and got a degree, just like you wanted (don't mention the attendant lifestyle) and here I am, thirty-fucking-two years old and you're still telling me what to do and what's more you tell lies about me and worst of all, my wife, behind my back.

I didn't speak to her for a year.

It was a war of nerves, a battle of wills, the whole classic mother-son scenario. Whoever picked up the phone and dialled the number first was the loser. If she was going to live to ninety (I'd be in my mid-fifties: there was a vast amount of time to be gone through before I got there) the balance of power was going to be altered. No way was I going to let her become any more like Mabel Snr than she already was. I was going to grind her into submission until she realised that if she wanted a second son, she was going to have to change: I didn't give a rats how old she was.

She was dying of heart disease. Eventually, a month before she went into hospital the final time, she rang me. She didn't know what she'd done. I can't remember now if I told her. I suppose I must have done. I'd won. But on January 17th 1991 she was dead. Tasha knew before we told her. Her little face looked up into mine and Louise's minutes before we were going to break the news.

'Nana's dead, isn't she.'

We were stunned by this and looked at each other in wonder. No way could she have found out from us, we agreed later.

The last time I saw her she was very pleased to see me and we didn't mention the classic, Candler Street-style row. It had always been like that at number nine: someone was always not speaking to someone else. In the end the winner was Mabel Snr, not me, who'd not long since gone to her grave laughing, no doubt. She ruined her daughter's life, though she wouldn't have known. Likely as not she would have cared if she had, but she never ever, no matter how hard anyone might have tried, understood. She made my mum, who as an adult had changed her name to Joan, leave grammar school at fourteen to take in washing. The first time mum had come back to Candler Street with homework and proudly or with trepidation, no-one now will ever know, taken her books and put them on the living room table, Mabel Snr, the cow, had swept them on to the floor telling her not to bring her fancy ideas into this house.

Joan's whole face now, fifty nine years later was so sickly it was yellow.

'This is no way to live your life,' she said. And I was glad at the thought that she may have been preparing herself for her end. This was indeed, no way to live a life any more.

I still had a sneaking suspicion she was indestructible. So when I kissed her goodbye I thought there was no doubt I'd see her again. Now, after hiding the truth about her symptoms for so long, probably because she was terrified there was something seriously wrong with her, a reaction typical of her generation, she would be getting appropriate treatment. With my mum surely anything was possible.

Not this time. The years of caring for my father, the deluge of grief that followed and four decades of committed smoking had done irreparable damage.

So I got the train and met Keith and we replayed the scene from six years earlier at hospitals, funeral parlours and awful, anonymous brick buildings where death certificates are dished out and I hoped all the while I could get away back home that Friday night. We were away at Hartlepool the next day and I was going to go if I possibly could, without offending my brother (Who am I kidding. Of course I was going to Hartlepool the next day). The evening before, I'd met Keith's new partner, Tracie, who was much younger, much younger than me even, but mature and down to earth and very likeable. I really liked her. Mabel hadn't approved, but she would have objected to any woman Keith brought home as a matter of principle.

Within two years they had married, and now they have two very fine daughters who never knew their father's mother, and I have to say, that'll do them no harm whatsoever. Their other grandmother will be some photographs and stories, some funny, some not.

In my cocky university days Mabel was at her best. Dad worked too hard but was fine. They had more money than they'd ever had and one day they would be retired and very, very content, just to have each other. My friends thought she was a tricky customer alright, but she could be a laugh, especially when she didn't mean to be.

Once in the kitchen with me and Steve she turned to me and said,

'Son, if I ever find out you've taken drugs I'll swing for you.'

'Mum, they've abolished hanging.'

'I don't care, I'll swing for you I will, I'll swing for you if you're taking drugs.'

'Mum. They've abolished hanging.'

'I don't care, I'll.........'

Steve, who was in pain and cackling like a demented dentist, told all our friends and Mabel fast became a legend.

'Don't eat that gravy,' she said soon after, 'it'll grow maggots.' This time there was nothing I could say. We all stood there in the kitchen and our faces opened wide, but she was determined there would be maggots.

Regretfully, the story that weighs most heavily and comes most readily to mind when I think of my mother, is of her as Mabel Snr. Keith, between marriages, often stayed over with her. One night he came in to an empty house, and later she appeared.

'Hi, mum, where've you been?'

'The horticultural society.'

'Oh, right,' says Keith with a heart full of hope, 'did you have a good time?'

'Of course not, your father's dead.'

That's my Mabel Snr. May she be resting in a place of sunlight where flowers grow, and where there is education.

17

The Commentator

'And.....that.....was....liquid football.'

Alan Partridge

I heard someone on the Compton Street one Saturday afternoon, shouting at one of our more lumbering, impotent strikers,

'Grayson, tha's as much use as a cat's arse,'
And while we were all laughing, added,
'...and about 'alf as attractive.'
This pretty much sums up what I think of football commentators. If I'd had a brain when I was younger I would have become a commentator. I'd mastered the basics by the time I was nine, which wasn't difficult. Football commentating is for men who can't or won't grow up, let's face it. I mean, listen to them:
'Beckham. Lovely ball out wide to Gary Neville, overlapping.......plays it in.......and Cole!! Oh, all-most got there. United unlucky there Ron...(?)'
That's it. That's all it is. That's all they do. It's easy. A fool could do it, and down the years, well, they have done. Nothing, but absolutely nothing makes me more angry than to hear someone praise a television commentator. Most of them are actually bad at it, which should be virtually impossible. But either they have a hopeless vocabulary (Motson), wail like self-righteous old Tory women (Davies), scream like total idiots where it isn't remotely appropriate or enjoyable (Jonathan Somebody or Other), have no vocabulary whatsoever and sound, well, ludicrous (the now sadly departed Mr Moore) - the list goes on and on, I do apologise - or spread clichés everywhere like a plague (Tyldesley, who started out well until he was tamed), which is easy to do, that's for sure. If I hear one more of them talk about a player reading (or not reading) the script I'm going to dig up Larry's dead body and throw it at Martin Tyler. I swear.

And as for professionalism. To address the problem of pronunciation of French footballers, one phone call to any secondary school in the country with a request to the switchboard to speak to a French teacher would enable the potato headed English commontater to pronounce Lilian (Lily-on - drop the final 'n') Laslandes (La-londe). I mean to say, I have heard recently 'Laz-londe' (aaagghh!) and even, from the splendid Tony Cottee, 'Laz-landiz.' Dipping into history, I still have not forgiven Mr Motperson during the so-called 'Euro 96' tournament, for pronouncing Kristian Karembeu three different ways in the opening twenty minutes, all of them wrong ('Karemboy', 'Karemboo' and 'Karemboe' - it should be 'Karembur', but hold the 'r' a little so it sounds like the sound you make in the middle of 'hurt'; see? it's easy).

Still things don't change. As I write, Sven Goran Eriksson - that's 'Yoran' as we all know - has just been referred to as 'Goran' by Garth Crooks, and Motperson, who both only work for the national broadcasting television station so why should they bother to get it right. And to listen to an Arsenal game on Radio 5 is to hear the French language torn and mangled to death. Why are we so parochial and ignorant in this country when it comes to foreign languages?

Straying further into hostile territory, why don't these guys have the good sense to be self-parodying? Did they never hear Steve Coogan's mirthmungus Alan Partridge on The Day Today satirising them with a bouquet of exclamatory remarks over a melange of obscure goals from the European game: 'Eat that!' as a shot crashed in; 'Shheeyit! Did you see that!' as another whams into the net from twenty-five yards. 'That was liquid football.' Why can't they get something close to this? I'm sorry. I'm sure they're all really nice people, and good luck to them for doing so little for so long to deserve their nice, comfy salary. I doubt they give a fourpenny fuck what I think anyway, so why am I feeling guilty here?

I often turn the sound down when I'm watching football these days. It's much better, you should try it. Sometimes I put some music on over the top of it, and although you'd think this sounds a bit like having chips and custard, it works, believe me. Or I sit and talk to one of the family and watch at the same time. You can very profitably kill two birds with one stone here, chatting amiably with wife about this and that: the day at work, the new sofa you're going to buy, who in the village has been moaning a lot about their piles, whatever you like. You can do this and catch the goals from Arsenal-Chelsea or see if that mad tackle from Viera really did deserve that fist in the gob from Jimmy Floyd Hasselbaink.

When you're watching a live game, you fare much better without some nitwit droaning on like the plank on the train with a mobile telling his wife she'll have to leave the house to pick him up ten seconds earlier because the guard was busy scratching his nuts at Reigate. You find yourself starting to relax a little more, if you're on your own that is, and without doing anything to force the issue you'll suddenly realise after a few minutes that your brain has begun to pick up patterns of play for you and you can see a goal coming five minutes before it actually arrives. It's very pleasing. Do this for thirty minutes and you find yourself rather soothed all round, while you're realising gradually that Tony Adams is an exceptional player after all and Peter Reid really does look like a monkey. You notice players' haircuts, players playing great passes, players picking their nose, all sorts of things without commentators bothering your mind with their inane drivel.

So you're thinking, right, where do you get your front from, shooting your gob off at those nice professional lads who do the game such a service climbing up all those ladders in the wind and the rain? You try it and see how hard it really is! Well, listen here: I have tried it, and like I say: it's easy.

I started young, at seven, soon after I got a Subbuteo set for Christmas. I woke up in the middle of the night, like kids do,* rushed downstairs and into the living room and switched on the light. The room opened straight on to the little dining room and there stretched out on the table was the most wonderful thing: a luscious bright green baize football pitch glued immaculately to a thick board, with two teams placed carefully in their positions, one in red and white, the other in blue and white. The goals had nets (this was so fantastic, I can't begin to tell you: whenever we went over the park to play football, there were goals there, but never with nets. I was always disappointed)!

I didn't like playing the game with people because I was such a bad loser, throwing tantrums all the time, and my obvious day to day opponent was my brother and he was older so was bound to be better than me. So I worked hard at not giving him the opportunity.

I managed to persuade my Dad to let the board become a part of my bedroom furniture and proceeded to play the game on my own, performing the player function for each team in turn. And I played for hour, after hour after hour, week in, week out, for year after year after year. I had cup competitions, I staged bog standard league championships, I played internationals. And for each match I played I carefully selected one of my growing collection of programmes, propped it up against the wall at the half way line, and commentated, with enthusiasm and great style (or so it always seemed to me), my days and nights away. I had a brilliant kitchen timer that rang after any period up to an hour I wanted. It also told me at a glance how long there was left to play ('Colchester on the attack now, one-down with only four minutes to go: can they produce a goal?')

I did this through my primary school years and way, way into my sec-

---

* That's the middle of the night when you're a parent, 6.30 am if you're still knee high to a snake's back leg.

ondary school years. At times I wondered when and how I was going to break it to a future lifetime companion that I liked to talk to myself for a hobby. Eventually, the worry drifted away into a mist of time. By the time I was, ooh, seventeen, I'd finally given up, apart from the odd cup final for old time's sake.

But a long time later when I was on a coach bound for Blackpool and one of the supporters' club committee right in front of me was telling someone right behind me that they were going to be making videotapes of Town home matches next season and were looking for a commentator I looked the feller smack dab straight down the middle of both eyes and said, 'I'll do it.' And he looked at me for the merest quizzical instant, then in a flash saw the look on my face of total certainty and resolution and made the tiniest smile at the corner of his mouth and replied, 'Alright then. The cameraman's having a try out at the game Toosdee. Be there for ten past seven.'

I grinned. A chance to turn all those hundreds of hours of practice into something that would do me a bit of good at last. See, I'd sussed this out as soon as Ian told me that from next season they were going to video every game. If I was going to commentate, there was no question about it: I was going to get in free.

And there was no doubt in my mind straightaway that this was another step inside.

On a balmy Tuesday end of season evening (this was almost the end of the first failed Hart miracle campaign) I stepped beyond the prison gates of the football fan for the very first time. I was shown through a turnstile at the main stand by a lone steward and met Ian and we walked through a door, normally a total no-go zone for the likes of me, which let directly on to the cinder track next to the pitch. Even empty save a few players from each side still having a leisurely kickabout-cum-warm up, Saltergate was a picture. My stomach turned over at the sight of it.

There was no-one to notice, but I still felt I'd entered a charmed circle as we walked alongside the main stand, the dug outs (I could reach out and touch them if I wanted to!), then the players door passing me on my right and the empty, now wide-looking away terrace of Cross Street ahead of me. Take a look at that excellent castellated wall at the back which I've now read about in the Bible of Football Ground lovers, Simon Inglis's Football Grounds of England and Wales, then swing round behind the goal. You notice for the first time, though not the last, how many bumps and undulations there are in the pitch near the touchline, as if the groundsman down the years daren't touch it in case they dig up buried treasure only they know is there and be cursed for evermore. Why has this never been levelled? Are we that poor a club? Have we always been? Why does Dave Waller have to dribble up and down a hillside as he slaloms defenders in an effort to notch a goal?

Finally a gate is opened on the Cross Street side in the awful fence that circumnavigates three sides of the ground and we pass through the no-man's land between home and away supporters to find a small door in the back wall, like a trap door on a stage into...someone's back garden? There is a path about nine inches wide between one of the ninety-two most important historical sites in England and Wales and someone's stinking compost heap, a mound of noxious dirt which smells as though the contents of the devil's own jockstrap have been emptied on to it after he'd just played his part in the First World War. We struggle through to some steps which bend at a right angle back up to a door which takes us into a box structure build on top of the low terrace roof: a commentary box no less. I smile a smile of small but satisfied triumph like Mussolini surveying the crowds in St Peter's Square after having spent a long time on the Vatican toilet, and think about what I am about to do. Not only am I trying out tonight for the supporters' club commentator's position, but I am recording my entry for the Radio 2 Fosters Search For A Commentator competition of 1990.

I'd heard about the thing on the radio and had noted down the address with a feeling of no more than idle curiosity, but the more I thought about it, the more it seemed an interesting thing to do. I wasn't going to do this professionally if we won, even if a victory opened up the opportunity, but wouldn't it be a hoot if I won and it'd be my name in the papers, and a mug shot and ooh, that would be grand. It was regional rounds first and here I was anyway about to yap for the Spireites so why not? Why on earth not indeed.

I switched on my little tape recorder when the game started and perched it on a ledge right where I could talk into my microphone from the camcorder and off I went on my live commentating debut.

Well I told you it was easy, and even though over a thousand hours of Subbuteo was a lifetime away, about the same of listening to Match of the Day, the Big Match, seven World Cups and who knows how many Saturday afternoons worth of radio commentary it was no harder than breathing. Plus, a wife and half my friends would go on the record for nothing and swear I've always had verbal diahorrea since they first knew me. So.

'Arnott. Lovely ball out wide to Bryn Gunn, overlapping.......plays it in.......and Waller!! Oh, heads it just wide. Chesterfield unlucky not to be one-nil up with five minutes gone.' Unfortunately no Big Fat Ron of the chunky jewellery beside me, but you can't have everything.

My bosses on the committee looked at me a trifle strangely when next they saw me. Thinking, 'who or what is this crazy bastard cockney who talks to himself with the ease of a lawyer sliding his arse on to the front seat of another BMW?'

'Was it okay?'

'Yeah,' says Pat, the chairman of the committee, thoughtfully, 'it was very good.'

'Thanks,' says I with a smile, 'so I've passed, then?'

'Well put it this way, we're thinking of doing away matches too if we get a decent run goin;' would that be okay?' I snorted to myself in mock contempt: would that be okay.

'Fine by me.'

The Midland heat of The Competition was in Birmingham, and I had my pushbike nicked from Whatstandwell station, which was a bottomer because I'd only just bought it and that was the first time I'd ever left it anywhere. Otherwise, it was a good day. I won it.

It couldn't have been hard; I mean, how many nutcases can there be in the midlands region? My defeated rivals were a mixture of rugby and horse racing oddballs (I nearly called them 'enthusiasts,' but we all had to be way beyond that stage), and I think one other Motperson besides me.

I've long since thrown a lot of the details of the event into the memory waste disposal, so what game I talked about, forgive me, I couldn't tell you. I can only just recall the fact that the talk-off was staged at BBC's Pebble Mill studios. We all took our turn, alphabetical order, and went into a booth with a TV, a chair, a mic and a pair of headphones, and did our own personal thing at the appointed cue. Were Everton one of the teams? I think so. A real radio commentary faded out and in I jumped with the usual confidence that spilled out of me because how many of my rivals have the equivalent experience of fifteen years work on Rochdale versus Chorley and another two thousand matches live from my bedroom? Self-belief is half the battle. Sound as though you know what you're banging on about and you'll fool everyone bar the experts.

That said, the main judge and presenter of the 'award' of Midlands Regional Winner of The Sports Equivalent Of Stamp Collector Of The Month Award was none other than Steve Rider himself, a man I must say I had no respect for whatever. I practically screamed whenever his anodyne face appeared on my screen. And who knows, perhaps I took off to football all those Saturdays because subconsciously I couldn't face the thought of watching him on Grandstand for a nine year stretch. Nevertheless, I had to chuckle minutes after he announced from a tiny podium that I'd beaten the rest of the field by a short head or something, because there I was with my back directly touching his for a scrunch of hammy publicity shots for the sponsors who hoped that the Derby Evening Telegraph and Derbyshire Times would replace photos of a Mrs Doris Johnson of Ripley, disgusted at the local constabulary's inability to catch the thief who stole her washing, with Beeb star Rider and a stupidly grinning nobody. Whether they did or not, I never dared to find out. However, I was less than gruntled weeks later to find a copy of one of these photo-disasters appearing in no less hallowed literary organ than the Chesterfield Football Club Official Programme.

Time has not been kind to this souvenir of time. Not only were my glasses clearly borrowed from a giant owl, but my headphones can only suggest that I went straight from Pebble Mill to the nearest aircraft carrier to guide in a load of Harrier Jets from their latest training mission. Sadly, for one of the last times in a somewhat chequered but by no means unhappy existence, I am wearing a tie. O dear.

I was quietly absolutely bloody full of myself between the heat and the final which was to take place at The Oval cricket ground, no less. This despite finding a space on the railing where my new sixty quid second hand racing bike should have been. Alexander The Great never had to walk home up a steep hill after his latest triumph over the Mongol hordes, or whoever he used to conquer for a living.* The last thing I'd ever won outright, on my own was, well, never. I'd got football medals at the cubs (Waltham and District, league and cup) and they asked me to join the Lord's Ground Staff, but there was no ceremony and no neo-press hoo-ha of a distinctly just a fraction above non-entity kind.

For the final it was posh London hotel the night before for finalist and partner, a pleasant and plentiful dinner at same with excellent wines, and Steve Rider again telling stories about celebs that only emphasized the fact that you were never ever going to join their ranks whatever you did tomorrow. This thought had troubled me a lot since the heat. There I was a mere Derbyshire supply teacher, my career going nowhere; I would have

---

* Which reminds me to tell you about the greatest piece of sports commentary of all time and don't you dare let anyone tell you different. Sid Waddell, darts commentator way-beyond-extraordinaire, was doing his stuff on an Eric Bristow procession to one of his many world championship victories, and whilst Eric was closing in on another leg, he switched his gorgeous Geordie dulcets to a subtle blend of pure passion and dignified reverence and waxed thus:

'Alexander of Macedonia had conquered half the known world by the time he was thirty-three: this man is only twenty-six.'

Enduring image, isn't it?

rather liked to have known just what stakes we were going to be playing for out there. Idiotically, I didn't make it my business to find out. Hindsight makes complete wallies of all of us, but before I threw myself totally at this thing, I needed to know what chance there was of an outright win turning itself into something a little, no: a lot more solid. Like a job.

Well, shit: I'd just moved up to Derbyshire from London so some sort of opportunity at the Beeb's sports department itself was out of the question. Unlikely anyway, why would they want to employ a sports reporter there anyway? Where did commentators live? If I was offered the chance to do match reports for them I could cover the north and midlands from where I was. Was that the sort of job I was looking for? No. Well, I didn't think so. Did I? And anyway, what were they going to offer the winner?

Why didn't I bother to find out? I haven't practiced for this. I meant to but I didn't. Not once. Not for a minute. At Saltergate I worked with moving pictures attached for the viewer: this competition was for radio commentary, which was different. I needed to tape some TV football and polish my technique for hours. Then tape it and listen to it back: hear my faults and eradicate them. In other words, prepare professionally for the event. Then I might have a chance of more glory. But no. I won easily in Birmingham, why was the competition here going to be much different. I would wing it and still win. Maybe.

I was enough of a student of the game of cricket to appreciate the hiring of no lesser historical landmark than The Oval for this glorious festival of the spoken word. However, it typified the event. It was good, but it wasn't quite Lords. Then again, the hallowed turf-environs of the 'not far from the' home of cricket was cheap enough to allow its history to be swallowed up by an Australian company that flogged cheap beer to people who didn't know the difference between fizzy, processed, falling down water and a pint of Foxnadger's Old Scrote, which gave the thing some glamour at least.

The second class nature of the event - John Inverdale turned up late looking like a rugby playing overgrown student for the judging, as if this was a break between two more pressing engagements - didn't bother me particularly: my lower intestine was too busy filling up uncomfortably and my stomach building up enough fire for the biggest ceremonial book burning in world history. I was last of nine other hopefuls and had to wait two and a half hours for my turn at the coconut shy, a time that passed more slowly than Christmas eve when you're seven and there's nothing much on TV. I went out for a walk around the ground.

It was a beautiful late winter day, with the sun steadily melting a sea of grass as it rose above the gasometer and dreary blocks of housing I'd seen so many times on the box watching test matches. On a day when I wasn't so nervous I felt I was going to fall over in a faint, I would have loved being there. I'd sat in the seats that spread out emptily all around me a few times and would have enjoyed hugely the fact that I was walking on the grass edge of the famous arena feeling that, however dubiously and briefly, I belonged here. Perhaps I would be walking round again later in the afternoon with Louise in a quiet lap of triumph, savouring the moment when I'd at least earned the right to consider a career change, even if I turned it down ten seconds later. If I could only get myself up for this and show them I've got a brain and a better and more colourful vocabulary than all the pro-commentators put together; if I can only calm down and get into my stride quickly. If I do that, the lack of preparation won't matter a bugger. I can do it. Yes, I can do this!

I was hopeless. I must have come last. I performed like an old nag in the 4.30 at Chepstow. I got the 1989 Liverpool-Forest post-Hillsborough cup semi final, real juicy stuff, with a penalty and loads of other stuff happening, and I blew it completely. My words flew out of my big mouth in a cascade of soft feathers instead of being crisp and tidy and economical. I sounded like a stuttering make-weight who the organisers had hauled off Kennington Road an hour before the off and Steve Rider, bless him, in the public de-brief, tore me to shreds in front of a hundred people just before the celebration lunch in the Long Room. I was among the first to shake hands with the winner, a young feller who'd specialised in Under-Water International Camel Chasing, and ran out of the place in a gust of self-loathing dragging Louise behind me. Instead of slapping me hard and telling me to go back in there and eat food like a grown up man, she followed resignedly. As Brian Wilson once eloquently put it, she knows me so well.

I'd never been found out like this before. The field had been much better than I'd expected. There were two weirdos into horse racing who found each other the previous evening and were now inseparable. They were so in a world of their own they seemed disappointed to be separated just for five minutes to go into the appointed room to commentate. One of them had already been doing some work for Radio Wales, someone said. Another was already working for a station in Scotland on football. These wouldn't have been going in on a wing and a prayer like me: they'd have been nerding their way through reference books and making practice tapes, no question. These grafting amateurs had given my butt a good kicking and it was no less than I deserved. Rider had taken a black jack out of his well-made suit and smashed it into my face but, I thought as

Louise smiled hopefully at me coming back from the buffet with a cup of coffee, maybe this is what I needed. Perhaps this would wake me up. Trouble was, pained though I was to have had my trousers well and truly taken down, I looked deep into my heart and saw the truth that had been sitting there on a stool, idly smoking a fag and waiting for some attention: 1. I was 33 and too chicken to compete properly in case I lost and it was proven that I wasn't as good as I thought I was - in short, I was a loser. 2. I didn't want a new job. I didn't want to be on the radio, or graduate to Motperson Land one day: enough. What I wanted more than anything in the world then, was to have my Saturdays free: to watch the Town, wherever they were playing.

18

Being Benaud

'..and that looks like a Grade A worm place!'
Richie Benaud, responding to picture on monitor of
a pigeon ducking its head into the grass in search of lunch,
Trent Bridge 1977.

So I went back to my commentary box at homely Saltergate, selling the fanzine on the street til ten-to-three then rushing round the corner up St Margaret's Drive to the club's front entrance, then through a door on the right and along a corridor to the players' tunnel next to Paul Hart's office. I usually beat the teams to the tunnel in the early days, though once I walked through when the tiny passage leading to the pitch was filled with twenty-two men in bright clean kit with clacking boots on the stone floor all of them seeming to tower above me. I suddenly felt small and unimportant, though Mick Leonard, our keeper, who I now knew, nodded seriously at me as I hurried past and out on to the pitch side before I was crushed by a heaving throng of professional sportsmen.

How exciting was this? It was what I wanted, was it not? Amazing, though, how blasé you get in life. The first time I walked out on to the pitch through the players' door it was as exciting as almost anything I'd ever done. The tenth time I walked through I still felt oh-so pleased with myself at being so privileged. The fiftieth time I was just rushing through in a hurry to get to the microphone before they actually kicked off because the most important thing to me then was to sell every possible copy of The Crooked Spireite I could. And as there was always a last minute rush down Saltergate to the Kop turnstiles when I might sell another five copies, I would pick up my bag at one minute to three and leg it like a criminal with a dole card exiting the scene of a crime round to the club entrance quick enough to get my voice on to tape to accompany the first kick of the ball. There were times when I wouldn't make it.

But that was later, after Paul Hart and promotion chasing seasons, when the shine was wearing off the silver of the trophy of Being There. The first season I talked my way to freemans I did the best I could, not least because the people who watched and heard the most was the Gaffer and his players and I wanted to make a decent impression. So I was as thoughtful and as professional as I could be, even making notes about all the players from the away side and making it my business not to be like the twerp I'd heard on the copy of the previous season's huge 3-1 result at Bramall Lane when the home commentator whined and whinged like a baby just because his favourites couldn't beat the local team anchored to the foot of the table. As a matter of pride I was not going to fall down that hole. If a team came to our place and gave us a hiding or sneaked an Arsenal and later requested a tape, they would hear a voice on the play who spoke dispassionately about what he saw and showed a creditable knowledge of the game - for an outsider, naturally.

As the first few games passed into the autumn and I relaxed into the job, I began to be a little playful and take a few chances. Mostly I wanted to try to emulate my hero in the trade, the only man I looked up to really, the Daddy, the Maestro, the Master Craftsman: Richie Benaud.

Now, the initiated reading these pages, may well be somewhat bemused by this, as Mr B. is an Australian who has commentated on the fairly noble game of cricket since around the year 1960. And they are probably thinking, 'only a complete idiot with a wooden leg is going to try to model a football commentary on the style of a cricket specialist. Well, yes, you may indeed be on to something there, but I was determined to do my Rich impersonation, just for the sheer fun and hell of it. So, when a Town goal went in, instead of raising my voice to the level of someone announcing a fire in a crowded building, I paused, let the sound of the Kop or the Compton crowd just below me fill most of the audio tape for a few seconds, and then almost ironically pass comment or do the unexpected:

'Well, the Halifax defence have only themselves to blame: Waller's been threatening to do that for most of the first half, and he's crashed in that cross from Ryan and it's now 3-2.'

If I remembered to, I might try to recall an exact piece of Benaud I'd heard before, analysing a fall of a wicket, say: connoisseurs of the man's genius will be familiar with his taste for the pause and the avoidance of cliche. So, instead of ranting and raving about what is always a significant moment in a team's innings, he'd keep talking in exactly the same way as he'd been doing the ball before when a batsman had just idly let a widish delivery pass on by to the wicketkeeper. So someone's stumps might just have been flattened and fielders would be rushing to congratulate the bowler, but Il Maestro would be saying, 'Now, you won't see a better yorker than that all dai-eee.' Or if a late order batter lost his wicket in the same way at a time when nothing much is at stake in the game, or better, when it is, and everyone on the field and the box is getting tense, he'd go for the understatement jugular and just say, as I once heard, 'Bowled........him,' in that laconic, south Australian drawl. It might have sounded as though he was sitting up there in a dressing gown sipping Chablis with pretty girls carefully manicuring his toenails while he took the occasional disdainful glance out of the commentary box window, but if you followed his career you knew this was Richie at his imperious but still totally focussed best, Oh, yes, that was the way to do it: the plodders in his trade across all sports might do the normal everyday bleedin' obvious and tell us what we've just seen with our own eyes thank you very much, but not this man. This was the commentator who, towards the climax of the 1979 World Cup final, first innings, saw Viv Richards, in masterly but physically damaging form, absurdly moving a careful, but almost unnatural predatory step towards the square leg umpire, in order to explode a rising off drive from a good ball towards bowler Mike Hendrick's head (who ducked while the umpire lowered his own napper and hoped he would still be around to begin enjoying the rest of his life) and observed, in two sagacious words, his voice rising on the only syllable of the second word: 'Very wise.'

I doubt whether two words in the history of language have ever conveyed so much meaning. Certainly no-one in the history of sports commentary would have approached the situation from such an oblique, yet quietly, subtly hilarious angle. Sid Waddell you enjoy hugely but laugh at: Richie Benaud you laugh with. There was no-one, no-one remotely within a country, if not outback mile of the man (and neither is there to this day).

So I'd try to match his detachment and dryness, his refusal to wind himself up like an amphetamine alarm clock when a moment of high drama erupts in front of him (though he would allow himself the luxury of letting go if he felt like doing so). If a winning goal went in with seconds to go, just to entertain myself, I might even just yawn loudly as if to say, 'you don't need me to tell you what just happened: you saw it for yourself'.

Naturally, though, seeing as I was watching my own team playing important matches sometimes, I would happily lose it and take a few chances. In 1990, in the first leg of the Play Off Semi Final, a game which led to disaster at Wembley, our winger-turned-striking replacement for the injured Waller, Calvin Plummer, scored twice in the first half to scenes of vast, leaping and arm-thrusting joy around three parts of Saltergate. Now, Calvin was black, and I'd always loved that scene in the American movie *Animal House* where the lad who was later the lead in *Local Hero*, Peter

Riegert, goes into a roadside bar and makes a complete fool of himself shouting 'Otis! My man!' at the lead singer of a band that played r n' b gigs at his frat house. Otis looks across blankly, thinking, naturally, 'what the holy fuck is this shithead doin' in a bar exclusively reserved for brothers?

So anyway, Calvin makes it three-nil to Town on this mighty big occasion and I have to let it go, 'Calvin, my man!' in honour of his putting us halfway down Wembley Way before even a ball is kicked in the second leg. I was happy, and this was fun - a perfect grandstand view of every game for free - so why not mess around? Better to go down an individualistic idiot than a commentator drone clone.

Calvin Plummer may well have a copy of the game on our supporters' club tape and for all I know, sits back and watches one of the most important performances of a career most noticeable for its underachievement. And if he does, I hope he has the good sense to think, or say out loud, 'Who is that shithead-whitey talking like a total prick about my goals and who does he think he is?' Mostly I thought I was Richie Benaud, but not that time.

Neither did I hold on when Dave Waller scored a spectacular injury time winner against Halifax Town that first season to complete a 4-3 scoreline where at half time we were 1-3 behind. Here's what I found myself committing to tape:

> Throw in to Chesterfield. Desperate rearguard action from Halifax Town, no doubt. Gunn [takes throw-in]..Again the header from Bramhall, he's won so many headers tonight. Ryan..holds it... wide to Hewitt..sweeps it out wide to Waller. Can he keep it in? He does, superbly. [Sucks in defender then leaves him in the dust, dribbling past him and in from the touchline towards goal]. Oh, [Richie-like pause] magnificent play by Dave Waller.... [pause as DW, just inside penalty box, tries to throw defender on wrong foot to make space for a shot] ..tries to curl the goalkeeper..... [crowd and commentator hold breath as Wall attempts arcing shot around the goalkeeper and in at the far post] ..and oh! [slight pause] you dream about finishes like that to a match: you dream about goals like that...Poor Halifax Town. They murdered Chesterfield in the first half. Murdered them. 3-1 up...Dave Waller had scored an unbelievable, and un-bee-leeevable goal and it's pulled some miracle out of the fire for Chesterfield - and un-bee-leeeeeeevable shot with his right foot and it's Chesterfield 4 Halifax Town 3.............

A couple of dozen too many unbelievables there no doubt, and I'm sure Richie would have pulled off some sort of verbal triumph with such raw material, but that was me eight matches into my new hobby and I'd put that up against anything Piggy Motson's ever breathed into a microphone down the years: at least I didn't resort to a stale trademark 'would you believe it?!' In fact you can put that on my grave stone.

Here Lies
Craig Wilfred Thomas
Died 23 April 2066
Aged 109
Deeply Missed.
Better Than John Motson.

19

Carlisle And The End Of The Line

'Nite and Fog are my days..'

Mercury Rev

My commentaries may not actually have been that bad, because one day at work I got a call from the presenter of the Saturday afternoon show on Radio Hallam, one of the BBC's two Sheffield radio stations. He'd had a recommendation of what I did at Chesterfield from their usual reporter, a guy I knew called Phil, a Town fan who would have owned a video or two of important home wins. The situation was this: Hallam were short of a reporter from the area for Saturday's game at Carlisle: did I want to do it?

Hmm, I thought, this would normally be a bears shitting in the woods type of proposition, but did I want to be going on the train there and back: the coach would be gone by the time I'd finished with Hallam? Freezing, railway platforms in February are not my scene, frankly.

I knew too that this would be serious business from what the man was saying: three times each half I would have to give a live report on the game as it developed and a summing up at the end. Then, I would need to do an interview live with one of the players afterwards, about a quarter of an hour after the final whistle. That might be nice, though, especially if we won.

The feller said 'think about it and I'll call you in a couple of days,' the undertones in his voice of which suggested, 'there's no-one else, we're desperate.' In the end I had to do this, because for a boy who's misspent youth consisted of kneeling on a hard bedroom floor flicking plastic around a green baize to the sound of his own voice, this invitation was akin to a rubber-brained skinhead screaming 'CUM ON 'NEN!!!' to a different brand of same across the street outside a football ground in the late sixties.

So when Radio Man rang back the next day I knew he was in trouble and that I was his last hope, which made it easier to agree to the assignment. So I get my brief there and then: again how many match bulletins I'll have to send down a telephone that will ring when it's time and connect me to the programme presenter, a pass to get me through the usual jobsworth on the door and an interview is all arranged with Sean Dyche, our ginger-haired rising star of a right back.

The Saturday a.m. sees me crawling around a dark bedroom fishing clothes out of drawers and off out into a grey dawn before anyone else in the house stirs, which is early as anyone with a passing knowledge of the waking hours of small children will tell you. Outside it was raining already, so I pulled my hat down tighter and set off for the bus to the train. Many hours later I arrived at Carlisle station in what still looked like a grey dawn and in weather perfectly suited to wild romantic walks across windy moorland and suicidal depression. You could, I suppose, finesse that further by adding 'and an afternoon of lower division football.'

I was there so early I had time to fuss and fret in the tiny press box about which was my phone and was I sitting in someone's regular spot. However by twenty-past two I had a working phone in front of me and was ready to deliver my spiel about how significant it would be for the Spireites to win here to keep their play off hopes alive and so on. This I duly did and feeling I had done okay and that I hadn't sounded too nervous, I blew an express engine sigh of relief out of my mouth when I hung up. This then made a circle of condensation on the glass ten inches from my face, still taut with tension. Whatever the sky was going to send down in terms of weather, at least in here I'll be warm all afternoon. Apart from that it was hard to think what was good about being here in a dirt hole hundreds of miles from home, on my own and with only the faintest idea of what the frig I was doing. For the first time since I took my space helmet off on Planet Football, I thought there might be life away from all this.

The thought that I was going to register a 1° blip on the Local Fameometer nourished me though. It was also, I knew, a challenge. Live, could Mouth Almighty cut the mustard as he'd always thought he would, if given the opportunity. I usually liked a quiet life rather than to be placed into any place remotely whiffing of difficulty, but I'd not resisted this. Perhaps I could be grown up after all.

I also took heart from the fact that at a quarter to three I realised I was sitting next to a former England international. The bloke who'd recently moved into the patch two to my right - we all had to stand up and squeeze ourselves into the wall behind us when someone came into the box like a row of cinema seats - kept calling the man whose sleeve was brushing mine 'Ivor' and a bell rang from a newspaper article I'd seen a year before about England star of the 50s Ivor Broadis writing for a local rag up here on one of his former clubs doing match reports and the like. The little man in the nerve centre of my brain sent a power surge to the rest of it and down into my spinal column;

I suddenly felt more awake as I realised with a start that this man had played at Wembley with Stanley Matthews, Billy Wright and Tom Finney, absolute legends of the game. Now this was something to warm the old cockles of the football heart on a dreary day.

I suddenly felt better and smiled at the thought of something Danny Baker had said on the radio the week before. He was in New York for the first time, about twenty years of age, full of energy and himself with that Big Apple Manhattan buzz every foreigner talks about. He was also with a bunch of mates who'd saved up for months and months to be there, so he was flying high, when he saw none other than John Winston Lennon walking past him. He did a double take, and realising this was too good an opportunity to waste, dashed back towards the icon of the twentieth century and said, 'Excuse me, didn't you used to be John Lennon?'

Chuckling quietly to myself I felt like doing the same thing here but I thought 'didn't you used to be Ivor Broadis?' might be too near to a lot of fun for my own good, so I just cleared my throat a little to prevent a squeak coming out and said, with as big an air of respect as I could muster, 'Do excuse me, but do I have the pleasure of sitting next to an England international?'

'That was a long, long time ago,' came a response, the speaker barely sparing me a sidelong glance. And he took another pull on a small cheroot and looked thoughtfully through the grimy glass again, perhaps thinking of the 100,000 crowds watching him at the home of the Twin Towers for a fleeting second, perhaps thinking about his mortgage or not being able to perform in the bedroom any more, never mind Wembley, who knows.

'What a modest bloke,' I thought, and was beginning to conjure up images myself of immaculately white international shirts, lush, extravagantly green turf and the expectancy of a vast crowd before a battle against the Scots, when suddenly the phone rang in front of me. Hello: ten to three said my watch; I wasn't expecting to hear from Hallam until a quarter past.

'Hi, Neil again, you're on with your team changes and final pre-match stuff in twenty seconds.....'

What? No-one told me about this, what was I going to say? I had a team sheet in front of me, but before I could send my mind out to grasp the difference between the team that had beaten Colchester United the week before and the one that was about to come out here, I was on with a 'and now over to Brunton Park again and our reporter Craig Thomas.....' This had actually sounded pretty cool the first time but now it was just the immediate prelude to a load of mouth guff. I spluttered something about nothing very much and this clearly sounded like 'HELP!!' because the anchor man rescued me pretty sharpish and rather professionally I thought before wailing with grief inside at another Thomas microphone disaster. Still, I told myself, there's nowhere to run, you just have to get on with it and hope you can pull a professional sounding job out of the fire when the game starts.

Never has a football match passed in front of my eyes so quickly. The phone seemed to go every two minutes but was in reality every fifteen, and each time I tried to describe what I'd been watching and how the game was unfolding. I garbled some stuff about the opening quarter of an hour at 3.17, then at 3.31 I was back talking about Andy Morris opening the scoring for Town when a free kick to the home team was nutted into the net and I had to pass on this news to the listeners instantly. So I did. It still sounded like garble to me and I couldn't get the phone down quickly enough so I could collect my thoughts.

What I couldn't work out was whether to quickly write myself a script to read out as each quarter hour moved towards me or think on my feet and trust to good fortune. I'd started out doing the latter, and was in the process of changing my mind and starting to write a half time report when brrrringg, brrrringg, we were off again and I was making it up. I got up and tried to find the press room for a cup of tea but couldn't find it I was so flummoxed by this whole reporting business. I thought I'd get back to my seat to work out a second half strategy, but my mind just wouldn't work. I felt like I was on a roundabout going round and round too fast to get off; the afternoon was completely beyond my grasp it seemed to me, and the harder I reached out to grip it, the further it moved away from me.

The second half began and it started to occur to me that I was so busy trying not to be the worst radio reporter in local radio history I was hardly noticing how my team were doing. It only rammed home to me how little fun all this was. So more ringing phone and more feeling as though I was trying to shout a clear picture of a football match from a mountain top to a bunch of people ten miles away in a force ten gale. By the time of my last report, the wind felt as though it had died down somewhat, and that the crowd had actually crossed the hillside to get within earshot of what I was saying, because what I was telling the mouthpiece about time slipping away from Town, now 3-1 down, and if they were going to get something from the game they would have to do something in the next couple of minutes, actually made sense to me.

Ten to five, it was over. I hoped my summing up got across the point that we'd been stuffed and that we might well be forgetting promotion for another year, and I went down to the dressing room area to see if I could scare up Sean Dyche. The door remained firmly closed. Perhaps they were getting a hammering from Chris McMenemy, the manager and wouldn't be coming out for a long while. I went back up to empty stadium wondering whether I was about to screw up the final part of the assignment. Maybe I should go back down and find him. The phone rang. No Dyche, I said. Ring us if you get him, they said. Minutes passed. I was fed up. I'd let myself down this afternoon. Clearly I wasn't the genius with the microphone I thought I was. It had been bloody difficult, though, the hardest thing I'd ever done: harder than exams, harder than asking girls out, harder than grief. My train left at half-five and I couldn't afford to miss it. It was five and Sean was nowhere in sight. Let's leave this bloody place behind and get home, I thought.

On the train I gradually sank into a worse and worse mood as Town's awful performance hit. I spent all week every week thinking about the team, my mood usually reflecting my team's last result like millions of other losers. Now I had my own personal inadequacy dumped on the regular pain and bereft mind of defeat. The 'how could we possibly have lost?' mystery about to be considered for the first time: a hundred or so hopeless conversations with myself would follow until the day of the next game arrived on my doorstep.

It was dark again. It was still January. It was another five hours and more to get home, most of it under the unremitting glare of strip lighting. It was bloody awful.

The following Monday I was called to the phone again at work. It was the Hallam Anchor again. 'Hello' I said sheepishly: this must be my debrief. Look out.

'Hi, Mike here. Thought I'd give you a call about Saturday. Here's what I thought.'

No nonsense, these media types.

'It wasn't bad...'

Phew, that's a relief,

'...and it wasn't good.'

Oh. Right.

'You sounded very nervous to start with, but you got a lot better. I think you're worth giving another go, it gets easier. Look. We have a weekly team meeting on Monday nights, if you want to come along....'

Another go. Was this an invite to join the team? Did he think I could do a good job? Not *that* bad, then Why is it when I know I don't do something that well I kid myself I did? All day Sunday my performance the previous day got better with each passing hour. I had to admit though that Phil, whose reports I heard down the line from the station from Bramall

Lane sounded slick and professional even though he was a part-timer like me. Not that good then. Why did that hurt? Because I was the long lost son of Richie. Because I'm vain. Do I want to do this on a regular basis? It wouldn't be doing Town every week: that's Phil's prerogative. Do I want to go to Rotherham and Doncaster once a month, when I could be watching Town? Nah.

'Thanks very much, Mike, but I don't drive, I can't get to Sheffield for meetings.'

'Can't drive?' he's thinking, 'thirty-what and he can't drive?'

'And anyway, sad as it sounds, I wouldn't want to miss Chesterfield matches, and my wife's expecting twin monkeys in July, it's going to be a media circus....'

'Okay, I understand. Well, if you change your mind, let me..

'...let you know, yeah, I will. Thanks, 'bye.'

And with that went the end of my broadcasting career.

20

The Reins Of Power

'I must follow the people. Am I not their leader?'
Benjamin Disraeli

By the time The Crooked Spireite was a mere four years old, the editor was suffering from Knackered Fanzine Supremo Syndrome, and was thinking of quitting. This can't be true, I thought and told him. To be a fanzine editor must be one of the most satisfying jobs in the world. The happiness you spread into people's lives, like hot, melting garlic butter - how could the pleasure of doing that for folk be foregone? The importance of it! People loved the Spireite, I knew: it meant the world to them. The prestige of the job, to me, was higher than anything else I could imagine, on the fans' side of the fence at least.

Managing a team to a league championship undoubtedly wins you a certain amount of credibility, I admit: the love and admiration of possibly a quarter of a million folk in your city, a lot of favourable media coverage and a place in the games' historical literature - this is something to be proud of. But to be a fanzine editor! To actually carry the stick of dynamite around in your pocket! Working class terrace guerilla, actually making football fan culture as part of your every day life; well to do that is incredible. If you never had the talent to be paid to kick a ball or kick players, this surely was the next best thing. And here was Stuart considering giving up his baby to an orphanage: I was dumbfounded.

Stuart had lovingly produced thirty-three issues and they'd all been gratefully welcomed in return by almost all its buyers (you never can keep everyone happy). I knew that it had won a lot of respect and acclaim even across the country from the numbers of visiting fans who came up to me in the street and bought it with smiles on their faces saying, 'Crooked Spireite! I've heard of this!' while shoving a nice fat coin in my hand.

They had all been lovingly crafted too and they were still excellent in my opinion, whatever Stu was now saying about the content becoming stale. A life without the fanzine was an intolerable thought. The obvious solution was the main chance: if Stuart hadn't asked anyone else to keep the train afloat or pick up the baton and run over a policeman with it, I'd tell him I'd do it if he'd let me.

I was nothing short of desperate to keep the CS going. It had become a part of me. I loved what it was and what it stood for: a sort of Literary Terrace Culture Marxism With Jokes; an avowedly piss-taking, anti-establishment, take no bullshit from rich football directors rag that would hopefully shape fan thinking on club issues. Whether it influenced thinking in the boardroom was quite another matter, although Norton Lea, now millionaire chairman (though old enough to be collecting an old age pension) certainly knew we were there. Some fanzines fought their clubs on matters of huge importance and sometimes won: a Charlton mag led the campaign to get the club back to their old ground, The Valley, which they eventually did against all the odds. Some fanzines were just about having as much fun as possible, making jokes about players and rival clubs while avoiding politics altogether. We were in the middle.

Our campaigns consisted of sustained bouts of moaning and satire on the nuts and bolts of being a Chesterfield fan. By the late 80s almost all the 92 clubs had erected horrendous fences to keep fans off pitches. Everywhere these were resented, for the attitude towards fans they represented and because they spoiled the view, sometimes ludicrously. But after the Hillsborough disaster in April 1989 (the day I interviewed Andy Morris), the fences came down at one ground after another until Saltergate was one of the last to have them. We nagged constantly about that. The catering had always been abysmal at the ground: we whinged and whined for ages about that. We were the most generous club in the country in terms of the amount of space we allocated to visiting supporters: so we droaned on constantly about the need to give fans the whole of the Compton Street terrace again so we could watch our team attack both ends of the pitch from close quarters. Naturally we lobbied on football matters too: the chronic under-investment in the team being the biggest complaint, as at most clubs.

Though we were neither energetic nor brave enough to really get under the Chairman's skin with red card protests, boycotts and back turnings at matches to try to mobilise the crowd, or 'the mob' as he would have seen it, Norton Lea - imperious Monty Burns caricature that he was - hated us with a 'how dare fans try to exercise freedom of speech in my fiefdom' sense of outrage that was as hilarious as it was totally nauseating. He could have played the absolutist monarch idiot and tried to ban us from the ground, but he was too shrewd for that. If he could keep us just a little sweet, perhaps he could keep us from swarming all over his back. But we waged a war of ridicule in words and pictures in what we hoped was the classic Private Eye tradition, though for the sake of our personal livelihoods we did try to draw the line at out and out libel. To keep doing this was one of the major reasons The Crooked Spireite was worth being invited to take over.

The principle one was ego. I would receive the kudos that would compensate for my being a foreigner. I would work hard, do a good job. I would print all manner of views and try to be as nice to everyone as I could. But this was my big chance to open my big fat gob and pontificate on a soapbox to anyone who would listen; and I was about to inherit a captive audience of 800 buyers and between three and four times that number of readers. In my mind that made me a mighty big person with a mighty big opportunity.

It is extremely easy to say that one of the biggest compliments I've ever received - top five easily - was when Stuart Basson let me know that he considered me worthy of carrying on the name of The Crooked Spireite. Next to all the green lights I'd had of a romantic, and dare I say it, sexual nature (every one a precious friend) and being called an 'honorary woman' once by a Sociology teacher, I think this was the crowning moment of my career.

So one worn out looking Sunday afternoon in February 1992 I plonked my rear end on my scooter and rode off towards Stu's flat in Chesterfield near Saltergate (where else?). I was passed a document containing the names and addresses of subscribers and the routine for getting the 'artwork' - the magazine as it would make its way through the machinery - to the printer. Most importantly, he showed me how to prepare the artwork for the printer, because the technical side of anything interested me about as much as the Luxembourg take on the Common Agricultural policy. Because I couldn't draw, couldn't fix and couldn't mend anything, and I mean anything, I had to listen carefully and mentally get my backside in gear. Fortunately for me and any readers I managed to satisfy over the next few years, this was stuff an advanced ten year old could do. Stuart had never seen me with scissors and glue though. If in doubt, I thought, Louise can do that. So, I left a new man. I could now call myself 'football fanzine editor'. Feeling proud, slightly daunted and suddenly lonely, I buggered off home.

I was lucky about one thing from the off: Stuart was going to keep doing the front covers the readers loved so much, which was a huge weight off my back. If he could keep the standard going there, and I could badger a few people whose work I liked to keep writing, then I'd be okay: no way was I going to preside over a magazine which quickly declined in quality, accompanied by the inevitable falling sales and disintegrating interest. Stu was going to keep the season by season history on the go too.

This had now run to thirty two installments, and although it was an acquired taste for a lot of readers, i.e. boring, it wasn't to me. Indeed, it made the fanzine unique as far as I knew, for in no other could be found a scholarly, yet entertaining club history that no-one else had ever researched. Apart from the in-depth interviews, it was the only thing in each copy that had lasting value and wasn't just fan opinion. Furthermore, that was four pages of space filled every time.

The first thing you have to worry about straight away when you think about the next installment is this: will the pages fill up with stuff? One decision I made on the way home that evening as I trundled my way home through country lanes on my polite blue, suitable for ladies Honda (couldn't afford a Lambretta) was that to counteract the expected disappointment of the changeover from me to Stuart, I would give the punters four more pages. I figured if the quality was going to dip slightly, at least I was going to give them more of it to read, if you see what I mean. So up we went to 36 gorgeous pages. And somehow, before I knew it, without making the print bigger to pad in space, issue thirty four was full. The cover was excellent, tearing to shreds the new shirt design we'd heard we were doomed to face the following season, which promised to have Toblerones and teepee shapes all over the front and back. Such an historical and emblematic creature as the club shirt has to be right and as traditional as possible. Though shirt culture has shifted in a retro direction in recent times, the early nineties was an age when chairmen listened to marketing men who told them that a top which was as far away as possible from looking like a football shirt was the way forward. This was particularly true of the then current Arsenal yellow and blue away shirt, the pattern for which Hawaiians rejected as too wild.

I always had too much to say for myself about everything so there was yards of white paper taken care of straight away. I could let it go on the subject of Doncaster Rovers' floodlights and how Liverpool were never going to win the league again, any damned thing I pleased. This was the beauty of never having any stuff I submitted to the new editor turned down. The CS could become my laxative.

Perhaps fans were worried about The Spireite at the Basson departure, because for a while every time I came home there was something in the mail being offered by a fan for publication. To start with I put in some stuff that bored me to tears, but I had to be polite, at first at least, so that was more space gone. A bloke called Chris who edited a Doncaster fanzine let me use some excellent material he'd put in his magazine originally about a now Town player and responded enthusiastically to my suggestion to do another article.

So, filling space was proving to be the least of my worries. Regular contributors from recent issues rallied round and Stuart himself seemed to gain a new lease of life from having less responsibility and more time on his hands and sent in some cracking material over the next few months. His April '92 cover, my second issue, showing a naked baby about to be dropped into a vat labelled 'PIE MIX' under the headline, 'NEW FANS' FODDER SHOCKER' was a particular tour de force. Undoubtedly, the transition for me turned out to be smooth and easy. The relief was so great I could have stuck it in the fuel tank of the scooter and ridden to work for a week on it.

Not only that but within a few months of taking over it appeared that the readers who parted with their cash, admittedly only 50p so it hardly knocked a hole in the pocket, were at the very least content: sales for me were as high as they had been for Stuart. I could go to bed at night now not only a hard core Town fan, but also resident supporters' club commentator, and best of all, editor-owner of the only fanzine in Town. Aaaah, I could sigh blissfully, and did. O happy days, O happy man. Now I actually meant something in the world. A tiny world, admittedly, but a world nevertheless.

And with that taken care of, the following season I tried to work on a strategy to shape the fanzine in a particular direction. I wanted, rather selfishly I thought, to gather round me about five like minded writers all in tune with each other pretty much and all capable of writing great material. To do this only took a few phone calls and a determination to win the argument if anyone said they were too busy to write stuff. One writer had done great things in the early days on being a manager of a Sunday morning league football team. His name was Dave Radford. The other was a guy who'd sent in a fantastic piece rubbishing the team completely for the first Thomas issue. I hated it at first because I was still in 'Crooked Spireite: The Fanzine That Supports Our Boys' mode, which was both daft and limiting. His name was Bob Wort (rhymes with 'shirt'). It was he who got me the first of something all cowards dread but which people who shoot their mouths off will always make: enemies.

21

The Enemies Within

'An enemy in the hand is worth an enema to the faint of heart'
Anon

Before I could even properly upset the board, I upset the team captain. He rang me up. I felt bad enough as it was that evening, having experienced one of the most excruciatingly painful games I'd yet seen the team play, and as by now I'd witnessed nearly two hundred in five and a half seasons, I'd seen a few disasters and indeed, felt like a veteran.

The very worst thing about supporting a football team is hope. If you're bottom of the league and you troll off to watch your team of a Saturday afternoon, you expect nothing because you usually get nothing. Even if you're attached to a dead team walking out of the league to the Vauxhall Conference, you'll have been clinically depressed for weeks if not months, so it won't be so bad: you'll have got used to the pain and become resigned to your dismal fate.

There will even be a light at the end of your tunnel. You'll be thinking of Lincoln City and Colchester United even as your team goes one-nil down, clubs who bounced like rubber cheques back from oblivion to the monumental history of the football league for another shot. United even made it to division two. A new manager and a bit of luck and you'll be dreaming of a glorious promotion campaign with three-nil away wins all over the place and a mayor's reception at the town hall at the end of it. It's a dream so beautiful you won't even see the killer second goal go in or hear half the crowd booing in disgust around you.

But when it's March and this is your last chance to put a run of results together to get you to the Play Offs: when you really must win, and you're 2-0 up and coasting so you think you're there and this is it; and then you concede two late goals, the second in the last minute: then, oh then it feels as though your mind is caving in under its own weight with despair. It's a mental Armageddon. And no amount of telling yourself that 'it's only football so grow up and get over it', I'm afraid, can change the way you feel. Whole hours pass by where you think you'll never be in a good mood again. Ever. In this state the determination never to smile again becomes your revenge on the fates for dealing you such a crapulent hand. When this happens, it's hope that's destroyed you, that's the thing. When you're a football fan you want too much, that's the trouble. To travel in hope for a football supporter is to walk along with a psychotic assassin right behind you armed with a large hammer.

So it was this way when the phone rang at ten past six and it was someone I admired, one of our own players, calling to tell me what a bastard I am for printing what all the players think is unadulterated trash about them. That I'd let them down. I feel terrible straight away but I also think, 'well thanks a lot for all the times I defended you when other fans were slagging you off'. And I think of Stuart who is going to find it hard not to chuckle at this and say 'welcome to my world these past four years.' All I want to do is get Mick Leonard off the phone as fast as possible. Just get me out of here: I'll admit anything so long as you go away, just tell me what it is you want me to say.

Then he's referring to the bit of the article which ever so slightly infers that the last manager - and this is the hoariest chestnut of all football myths - has slept with all the players' wives and I am crawling under the table like a cockroach with embarrassment. I apologise once. I apologise twice. Then a third time and a fourth, and gradually the hurricane winds of anger die down and he confesses to how stressed the players feel and how crushed they all are about today's result. Now I begin to feel sorry for them, and Mick but I still want him to go away and leave me alone.

An hour and a quarter after it rang, I put the phone down. Shit, shit, shit, what have I done (I so want to be loved)? I rush to find a copy of the offending diatribe and sit down to remind myself what I had printed. It's under the heading of a fairly regular feature called 'The CS Soap Box' and it's by a bloke I've never met called Bob Wort, though his work is printed under the pseudonym 'Pissed Off Of Stockport' which is suitably to the point if nothing else. Now what has he said that's done all this damage?

> 'Sir, I must admit that the purpose of this letter is unclear, even to me. They are, I suspect, shared by many and any rash-conclusions which I have reached through my own desperate thoughts are far from constructive. But frankly, the paucity of ideas both on and off the field would seem to indicate that someone is in need of having the bleedin' obvious pointed out to them.
>
> For the manager to blame a quite appalling home record, in part, on the fans who have begun to air their frustrations after being subjected to a succession of dismally tedious performances, is an insult to the appropriately small number who were prepared

to devote a large part of Saturday January 25th being humiliated at Ninian Park.

This was not the first dreadful display of the season and it will, I fear, not be the last. More worrying is the impression given by some of the players that this is a level of achievement which satisfies them. What follows might seem like the pessimistic rantings of a man with nothing better to do than kick The Blues when they're down, but something's wrong and I have got better things to do on Saturdays.

I don't like knocking Town: I've been watching them since the age of four. There have been some very good times, although not too many lately. Ten years to the day we must have been top of Division 3: just look at us now! For two and a half of the ten since, it's been good to be a Town fan, but I'm afraid the rest has been shite. I'm not the only one who thinks we're a Third Division club, but unless we quickly turn things around we are in danger of becoming a '4th Division Club,' not just in terms of league position but in overall status.

You could almost feel the lack of respect at Cardiff - you sensed we could be Halifax or Aldershot for all their fans cared. Even worse was the reaction of three Tranmere fans sat in front of me in purgatory corner. Their initial disbelief gave way to hilarity as the Blues' performance went from bad to worse. They practically pissed themselves when Steve Norris provided the grand finale to one of our few threatening moves by falling on his arse. Tranmere fans! Remember when we could laugh at them? Even the Sunderland fan who was equally inexplicably sitting behind me raised a smile, stretching muscles which had not seen service for many a year'.

Well, I thought, this was nothing for the players to get unduly camp about. This is sensible and measured stuff, and after all, we did get hammered 4-0, travelling over 350 miles in a day for the privilege. Surely footballers must take responsibility for their actions, like the rest of us who go to work: if we make screw ups, we often take bollockings. I wriggled down further in my seat: it was a good article, nicely written. I read on with a developing sense of injustice at the ear-blasting I'd just taken. Hang on though, what was this?

'The defence has in general been pretty good this season. Nobody can really argue with that, although we can quite rightly wonder how, given the deficiencies of some of its members. Mick Leonard, while one of the best shot-stoppers in the lower divisions, if not the football league, must be one of the worst cross-takers. Some of his limp-wristed attempts at punches remind one of Larry Grayson*, and you can see the defence shitting themselves at the sight of a cross. Given the Neanderthal nature of the fourth division attacking philosophy, this is hardly a manageable weakness'.

Oh, crikey, so that's why he's so upset,

And Leonard's captaincy credentials just don't exist. We all know what Mansfield fans are and what they should do, but surely it's up to us to tell them and what he did was a disgraceful example to set his players**. We need a keeper who'll dominate his box, not another in a long line of goal-line ditherers'.

O my sainted anus: that is near the knuckle, and a bit unfair on an extremely fine goalkeeper who wasn't that bad in the air. I'd forgotten though, what a well-chiselled piece this was, and O Mother! I'd forgotten this: he's going through the whole team pulling them to pieces:

'The improvement in the play of Lee Francis (although he would have been hard pushed to get much worse) and the softening of his homicidal persona has been among the high points of the season so far, although his ability to kick a ball straight remains in question...........Googy [centre half Paul McGuigan], while big and mad, is not as big and mad enough to compensate for his frightening lack of speed and his hippo-like touch on the ball........We rely a lot on TB [Tony Brien], although I can't help feeling he hasn't quite justified a fee that was incredibly high.⁺ It would have helped had he not had a psychotic Scotsman as a drinking partner/career destroyer..............Troy Turnbull [attack-

---

* To help out younger readers, Larry G. was a noted gay and very camp comedian of the seventies and eighties in Britain.
** Mick Leonard had been sent off in the 1-2 defeat at Mansfield earlier in the season for arguing with their fans behind the goal who had been taunting him.
⁺Though barely a Premiership player's spending money for the week these days, the £90 000 we paid Leicester for TB was only £10 000 short of the club transfer record, and Bob was somewhat prescient in his assessment. His promising career went down the toilet almost completely after he left Chesterfield, supposedly for a better club.

ing midfielder] must be the Bart Simpson of the fourth division: underachiever and proud of it.............. Cookie [John Cooke, now one of Peter Reid's staff at Sunderland] has obviously been the revelation of the season and the only man who looks capable of scoring in a brothel with a tenner in each ear'.

This was really turning into a disaster. When I proof-read the article, which is fanzine editor code for 'when I typed out the hand-written original,' it really didn't seem especially offensive, though it wasn't the normal house style, and I'd decided to balance the rawness of the tone with a reply immediately underneath defending the team. Suddenly it occurred to me that the players, or at least Mick Leonard, had taken not a blind bit of notice of this and had totally freaked out. I imagine someone brought this into the dressing room at training one morning and passed it round among the rest of the players. Or maybe one stood on a chair exclaiming, 'Listen to this, lads, get a load of this filth!' and read a choice selection of Bob's insults out to a seething first team squad. My sympathies were changing by the second as I chewed this over. You know, I thought, if you only lightened up for five minutes Thomas, you'd wake up to the fact that these packets of something nasty the dog left on the carpet is actually just what the fanzine needs. More of which he was dropping with considerable alacrity. Bob had turned his arc light back on to the contribution made to the campaign so far by one Lee 'Troy' Turnbull:

'Although the buzz of anticipation when he receives the ball has been downgraded to a vague mumble representing a slight easing of the tedium, he's still rated the man 'most likely to do summat.' Why? Take away his amazing goal at Rochdale and he's done precisely bugger all this season. The same people who made him Town's most overrated player..[in a poll recently] should now tell him he's playing like an arsehole'.

Well that bit's constructive, anyway, so there's a relief. I couldn't help a snort of mirth escaping down my nose at that one: clearly the man was really warming to his theme now.

'And then, of course, we come to the jewel in our crown: our posse of goal-hungry strikers. Surely there can't be another club in the country that could gather together so many forwards without finding one who looks likely to hit the back of the net from time to time. Obviously the loss of Fats [Waller*] has hit us hard, but surely we shouldn't have been relying on him after all this time, even if he was a total hero. Indeed, the only forward to really impress me has been loan signing Warren Hawke - pity he was hit by the Town jinx and got knackered just like all the rest. Dave Lancaster has been a real let down, although I don't think he deserves all the abuse he gets. He's not exactly a touch player, so when he has an off day he looks absolute shite.

There's also a lot of mileage in the argument that he got a lot more ball to his feet last season, rather than the mindless aerial crap being hammered towards him this year. Nevertheless, his goalscoring record is a disgrace, but that goes for the lot of them.

Then there's the great white hope, Steve Norris. His signing smacks of desperation. Seeing the ball ricochet about five yard away from him during the second half at Ninian Park only to find him engrossed in doing his tie-ups so his socks didn't fall down did not represent to me a moment of great commitment'.

Bob's sagacious assessment of the playing strength continued, full of pain and passion before ending on a very downbeat note as he let us know he was so ashamed by the performance at Cardiff that he walked out twenty minutes early, and that being at matches was now so painful he was seriously thinking of doing something else on Saturday afternoons. Which of course was his prerogative. My view of the whole matter was still shifting in my head as I finished reading. When I looked closely at what I said in response to Bob I could see that I had let him and the fans down badly. I had torn into him for being a coward to leave early and for thinking about ditching the club at a difficult time, but I could see now that I'd been doing something at least as bad if not worse. Bob's article was an absolute tour de force: was in fact exactly the thing fanzines had been invented for.

I had been interviewing players and now two managers for over two years and had given them nothing but praise: in truth, I'd been brown-nosing so I could keep myself connected to the inside. In so doing I had made a conscious choice to effectively avoid objective journalism. Stuart had always wanted the mag to avoid wall-to-wall knocking copy as a cheap ploy to increase sales but this was no excuse. Now I was editor it was time to change direction and Mick Leonard had all but done that for me. If he could get upset about one single article then it was definitely

---

* Dave Waller had been forced to retire from the professional game through a cruciate ligament injury just as he was about to sign for division one club Grimsby Town in the summer of 1990: not quite the big time, but a two division step up from where we were at the time.

time to open the windows and let the smell of bias out of the place. It would be the end of player interviews but what the hell, we'd done all that. I'd done all that. It was time to shake the crud off the morning blanket and move on to a more honest fan position, a more mainstream fanzine position. I could also see how this promised a lot of fun too.

So I'd made my first enemy. So what. It was time to scoop some of that yellow out of my back if I wanted to be a real fanzine editor.

Then a funny thing happened: the team, whose crime had really only been inconsistency that season, went to pieces. They lost the next three games, then won only two of the next seven. That made two wins in the ten matches that followed the Leonard phone call and a slide into the bottom half of the league table. The last of those was the club's worst home result for over ten years: a 1-5 turning over at the hands of mediocre Lincoln City. I was up in the box commentating, but was so shell-shocked I was reduced to mumbling incoherently into the microphone by the middle of the second half. Anyone from City who bought a copy of the tape must have thought the commentator had unfortunately collapsed with a heart attack near the end of the game because by injury time I was staring vacantly at the pitch unable to say a thing. They must have had a right laugh at that.

That night at six o'clock the noise of the phone broke into another post-match fog of depression and it was none other than Mick Leonard. This time he sounded ever so humble. He was either so embarrassed by today's farce he wanted to get my sympathy before all the contributors destroyed the whole first team squad in unison in the next issue or, and this was more likely, to break the hoodoo that the absolute coating he gave me in March had brought upon him and his colleagues. A contrite professional footballer apologising to me, a nobody, was very, very sweet. To a supporter of a Premiership team he might have been a nobody himself. To me it was the same as talking to Bob Dylan. However, it wasn't going to change the policy of strict neutrality. The days of hob-nobbing with players and managers was over.

22

The Barnet Affair

'Oy, mate: you want to get your groundsman to make the pitch longer!'

Stuart Basson to Hull winger, who kept chasing passes from his defenders over the top which continually ran out of play for goal kicks.

I sort of blame Frank for the beret and a weakness I'd always had for hats. I once saw him sporting a real kushti one, your classic French, and I thought I wouldn't mind a bit of that one day if I ever summoned up the nerve. Somewhere inside me must live a Soho actor.

One Saturday the following season, again somewhere in late winter, we were playing Barnet away and, as per usual, I caught the supporters' club coach to the game. As it happened, I was on my own this particular Saturday, which proved a little unfortunate as things turned out. However, I had always found it easy to keep my own company. Much as I always liked conversation, there's little I like doing more than having a read, so I was quite content with my little life that morning.

By late lunchtime we were in Barnet high street, a place I knew fairly well, because Barnet FC was the closest football league club to the place I grew up. I'd once bought Surf's Up in one of its record shops and the parents of a school friend of mine called Paul Tyler had a pub behind the main drag, which I'd worked in occasionally. Here I had heard Derek and Clive Live for the first time, a seminally filthy but magnificent recording by Peter Cook and Dudley Moore. As much as I loved my new life up north, it felt a nice warm thing on a winter's day to be back more or less on home territory again. I even felt a little smug assuring the driver that we'd made exactly the right exit off the M25 and were, as certainly as anything could be, safely heading for the ground as he dropped me off at the shops for a poke round.

There is nothing much in the way of excitement for the shopper in Barnet, as any local resident will doubtless tell you, so it was hardly difficult to ease my way down the long slope of the main London bound road to Underhill, the home of Hobbits and the local football team. At the away end I found the cameraman Alan, stood at the front leaning on the fence, so I leant on it with him and we passed the time for a few minutes waiting for the teams to come out. Then all of a sudden, the typical basement division quiet was, I won't say shattered, disturbed, perhaps, by the sound of blokes chanting the name of our recently successful striker Dave 'Burt' Lancaster, who in the week had netted the first Town hat trick for over four years against Burnley, despite Bob Wort's assessment of his worth to the Spireite cause.

'Lancaster, la la la, Lancaster, la la la,' they went. Then, 'Oh, Lankie, Lankie; Lankie, Lankie, Lankie, Lankie Lancaster.' Then, 'Thomas is a wanker, Thomas is a wanker, la la la-la, la la la-la.'

I swung round immediately to clock who it was, my guts already feeling as though they were going down with all hands, because this might be for real and not a few of my wittier acquaintances messing about.

About five rows behind me, a tall bloke, young, about twenty, who I knew had zero time for me, his name was, um, Andy Pratt - or thinking about it it could have been Mick Turd - and the two brothers he hung around with, were clapping and grinning all pleased with themselves and looking vaguely in my direction. Another accomplice I didn't know was doing the same.

This was truly dreadful. I knew fanzine editors occasionally faced boo-boys and even physical threats, but it had never occurred to me that I'd ever get myself into such a position. I turned round to face the pitch and tried to work out why this was happening. I'd given Lancaster some stick in a recent article: that had to be the connection between the two chants, but it was obvious this was more personal. It wouldn't last long though. It would blow itself out as quickly as it started.

'Thomas, take off that silly beret, you prat.'

And there was me thinking how damn fine I looked in Louise's black felt French number. I'd seen Frank wearing one once and thought what a hoot he looked in it. So I'd slapped it on that morning as cool as you like. Or uncool, apparently.

'Thomas you look a right wanker in that hat.'

It was time to retaliate. It wasn't so hard, I had as much time for them as they had for me: something less than zero, so..

'If you lot had any brains you'd have stopped doing that by now.'

But they sneered back at me, this didn't stop them, it only encouraged them.

'Oh we hate Thomas and we hate Thomas......'

I was red raw inside with the most furious, acid rage. The injustice! Who did these people think they were? Didn't they know I was much cleverer than they were? The sheer impudence!

How does that saying go about power corrupting? I used to think Stuart Basson was a King among Chesterfield fans, and now I had his crown. I had never heard him treated with anything other than pure respect. I didn't realise it was him they were showing it to, not his title: fanzine editor. I expected the same from everyone who followed Town, or from those who knew what The Crooked Spireite stood for anyway. And I knew some of these bastards read the magazine regularly! What had I done wrong?

One thing wrong with me was that I wasn't a local. I'd had a brief run in with one of them at Wrexham a few weeks before now I came to think of it. We went a goal down in the first minute and some fans near where I was sitting immediately started shouting abuse at the players. I was appalled and muttered quite loudly, 'I'm not sitting with these jokers,' and turned to move up the stand to find some peace, and as I turned, this voice immediately to my right returned, 'At least they're from round 'ere,' without making eye contact, looking stonily ahead at the pitch. At the time I thought little of it because I thought he was a prat, but now I saw that xenophobia was part of their grievance as well as having the annoying tendency to talk and write as though I knew better than most of the fans, which I indeed thought I did, a lot of the time.

But this brings up a strange thing: the fanzine movement had been on the go for six or seven years now and new ones were springing up like boils on a malnourished sailor all over the place; but at Chesterfield there was only one and both its editors weren't even from the northern half of England, never mind north-east Derbyshire. Stuart was from Portsmouth by way of Luton and me from London. It was the strangest coincidence, but both of us had become besotted with the blue and whites, me spending my waking hours thinking of little else now as second editor and Stuart, fanzine founder, now busy establishing himself as the foremost historian of the club.

In rational moments I knew there was something very wrong and unnatural about this. Ever since I had started writing for the CS I had felt a sense of being an outsider and now I was editor I felt it ever more acutely. Not that it was going to stop me; I was way too far gone down the road of obsession for that, but it bothered me all the time, every time I wrote an article, every time I stood on Saltergate selling. However, I didn't think it gave these turds the right to strip my ego to pieces fully in front of the ninety or so fans within earshot.

So I stood there trying to watch the game, and failed. I tried to work out what to do as they didn't appear to have had their fill yet with twenty minutes gone: the chants and comments went on sporadically but regularly, like the symptoms of food poisoning. One thing I wasn't going to do was retreat. That would be giving them too much satisfaction. I went to the tea bar to try to collect my thoughts, then disaster: we scored. Normally that would have been more than okay but wouldn't you just know it, that leaden footed klutz Lancaster went and headed us in front from a corner.

If I'd had one grain of sense I'd have put myself to rest there for the rest of the game, or somewhere else out of the way, but, no, I was still trying to be clever. So I went straight back to my place and tried to look pleased with life. Sadly, there were three steps of space between me and the rest of the Town support forming a nice little stage, so it was an easy day's work for one of the enemy to trot down the steps as I walked to my place and pat me patronisingly on the head while his mates all had a good laugh at my expense.

I tried to produce a wry grin to show how little I was being affected by all this, but I must have looked about as cheerful as Marie Antoinette about to be guillotined. I stood there and tried to watch the match but my afternoon was about as mendable as a dozen eggs dropped on a hard floor. At half time I went and chatted to a policeman who was standing on the away end behind the goal and actually asked him whether what I'd just been on the receiving end of amounted to verbal harassment, breaking some law or other. He said it might well be and asked me who they were and I very subtly waved an arm towards them like a cop directing traffic on Hyde Park Corner, knowing that they could easily see me. I also knew they were about as brave as I was individually and as umbilically connected to the ritual of attending every Town game as I was and wouldn't want to have been doing anything that would have risked getting themselves thrown out of the ground.

Minutes passed in a daze. My mind was a dodgem car, continually bashed by a hurt I just couldn't control. I was shocked at how thin my psychological defences were, as if my peace of mind was a thing of porcelain held together precariously and roughly with cheap glue. Here it was on the floor again and here I was kneeling down holding some of the pieces, unable to do anything more constructive.

In the second half, things improved and the chanting stopped. But if Lancaster scored again, it would all flare up again, without any shadow of doubt. I held my breath every time we had the ball in the Barnet half, but fortunately this was becoming a less and less frequent event. Then better, they scored. 1-1. This definitely moved things in my favour. They'd started out attacking me high on the energy of an away day at the football. I knew how a football addict thought. This equaliser would be like pouring cold water over them; they'd be starting to fret about the result now, because whatever else I might say about them, they were Town fans right down to their sweaty feet.

What I really needed now was more goals in the Town net to really piss them off and completely take their attentions away from me. All the away fans were quiet as nervously we defended, trying to hold on to a point. By the time the home side got their winner, the game was almost over but it still made me feel better. Hah! Take that you bastards - serve you bloody right. Now you'll be going home miserable.

So would I though. The pleasure from the result was fleeting. I walked out of the ground still holding those pieces in my hand and all the long coach ride home I sat on my own with them scattered over me like funeral confetti. I ate out my pride over and over again and no mental trick I tried to play on myself could cure me.

There was one aspect of the affair that gnawed at my insides particularly as the M1 miles were gradually stacked behind us. When I had turned round to see who it was chanting at me at the start, standing just behind them was someone I thought I knew pretty well: someone with whom I'd often worked out jokes for the fanzine that only we understood. Looking at each other in a conspiratorial kind of way we'd throw our heads back and guffaw at our cleverness (either real, or imagined).

He travelled to games with his own circle of mates but sometimes we stood together and had a really good laugh, enjoying each other's company as well as the game (if we weren't losing). What I knew most about this man was that he had a brilliantly quick witted mind at football matches, and could have scissored Pratt and his gang down to size with a single sentence. I was certain of this because the gang knew the man and respected him. A simple, loud, 'Pratt, why don't you shut your fat ugly mouth and go back to school, you tw-eerrp!' would have ended the affair right then and right there.

He was one of those people for whom it wasn't so much what he said that got everyone in earshot guffawing happily, but his natural ability to inflect a sentence perfectly. Just one of these in my defence would, I knew, have cut them dead. Then I wouldn't have felt so lonely there at Barnet and so destroyed. If things weren't bad enough sitting there in the dark, I now felt betrayed as well.

The man standing behind them was Stuart.

23

Boy

'If I had a thousand sons, the first human principle I would teach them should be, to forswear thin potations and to addict themselves to sack.'

William Shakespeare

My son was born an hour and a quarter after my daughter. He wouldn't have come out at all without modern medicine, it occured to me later: he'd have died and so would Louise if this was 1886 not 1986. If you think too hard about parenthood you can waste a lot of time and energy going mental. There are so many decisions you can agonise over: the right or wrong milk at the start, the right or wrong food when they start on solids, the right or wrong colours to wear, the right or wrong television, the right and wrong schools, ah, it can just go on and on.

We both thought we should keep things simple: breast was best (but curry as soon as was practically possible), no pink for either of them, Neighbours if they wanted and the local comprehensive so long as we weren't living in Willesden or Moss Side. Louise and I were in the education trade so had none of the anxieties of my brother who still lived in the old Hertfordshire homestead after Mabel Snr died, and seemed to be surrounded by people who belonged in a home for loony parents as far as I could make out. In this old hunting county of a delightfully eccentric Scottish homosexual monarch (King James Avenue does a semi-circular dance around our very own Francis Bacon Street) - and I do advise you to stay well away from the place if you possibly can - there were exams to get into secondary comprehensives. Wh-utt? Insane enough having them for grammar schools. Kids of eight were going to coaching classes for entrance exams three years down the line. Pitiful. Some parents ought to be flogged within an inch of their miserable, superfluous existences.

Then it transpired that the whole south-east of England was going mad on the education front. A friend from our Orpington days rang up one night and confirmed that this utter madness went on in Kent too.

Thankfully none of this upper-middle class fast-track to one's own personal breakdown nonsense went on in Derbyshire. We both knew that bright kids do very well academically wherever they went. Landing in a village near Matlock it was a fair bet that the local primary school was okay and that the local bigschool wouldn't be full of drug dealers with mobile phones and knives. It was a mostly middle class area after all. If Lyall and Tasha had inherited the genes that had got bothof us to university then everything would plop into place and they'd grow up fairly normal at least. That to me was sensible parenting.

I don't know exactly why, now I know he'll never play for Scotland, but I was always out in the back yard or in front of the garage (which when the door was open made a fantastic goal-frame) playing football with the boy when he was little. Naturally, he loved it and would have had me out there all day and night if he could. He was good too: skilful with a hard shot. From these facts of the father-son relationship sprang an obvious question: when would I take him to his first game of football? I wanted him to have the same life chances as me so I thought, 'as soon as possible.'

A boy's first professional game is as important a rite of passage as his first smoke, his first kiss, his first album and his first serious slanging match with his mother: it was important to tuck it into his sock early doors, as you might say.*

One Easter I took him to a reserve game v. Stockport County and although the game was about as interesting as a documentary on the history of the fencepost, he felt entertained enough, and watched every ball being kicked. He was ready.

So a few weeks into the new season, I took him to Saltergate for his debut. He stood right next to me while I stood on the street selling some fanzines for half and hour or so, then walked round the corner with me to the front entrance, his little four year old hand clutching warmly on to mine.

Up we went to the commentary box where he sat on a plastic chair from which he could just see over the three feet wall of wood that stopped us from falling on top of the spectators below. He knew he had to tap me on the arm when he wanted to speak to me so I could hold the microphone well out of the way so it wouldn't catch our voices.

'It's so loud, Dad!' he said a few minutes into the match, raising his voice above the fans singing down below us. There were two thousand,

---

* A word about the phrase 'early doors.' It was not, as some scribes mis-believe, the invention of Ron Atkinson. On the Compton Street terrace in the late summer of 1988, a man I stood with for around six games from Worksop, whose name I've long since forgotten, used to say to me, as we watched Town getting butchered under Randall every week, 'don't worry, Craig, it's early doors yet, it's early doors.'

eight hundred and one paying spectators in the ground.

'Do you think?' I replied, wearing a wry smile.

Lyall saw Town win 2-1 that day, and witnessed, with his Dad, one of the best goals ever seen at Saltergate. Warren Hawke, on loan from Sunderland got on the ball just inside the Aldershot half, ran straight for goal, beat two men, then lifted the ball neatly over the advancing, diving keeper. Brilliant. Mind, I don't remember my two goals at my first match, the one at White Hart Lane in 1963, so I don't suppose Lyall remembers his. But I know he enjoyed it all, as I'd done, because by the time he was ten he'd been with me to fifty league grounds and seen over a hundred Town home games.

I then thought it appropriate to plant a commemorative tree, so to speak. At every professional game of football, and at all the senior non-league ones come to that, a team sheet is produced for the press and the managers, and I always got one for my commentaries. A month or so later, I sent the one from Lyall's first game to Chris McMenemy, the manager, who I knew from interviews I'd done with him for the fanzine, asking him if he could possibly get the players to sign it as a souvenir for Lyall. And being pretty much a decent bloke, he did just that a week or so later.

However, it is an unfortunately accurate statement to say that the boy's first game doesn't exist and officially didn't take place. Aldershot went bankrupt later in the season and failed to complete their fixtures. The ones they'd already played were scratched from the record.

But it exists alright. There is a picture in the programme for the Rotherham game two weeks later, covering a whole page, with the caption, 'Stevie Williams sprints into the Aldershot penalty area' below it. At the top of the photograph is the Saltergate commentary box, and peeping over the parapet on the far left is the head of a little boy with a fair-headed fringe, looking down on the frantic action in front of the Aldershot goal.

What exactly I did for or to my son that day I will never know, but I guess it might have been something similar to what mine did to me, because from time to time, Lyall will come into the front room when I'm watching TV, or put himself alongside me in the kitchen when I'm cooking and say, 'When are we going to go to Saltergate again, Dad?'

24

Twenty-Two Men Chasing A Ball Around A Field

'Football's all about 90 minutes on the day; it's all about tomorrows really.'

Glenn Hoddle

My enemies at football. Little boys with little toys playing silly games. Mind, it all seemed real enough at the time. Football, I knew, was some sort of make believe world, a reality created by each of us out of choice. Football supporting, the really serious stuff, the obsessional kind, was a form of submission. I knew what I was doing all along: I gave myself up, willingly. When you're in the midst of the addiction, it seems to be offering you so much, how can you not surrender? You want to surrender. When the time comes you get in the car with a beaming smile and it's you who makes the offering.

Football's attractions seduce you on so many levels. For a start, the slings and arrows bit hits the part of you that responds to the notion of pure winning and losing. Was this inculcated in me by my being taken to games so young or was I born with it? Is the propensity to be drawn ineluctably into taking sides watching a match or a fight part of what it is to be human? If the latter is true, then the fact is, attaching yourself to a team is validated, totally.

It's hard to argue against this when one of your players has crashed the ball into the net from thirty yards and the endorphines now hurtling around your head have just released you from all the sick neuroses you hump on your back all day long. There you are, for about ninety seconds, totally outside yourself, jumping and shouting, and pumping your arms in the air like a total prat for perhaps ninety seconds at a stretch and it's all very healthy, I've no doubts about this. It's the same shouting and waving of the arms on a deserted hillside the alternative therapists are forever telling us we should be doing if we don't want to end up at fifty on a trolley with a white sheet over our heads. Better try what I did at Carlisle a year after my broadcasting finale: striker Steve Norris had put us two-up and this game being anything but a local derby, I was able to run thirty yards or so along the top step of the terracing with my arms aloft as if I'd scored myself. I wasn't showing off, except to wind up some Carlisle fans perhaps and I wasn't trying to extract a laugh out of Radders. I was just relieving myself. I was so happy, and doing this was lovely, soothing. Ah, the relief of an away win.

This is not considered to be normal behaviour. It is possible that something fundamental and fundamentally important has been bred out of us as we in the so-called developed world have tried to lead supposedly more sophisticated lives. Perhaps such loss of self, in moments as far from stress as is possible these days, is something that we move to find as a matter of course, something we naturally seek to be healthy.

Are we not programmed then to find football?

There's also the tribal attraction of football, something already fairly well documented, and it's true: there's something primally wonderful about walking along surrounded by your own people, heading for your own area of the stadium, intentionally designated as being a space reserved entirely and specifically for you and your kind. And though goal and victory celebrations are individual, in that your own personal needs are met by the player or the team's success, there is of course, something absolutely warming about being among fifteen hundred like minded souls celebrating a last minute winner at Scunthorpe which keeps you on course for a bigger victory than one mere skirmish: the whole war of promotion. What light this sheds on the question of the species homo sapiens possessing a desire for blood-shedding conflict deep in its DNA is a question I would rather like to avoid, but the point is now made, I suppose.

If this is so, then it is possible that an evolving species developed organised sports like football so as to channel this dark side of the facts of human life into something safer than mutual mass slaughter. It must be significant then, that psychotic mass murderering politicians such as Hitler and Stalin weren't remotely attracted to team sports (I don't recall ever seeing a picture of Adolf wearing a Bayern Munich scarf). Perhaps damaged lunatics like these scorned football because they recognise it for what it is: a weak and weedy imitation of the real thing. If this theory all ties up, it's no surprise at all, is it, that grey skinned slabs of emotionally and socially afflicted humanity are drawn to the game to take their revenge on the world.

On the more positive side of the tribal attractor is the fact that we all love to belong, to be part of a community, something greater and larger than ourselves. Through adhering our loyalties to a football club we gain affirmation and validation of self, for we are not alone, we are not outcast:

we easily see among us men, women and children displaying the colours and symbols of our own tribe and we know immediately we are safe and enclosed and special: there is no other tribe quite like ours. Handily too, we can be members without it costing us a penny, though there will be a supporters' or members club we can join if we wish for a fee, if we want to feel just a little cut above the average tribesman or woman.

In the tribe we have our own territory, our ground. This is tall and solid, sometimes a hugely imposing roughly symmetrical cluster of buildings, towering above the local landscape like a vast futuristic craft. Or if you prefer, a veritable modern cathedral. Which brings us to our next attraction.

As everyone knows, football is the modern world's new religion. The grounds are our churches which we attend on a roughly weekly basis ('draw near with faith'). We light our candles - buy our programmes and keepsakes, attend service - the match, and sing our songs of joyful praise and celebrate our prophets - the players. Even if we have a bad day in church, we still know that we have made a lifelong commitment to our God - the club (or is it the game itself?), and, because we have faith, we will return. Between times we will outwardly show our friends, our neighbours and our family our continued devotion ('go in peace to love and serve the Lord').

Like all believers though, we have our moments of doubt. We may not bother to attend as regularly as we once did. That is natural and human. The devil is always on duty, trying to lure us from the true path. We may even switch religions, though this is rare. Usually it's one life, one faith, unto death. Neither is it unusual for believers to have their ashes scattered in the church or cathedral itself at the end of their lives.

Or do you prefer to see the lifelong nature of commitment of the fan to a club as a form of marriage: a substitute for a human marriage, in fact? The ingredients are there: the daily and constant presence in each others lives and thoughts, the seriousness and permanence of the bond between you. Like a marriage the pair of you will probably experience some rough times together: you may grow tired of your spouse, bored. You may feel attracted to others. You may consider some sort of separation. But unlike a human marriage, you will be able to reconcile your differences and live together again, in harmony. For your spouse will never be unfaithful to you and will always be there (even Accrington Stanley came back from the dead).

There are lighter attractions to going to football too, of course, some of which are not at all unimportant. Most fans celebrate their visit to the shrine with friends, even with life partners, and the appeal of a social event which enables them to spend time with those they like or love can never be underestimated. Football and humour have always gone hand in hand on the terraces, with one regular laughter-making wag to be found every twenty yards or so at every ground in the country. At the smaller grounds where almost everyone inhabits the same square two feet of concrete and chippings each game, a fan can go to the game alone, but find rich entertainment and associative-friendship with great ease. Indeed, so much comment is there on the terraces about the game, it's actually very hard to make match attendance a solitary event: it's normally an intensely social thing.

Here's another attraction of the game: it's not work. Literally millions of men and women will go, and have gone to football for over a century because of the contrast between the emotional and social involvement of the match experience and their everyday working lives. During my year at an inner city school in Derby, when the stress of trying to work productively with some difficult children within a poorly managed institution was constantly wearing me down, the only true escape from the pressure was to lose myself in thought about my club. This was particularly so from the first waking moments of a Saturday, when the anticipation of the match later in the day was considerable and the absorbtion of the mind in the ninety minutes of actual play total.

Just about all of us lead lives which are made up of routines, some of them desperately humdrum. There are fans who work five twelve hour shifts a week in factories for money only Philippino sweatshop workers would be grateful for. When Alan, my cameraman friend, got himself off the dole in the early nineties he worked such hours, at night, with one half-hour break and with canteen facilities recently withdrawn. Small wonder he used to follow Town home and away year after year.

And what of the estate agent, the accountant, the trader, stuck behind a desk and a computer in a suit all week long, talking God knows what shite about margins, Stamp Duty and the rise in the pound? We have to de-stress, we must find escape. So what would you have: lottery tickets, heavy drinking, hard drugs, television, bingo, building Notre Dame cathedral out of lolly sticks, internet porn?

Or football?

In addition, it is all too easy to underestimate just what a collosal thing a football match is as an event. There is absolutely nothing like it, apart from a rugby match if I'm trying to be generous, but that, crucially, doesn't have goals. Proper goals. Netted goals. Though it is possible to be there and close yourself off to it, the game is a collosally attractive thing, particularly if you are close to the pitch. There is noise, colour, laughter, drama: both in terms of the result on that day - which is sometimes so cru- cial it can make or break your week, even your summer - and the extend- ed Shakespearian theatricality of the season as a whole, the shouting of insults, food, anger, shared experience, frustration, argument, drink, singing, friendship, exultation, loss, the coitus interruptus of the goalless draw: all this with an intensity that you won't find anywhere else in this country, no matter how far and wide you look.

All this awaits you when you go to the match. Imagine. The final whistle goes, you've come out on top and won 2-1 to go fourth in the table with a game in hand. You clap your hands together in appreciation one more time, then turn up the terracing to begin the journey home, where mum's got the chips on for tea, the fire blazes and Saturday night telly awaits, with who knows what pleasure to follow. Oh alright then, you turn up the terrace to start the short walk to the hatchback to take you home, where you get a packet of chicken tikka masala from the freezer, stick it in the microwave and think about opening a beer and nipping back out for a video. Whatever, it's no wonder football spectating has risen again in recent years against all post-Hillsborough predictions.

Then there is that unique and precious thing: a goal. When the ball goes into the net at a football match, it doesn't matter at what end, it pro- duces a reaction somewhere very, very deep in the distant recesses of the brain. It isn't just the fact that the scoreline, and perhaps the destiny of the result, is changed when the ball goes into the net that makes the goal a thing of significance. It doesn't matter if the score is six-nil against you and they score a seventh, something deep and weird is going on and it's the netting that's doing it.

If there was no netting, the effect of a goal on the mind would be neg- ligible, it would, indeed, just mean the score had changed. But the net col- lects the ball, accepts the ball, encloses itself around the ball. The net is fulfilled. The net bulges. That image is deeply fulfilling for us too: that we cannot escape. The ball being shot or struck into the net is a completion and its satisfaction just has to be sexual; it can be nothing else. The ball is often described by journalists as being 'slammed home', 'rammed in', 'slid in', 'rifled home', 'hammered home', so it's not just me. This imagery is no accident. Consider the words of commentators: 'it's there!' 'it's in!' *Of course* it's sexual. No wonder men love football. It's pornography! It's not as if it didn't have enough going for it already. And it's addictive. For gay men - oh, I could easily become jealous of gay men, there's lust: the week- ly spectacle of rippling muscle and whole athletic bodies, right there in front of you.

Which brings us to women. The modern female, of varying ages, are going to matches in increasing numbers. The ratio of women to men is growing, all the time, and is it any wonder? Why should the female of the species be immune from soccer's siren call? Doesn't a woman want a marriage, a faith, an escape (now that more than ever they're working for a living - who's going to want to be a kept woman any more?), some spectacle, some emotional release, a hobby, something to talk about? All those taut, hairy legs thrown in extra, for nothing too. I don't care how many degrees you've got: men, if our teams were all made up of women (because they were better at the game than blokes, naturally), wouldn't we just love watching those breasts, those thighs, all that grunting and sweat? Come *on*.

It's only surprising that there's anyone out there who isn't going to go to football on a regular basis. Or would if it wasn't becoming so damned expensive. And wait: I haven't covered all the bases. What about the academic and intellectual aspects of fandom: the talking about the game, the analysing of tactics, of players' form and managerial selection, and changes of managerial, playing personnel. How about the politics of football: club finances, club chairmen, club going bust, club going to new ground, club putting up season ticket prices. All this and more to be picked over and discussed, hour after hour. Tie this in with friendship: talk on the phone about it. Socialising: go down the pub and talk about it. And, lest I forget, what about the writing about it, for a fanzine perhaps. The statistics of the game (the number of games the team has played since last conceding a penalty, most shirt numbers worn in a season by a single player, etc), which you may also write about, or just compile and pore over, for your own pleasure. And I almost forgot: the history of the game, which you may digest and cogitate over slowly or even lovingly create yourself, in the quiet evening, with just the tick-tock of the clock on the mantelpiece for company and a nice cup of tea at your elbow.

Football: it's a whole life.

25

The Road To Spotland

i
Out on the Edge

'Mrs Hall's toffee rolls are the best....'

If you were daft enough to try to write a text book about being a foot-ball fan, you would devote several chapters to the travelling fan. Somewhere in here, perhaps in the very first paragraph, you'd state in all confidence that you can't be a real fan unless you go to away matches. It's the full unprotected sex, your biting the head off a live chicken of the whole football fan thing.

It's a big macho number. If you can say you went to Plymouth on a Tuesday night then you're the idiot in the bar with the blonde highlights in a bad mullet making up sex stories that only happen to men who appear regularly in movies with lunchboxes like fat leeks.

'Did you go to Torquay, Wednesday? Yeah, I went. I was on a business trip in Warsaw the day before but no way was I going to miss it. I hired a car 'cos there wasn't a flight to Heathrow that would get me there in time - cost me eight hundred quid 'cos there was only one hire car firm in the whole city - so I drove through the night, and all the next day, no stops, pissed in my trousers four times, no food, no drink til I got on the boat. Hired another car at Dover and drove straight to the game, no stopping, got to Plainmoor at half-six and they told me it was fogged off. So I drove straight home through the night: next day they said I'd taken too much time off work and they gave me the sack. The whole trip cost me two grand. Brilliant. You goin' to Carlisle for the Albert Gribbs Memorial Trophy preliminary round game? I'll be there.'

This is what it's like with some. To others, round trips of five hundred miles in the day to see a 0-0 draw and your team have one attack are as much a part of an ordinary life as a trip to buy plant feed at Do It All. Many fans are introverted and just slip quietly away from work a couple of hours early at three o'clock, pick up a pal or two and drive serenely towards a motorway and their date with a sublime evening destiny. And if you pulled up next to them at traffic lights in the relevant town at five past seven, you'd never guess. There are folk out there, completely inconspicuous to the rest of us, who look totally normal, who haven't missed a Forest Green Rovers, let alone an Exeter or a Southampton match of any kind for more than ten years.

It's not the home games that hook you, it's the away games. You may be the sort of bloke who would never do a parachute or God forbid, a bungee jump and who would no more go on a three week holiday trekking in Ethiopia than stand on a big box to shave off their pubic hair outside Asda on a Saturday morning. But there's a part of you that still seeks the wild, the exciting, the abandoned. So when you find yourself walking along the streets of Swansea at two-thirty on a Saturday afternoon - it'll be your third away game or thereabouts - the thought will suddenly occur to you that this is it: that in your mind you're wearing the kit of a Superhero, going where no man has yet travelled, a Seeker of Truth in a distraught, dishevelled world. Your work mates think you're dull, leading an unremarkable life, but really you're an intrepid outrider on Empress Palalla's search for the Galaxy of Doom! While you're slipping nicely into your third hour of coy sleep next to your cosy wife, I'm still on the road with the accelerator down hard on the way back from Exeter: what do you think of that! I'm actually doing some living, here, mate!

So, having always had a deep disposition towards this sort of behavioural pathology, I was attracted to the whole idea of the away game as a passing mongrel launches itself at an in-season pedigree woofer that's got its head stuck down a rabbit hole, and even more so because I knew from the start about the 92 Club. Though there is actually a club for people who have visited all the professional football clubs in England and Wales to join, with membership card, unique enamel badge and secret handshake, for most ground-collecting fans it's a spiritual thing to do the lot. When I'd been to, aw, thirty grounds, I started drooling about the idea of completing the set just for myself. I would while away a good hour on a coach to Chester or somewhere, imagining how great I would feel, setting off from the house on the morning of travelling to my ninety-second ground; how I would savour the drive there, the thrill of reaching the point of closeness to the ground where the fans and the floodlights appear. I would have to decide upon whether I was the sort of fan who would alert the home club in advance that this was the final leg of a long, long sojourn, so that they might put a line in the programme about me, or even - and yes, I have heard this with my own ears - mention the fact of my feat over the public address system.

Thankfully, I didn't think I was capable of dropping to levels of human behaviour this low, but I'd done stupid things in my time as only I quite knew, and anything was possible for me where football was involved.

ii
Bilshaw's Battlewagons

'Mrs Hall's toffee rolls are the greatest....'

When I first went to away games on a regular basis it was only because my wife let me. I think she saw the demented look in my eyes when I talked about an upcoming trip and thought that trying to stand in my way might be more trouble than it was worth, given that she wanted to stay married to me on a more or less long term basis. It was like the key to the door at 21, a real coming of age. When I was totally overcome with football at the age of about six: got taken to games, joined the Manchester United fan club, and got two football annuals every Christmas, it never once occurred to me that one day, that ever, I would go to different grounds.

Though it makes me sound like a daft berk, football grounds were my first love. Soon after I'd been to Tottenham for the first time I copied my brother and sent off to a dealer in North London for football programmes from as many different clubs as my meagre pocket would allow. I chose names from the league and results tables I saw in the newspaper. I was only a small child, I suppose, but even then the names fascinated me more than anything has since: Darlington, Plymouth Argyle, West Bromwich Albion. What was an Argyle? And an Albion? And when finally that first parcel arrived with the programmes inside, it was like another Christmas, though if anything, actually better.

I don't think I can quite put into adequate words what seeing each football league club released by a programme meant to me. Which ones can I attempt which aren't too commonplace: special - no, they were much more than that. Magical? Possibly. Supranatural? Yes, that begins to take it close. When I picked up a Wrexham programme, say, and saw the Racecourse Ground pictured on the front, I would goggle at it for a spell, and was transported to a magical beyond.

I didn't pore over my programme collection for fun. Each one had supernatural energy, properties; If magic has something to do with the unattainable, then that describes how I felt about football grounds when I was small: they were there, I could see that in some way, but they were so impossibly remote from me, they couldn't actually exist in a place and time that I could ever reach. So to see a set of floodlights on the way to Scotland: ohugh! to actually stand outside Belle Vue, domicile of

Doncaster Rovers: well...there aren't words, truly.

The idea that I could actually go to Wrexham, or Middlesborough, or Coventry, to see a game, see the ground, stand or sit in it, was an impossibly remote one. I suppose when you're small, a country the meagre size of England seems bigger than the whole planet does now. Oh, to have that magic back now.

So, to board a coach bound for Vale Park on the second day of 1988, home of the mighty Port Vale, knowing that this might be the first of a practically infinite number of steps along my own yellow brick road was like having a gate opened wide in front of me to a broad, green hillside, with sunlight poured all over it like gravy on a roast dinner. And a voice was saying to me, 'Now, son, all this is now yours: take, enjoy. Away you go.'

And off I went indeed.

A Romantic notion, however deep is, in the end, only that: romantic, not real and therefore bound sooner or later to be doused in the sour brine of reality. Someone always shits in the custard eventually, as Einstein used to say.

We won one-nil, on a January Christmassy day so grey British Steel decided to sponsor it, and I was predictably beaming with delight at the end. As soon as the journey back to Saltergate began, the monstrous beast began to stir in the shape of Darrel, son of Les Bilshaw, the coach driver and company owner. Aged about eleven and as hyper-active as a wagon load of speed freaks at a Wigan all-nighter, he must have slept the way to Burslem after being awake til four watching his father's porn film collection or some such, but now he was in my ear and everyone else's come to that with the loudest voice this side of the Grantham Town Crier.

'Is this your paper?'

'No, it's Germaine Greer's left leg,'

'Can I 'ave this?'

'No, I'm still re..'

'I'm 'aving this!' and off went my Guardian down the front of the bus in his nasty little hands. I'd be lucky if it didn't come back covered in bogies. I hadn't read much of it either; the little bastard!

He seemed to go quiet then, for the first time in half an hour, so I closed my eyes restfully just for a couple of minutes, and must have dozed off because the next thing I knew I could feel something soft on one of my eyelids. I opened them fully and what did I see but a shower of massive snow-like flakes falling about my person: my bloody, fucking Guardian!

'Are you asleep, mate?'

'No, I'm building Noah's ark, what do you think you're......'

But he'd run up the back of the bus now and was now basking in the approving laughter of some young men who seemed to find a nicked newspaper being returned to its owner in ruins rather funny. I was seething with middle class outrage. How dare this little bleeder... I was used to putting such impudent little fuckers in detention - the impotent nature of my anger was the worst thing: where were the people running this organisation; how incompetent could you get? My beloved new football club letting me down like this. My crest, if not fallen, was definitely sagging at that moment. And what if blasted over-orange squashed Darrel was on board every away trip? I sulked my way back the rest of the ride to Chesterfield, feeling that a great day was ruined and that this might be my last trip with the supporters' club.

But it wasn't. I would need their services for a long while yet.

It was on a trip to Aldershot that the Bilshaw arse was next seen hanging out of its trousers, so to speak, though I got there for that particular Tuesday night game by train, under my own diesel, you might say. Aldershot FC's ancestral home, also named Recreation Ground by the way, rests in the middle of the town park, so I paid to get in and was immediately surrounded by rhododendron bushes and flower beds, which was a mite strange - then things turned even stranger. Had there not actually been a man there to take my money - and there were no other fans at the single away-fan turnstile - I would have turned back to the station convinced I had the wrong night. I had to grope my way along the path through the park to the ground proper because it was pitch black everywhere: there were no guiding lights in front of me on buildings - there didn't seem to be any buildings! Just darkness. No floodlights were on.

This was ridiculous. It was seven o'clock, a match in The Football League of England (and Wales) was supposed to be starting here in thirty minutes and it was like a game in the park down the road with no-one turned up yet. I didn't expect a fanfare to mark my arrival, but this was ridiculous. I still thought it was just faintly possible that right now someone was making their way to the pub with my four quid and I'd read the date wrong in the paper when I suddenly saw the light from a tea bar. I blew out my cheeks in relief, bought a coffee - rancid, like stained washing up water - and wandered off to try to find some terrace or seats for away fans. This was one weird place: the tea stand was being used by a couple of middle aged blokes in blue and red scarves as well as me: everywhere else I'd been so far you went into the away section and you were sectioned off from everyone else as if you were a wild mutt from the Clapton Home For The Canine Insane.

Then I saw a tiny painted sign next to a drainpipe saying 'Away

Supporters' so I followed it up a dark alley that seemed to lead nowhere when there was a click from somewhere and two floodlights came on so I could see. There was a doorway that said 'visitors seats,' so for want of some terracing to stand on, I went in there. There were about a hundred plastic tip up seats there, the first row right at pitch level. I wandered through to the rail, four feet from the touchline, where a steward stood: I thought might get some gen on the home team, find out if they had any form - it would kill some more time too.

The stadium had about twenty people in it and it was ten past seven. Then I looked up from my watch to see that a bunch of footballers in blue and white had appeared on the far side somewhat sheepishly I thought. Then they began to trot, then sprint together in our direction, before coming to a halt ten yards from the rail.

'Oy, lads,' shouts the steward to the players, 'your fan's turned up to see you.'

And by the time clever trousers here had finished the sentence two of them had looked over at me, seen the look of complete embarrassment on my face, made the same expression, looked down at their boots, then turned around to trot away again as quickly as they reasonably could.

'One loyal supporter: you want to give him a medal,' shouted the white coated comic genius. I walked away and tried not to feel like a complete and utter prat following a team of losers: we'd not long since lost ten-nil at Gillingham. He probably thought the Town travelling army had all given up except for the lifers - 'get a lifers', he no doubt would have thought if he hadn't been born with a plastic brain.

There were about ten of us in the seats at kick off, and about the same over to our right to one side of the right hand goal in what appeared now to be a piece of away terracing. Now that was a poor turnout, I thought. twenty fans. That's bad. I tried not to feel really bad for the players and watch the game. The ground must have had twelve hundred people in it and had the atmosphere of a warehouse with a bloke going round switching the lights off at the end of the day. Still, it was League Football nevertheless.

With half time sneaking up on us like fog and already one-down, I followed the play over towards the corner flag away to the right and there, appearing as if from a descending autumn mist was what looked surprisingly like a crowd! Forty or so Spireites had finally made it. There was even the semblance of a chant as the ref blew his whistle for the break. They'd missed almost half the game, taken four hours plus a breakdown to get there, but a battling Bilshaw battlewagon had made it. The supporters club paying customer would now watch forty-five minutes of top league football - Town went on to lose two-nil and had one more attack - and get back on the bus for another four hours to get back into Town for about two a.m.. Were we getting ready for non-league football or a BBC documentary or what?

Of course, this happened a good few times with me on it. I have to say we never missed a whole half, though we missed twenty-five minutes and two cracking Dave Waller goals at Sunderland later that same season, as I've already told you, but we missed some opening five minutes's which to me was bad enough. And it used to really infuriate me on a trip that, times many, to find the ground we would get to the relevant town and then ask directions. We missed the start of a Northampton game and a couple of others like this. I used to wish I had the bottle to march up to Les and say something like, 'Excuse me, but I have always been under the apprehension that when an organisation contracts a coach company to ferry their members, it's the responsibility of the coach company to get some accurate directions from the local police or the relevant club so we don't miss half the bloody game!'

But I never did because for one, Mabel Jnr had always brought us up to make snide remarks that the person responsible for our inconvenience couldn't hear rather than to stick up properly for ourselves, and for two, because I was still new and an immigrant from the south and for three, Les was built like a stevadore and would have either replied, 'Get off me fookin' bus' if I'd said this or knocked me down the coach steps onto the hard pavement and driven off leaving me to walk home. So every trip where the timing was remotely close I just crossed my fingers and willed the clock to slow down til we got to the ground. It knocked a lot of the fun out of the day, let me tell you.

iii
A Goal Of Our Times

'She takes strawberry milk from her breast...'

Relegation is a harsh mistress. She has a whip and a knuckleduster with spikes, and that's what she used to kiss you hello. Walking out of Field Mill on a windy day in the Spring of 1989 knowing I was heading for my first date with Madame R., I could at least baste myself with the luscious fact, that the following season I would be stepping out into the genuine, the absolute dead, measured heartland of The Game. We were going to the fourth division. For the freak, the head, this was it, backstage with Jimmy Page swigging a bottle of five star Cognac, taking a guitar masterclass with Steve Howe, shagging Janis Joplin in the back of a limo.

If the idea of Swindon and Carlisle were almost magical, then to go to the Victoria Ground, to Spotland and to The Shay, was a thought that was pure Lion, Witch, Wardrobe and Looking Glass. The world got ever grubbier, grimier and polluted. People were buying microwave cookers and heating up trays of congealed looking barn slop full of chemicals and calling it 'dinner.' Life was progressively a more plastic, nasty, materialistic thing - this was before anybody had heard of the word 'ciabatta' for pity's sake, before you could drink a decent cup of coffee north of Hampstead, when the word 'organic' meant something deep pink, pulsing and slimy residing next to your liver. If I was searching for anything in life then, it was for some sort of authenticity. Others sought it and got it on moorland and hillside, fishing in the wilderness of Sutherland, at steam rallies, or Morris dancing. I knew, when we went down, that I would get it at Halifax, and Rochdale.

I had to wait thirty-four games before we played at The Shay. It was an absolute dump. A bomb site. There was a horrendous speedway track around the pitch, so if you were behind the goal you were miles away. There wasn't even terracing there, the club were so perennially penniless, or historically mean. The home end had been declared unsafe by the Football Licensing Authority so it was empty; that always reduced a match atmosphere by a more than half. There was a tiny area of covered seating and terracing which we could stand under to the right if you were behind the away goal, which was barely fit for non-league football, while across the pitch from there was the plainest, cheapest, Sofia-esque, piece of covered enclosure you could ever wish to avoid. The Shay, a name which conjured up misty, dank but wonderful Yorkshire Saturdays where it was always half past four and winter with the Town in their blue and white stripes two-one down and struggling. What a disappointment. It was March and the rain was cold enough to kid the back of your brain it was December the thirtieth, Waller scored a crucial equaliser but it was still two points down the drain for a team and fans believing we'd soon be winning promotion.

I went to The Shay four times and we never won there. One year a strange thing happened. We were up against it as usual. Losing. This was thanks to an extraordinary backpass from Dave Caldwell, back on loan from somewhere, in his black designer bicycle shorts which had most Town fans tutting from the off. He received the ball on the half way line - he was a striker, remember - and sent the ball back the opposite way towards his own goal instead of turning and hurtling up the pitch towards their goal with it as he once did to great effect. He played the ball all of thirty five yards directly to a Halifax forward, who scored. If this was not remarkable enough itself, I should tell you that in the last game he'd played for the first team a month earlier, he'd done exactly the same thing, and we'd lost to Walsall one-nil.

I was still grieving over the goal a couple of minutes later, when I looked up and saw one of our fans walk casually along the touchline to our dugout where manager Chris McMenemy, his two assistants and the subs were all sitting in a line. He then began haranguing McMenemy with a wagging finger and an angry expression that wouldn't have looked out of place in the front line of a war.

'If you ever pick that ....' I heard some of it but I was twenty yards away and there was background noise; '....again, I'm gonna............' No, I'd lost it, but you could tell he'd got to the crux of the matter very quickly. It staggered me too that he was allowed to amble further along the pitch side and place himself back among our fans without having a policeman or a couple of stewards all over him like a pint of vodka.

At the time I was talking to the manager for the magazine regularly so thought initially that this was a disgrace, how bloody dare he interfere with a professional doing his job in the service of the Town. It wasn't Chris's fault if Shagger was a lunatic. However, as the years passed and I thought more and more about this amazing incident, I thought it quite the most brilliant piece of fan initiative I'd ever come across and wished I was as brave.

Victoria Ground belonged to possibly the most depressing football town I have seen: Hartlepool. I so loved it though. It had a collection of huts along one side - I could not believe that: not even terracing along one whole side of the ground - and a dinky toy of a cantilever stand across the way. The home end had a low roof, about ten steps deep and our away end just plain uncovered terracing. To most eyes it may have been another ugly place to watch football, but this was Hartlepool United and I felt I had really and truly achieved a life's ambition to be there.

As a lad I had always had a second team, as almost all fans do, one either in a much lower or much higher division, and from the age of six, mine was Hartlepools, as they were known then, United. There was something about the word, the look of it on the page, and they, I quickly gathered even at that tender age, were synonymous with laughable failure*.

---

*In those days there was no relegation from the football league; the bottom four teams of the 92 had to seek re-election from the other members of the organisation, to stay in it and avoid the drop to oblivion. Traditionally, they were almost certain to be safe, but in more recent times, Barrow, Workington and Southport had been dumped in favour of Wimbledon, Maidstone United and Scarborough.

They were always bottom of the fourth division, always applying for re-election and I adopted them as my other team. The day my first Hartlepool programme arrived in the house was a cause of much warm internal cele-bration.

But If there was a quintessential home of the romantic loser football club, for me it was Rochdale's Spotland. How could it fail when it had the head start of a name like that, and a history of mills, men in clogs and Gracie Fields. To get off the coach at Rochdale was to have the rib-spread-ers yank the game's chest wide-open for you so you could stare at its throbbing, central organ. Forget Old Trafford and it's like. To twist-quote an old saying John Arlott was fond of repeating, 'what did they know of football who only Premiership football knew.' If you're reading this and you go to watch a big club regularly, or occasionally even, get in your car now, and drive there, to Spotland - you can't really take the train these days, though that would be even more authentic and marvellous - it does-n't matter if there's no game, they'll let you on to the pitch, and take a look around you. This is what you have been a fan of all your life. This is what gives your football life, perhaps your whole life, its meaning.

Without this place where you are now standing, there is no FA Cup, no League Championship, no First Division (let's forget silly names for a minute, shall we). I know, there are only four small, perhaps insultingly, excruciatingly small covered ends and stands here. But there are four floodlights which will signify that you have arrived at the centre, the home indeed, of football. You should bow your head for a moment and think of all you have enjoyed at your usual ground, all that you have enjoyed about football in your house, down the pub, at work, wherever you have talked about football. This is the well from where all that fun, all that pain, all that love, comes from. Naturally, whenever Chesterfield played at Rochdale, they got a right stuffing.

Except for one year. 1991. 1,852 fans in the ground that day in autumn. It wasn't my first visit: it was my second, but last year we'd done some commentary, and I'd been over on the main stand among the home fans. Terrible - lost three-nil.

This time I was on the away end, just a dozen gently sloping terrace under a very simple, but effective thank you very much, roof. The pies at Rochdale were famed. So about twenty minutes in, I went to a little wood-en hut, across to the right, still facing the pitch and waded in. The pies were there alright, and they were small. They came with mushy peas - no tins, the real thing. They'd probably been serving this here since before the First World War. And gravy. So I took my paper plate, and my little plas-tic fork, turned around and watched the game for a few minutes under a little awning that covered up the serving hatch when the hut was closed. It was raining. It was the sort of stuff of which we normally say, 'it's set in for the day': sheeting down in straight lines. Drip, drip went the awning as I cut into another section of pie*.

Looking up, chewing in a pleased sort of way, I saw Lee Turnbull, a beautifully elegant player when the mood was on him, on the break, take the ball over the halfway line, and play the ball fifteen yards forward to Warren Hawke, who shielded it well, his back to the goal thirty yards behind him. Lee, or 'Troy' as we knew him, for he looked like the sixties puppet Troy Tempest, had made fast, ish, ground forward and called for a return pass from Mr Hawke, who duly obliged, laying it off gently into the path of his team mate, who, head classically over the ball, met the said orb of leather with a majestic swing of his right leg. The ball - I was right behind the line of it - made a winded cry of pain as it left Lee's boot and screamed like a missile into the top left corner of the Rochdale net. What, and I mean, what! a sight that made. It was not a goal of the month, or of a season: it was a goal for all times. A goal which said pretty much everything about why people went to football matches: that once in a while, perhaps once every two years, you would see the game in it's full peacock feathers of glory. I had been going for about four years seriously then, and this was the first time I had seen a Town player smack one in from outside the penalty area. At last it had happened. At Spotland.

I should have finished my pie and peas, taken a final sip of coffee, had a last look at everything, then turned away and gone home. That should have been the moment when I was happiest at football. It would have been the perfect out.

I never was one though, for knowing when to quit.

iv
Punk and Pink Mohicans

'And her husband does the rest.'
                    Chesterfield supporters' chant from the 1970s: Anon

Travelling to games in the end, I'm happy to say, involved friendship. Was this the best thing about away games? Very likely. Radders and I had

---

*The real meat and potato pie was one of the supreme pleasures of football. Some grounds did great ones, but a chip shop near The Shay did Ninety-Nine Pee Specials: a pie with peas and a half portion of chips. I stood in the rain and ate it with a couple of like minded souls. I'm sure Gordon Ramsay's food is fabulous, but...well, the Halifax 99p special: go there too if you can. In winter.

some great times together. But we'd both agree, that the powerhouse of football companions was the man who told stories of punk and pink mohicans.

His real name was Rick, but in the magazine he preferred to be known as either the Chairman of the Bored, Doctor Disguiso or Hasland Harry, after the Chesterfield suburb in which he resided when first we met.

The first time I clapped eyes on him, I was becalmed on the hard shoulder of the M1 two miles south of Watford Gap services, waiting for the AA to come and get me and my Fiat Tipo out of jail so I could get to Northampton in time for a three o'clock kick off. This bloke, as thin as a whippet on a strict diet, ruddy but boyish complexion, pulled over in a company Astra and asked me if he could help in any way. 'No,' I said, but thanks for asking. His wasn't the first car to have stopped: one or two others, recognising my fat face from selling fanzines on the street had ground their motors to a halt behind mine to check that things were in order, and one lad was already ferrying Stuart and Radders to the County Ground. The odd thing about this character was the fact that accompanying his blue Town peaked cap* was an accent everyone north of the Angel, Islington would have immediately labelled 'cockney,' and would only have failed to pass muster if put to the test in conversation with a group of Barking costermongers.

I was too preoccupied with the thought of another missed kick off to think too deeply about the existence of another misplaced accent in the wilds of north-east Derbs., and mentally filed the encounter away under '?' for future reference.

We eventually met through The Crooked Spireite. I was trying to build up a crack squad of writers so as to produce the best possible piece of pocket gelegnite I could, for no other reason than if I wasn't in it for the money or the glory - incidents like Barnet had put paid to that idea and there was never any money - there needed to be something else to strive for. I'd been sent a piece of writing by someone signing themselves 'Hasland Harry' which consisted of linking each member of the playing strength with a suitable make of cigarette, assuming they were smokers, and it was more than useful. Not that any of the entries on its own was in danger of causing a rib to crack under the strain of incessant laughter, but

---

* I won't say baseball cap, because it wasn't made from materials of sufficient quality for it to qualify for that epithet. That a man as rabid about wearing the 'right' clothes as the Rich I came to know could wear such a miserable accessory as this, this thing which typified the cheap, niggardly and amateurish way the club shop was run at the time, says just about everything you need to know about the game taking complete possession of a, can I say this?, man's whole being.

every one of twenty four of the Town personnel had been assigned a clearly appropriate brand of smokes* - the author had given the matter plenty of thought - and the cumulative effect was of this somewhat unusual
extended metaphor for a bunch of supposed athletes was very satisfying
and added up to something far funnier than what passes for football
humour these days. There was a joie de vivre and a cheekiness about it too
which you couldn't help find attractive*.

However, the double-H had failed to send in his real name, and I
needed to know who he was before I published. So, as I knew the matchday announcer, I got him to send out a half time call for 'Hasland Harry'
to get in touch with me asap, and as luck would have it, he did. Then we
met on the terrace at Spotland (appropriately enough) while, in immaculately tailored shorts - it was August - he struggled with what looked like
a three year old boy in his arms. It turned out that Rich had been a fan of
the CS for some time and liked the cut of our jib, to wit, the house 'flavour'
of giving it to the board for continuing to treat the fans as mere turnstile
fodder and to the current manager for playing dreary, hopeless Route One.

Despite our shared geographical background and football values, it
was some months before we went to a game together, an obvious route to
go down in the circs of his driving to games alone and me with maybe one
other passenger, and I could hear his story. But eventually I did;

If you join the M25 near Potters Bar, four miles from Mabel Jnr and
DimbleLand, and drive anti-clockwise for about ten minutes you'd get to
the Rickmansworth turnoff, the land of Harry's birth. As the crow flies, it's
a mere ten miles, but it's that radial London thing operating again: I'd
never been there anymore than Rich had been to Cuffley. He and a brother had been brought up by his father, his mother dying when he was five,
and maybe for this reason, perhaps for another, Rich was a troublemaker
at the grammar school he'd got into easily enough, and was not remotely
interested in a berth in the big square world when he came of age.

Indeed, in his early teenage years he had become totally enamoured of
punk rock, and at eighteen, arrived at a difficult fork in the road. It had
been Rich's ambition for some time to be the owner of the most massive
and best kept mohican hairdo in the whole of the western world. This
arrangement involved the complete shaving of the bonce, excluding a
wafer thin but completely extravagant foot high plumage which took
flight in a vertical line from the forehead to the back of the neck. Not quite

---

*To give you a sample, 'David Moss - Camel...not, I hasten to add, because it's the
nearest thing to a donkey, but because a camel just keeps on going and going in all
conditions. I hope he doesn't get the hump about that [That last joke © Jimmy
Tarbuck 1804]'

the destiny the father imagined for the son when he held him in a Hertfordshire hospital for the first time somewhen in the year 1966.

'Either you stay here and drop this mohican idea, or you leave.'

He left.

The next few years were gloriously free. But poor. Rich grew the mohican and dyed it pink and followed punk bands around the country and played in punk band, The Soldiers of Destruction. He had no money and had to sleep in ditches and bus stations when he couldn't crash on a fellow punk's floor. He became a hunt saboteur. He'd tell you stories you could hardly believe, but this bloke was the truth alright. No question. Christmas day, when the rest of us were tucking into turkey, pud and custard, Rich was apt to be hurling a brick through the plate glass window of a country butcher in full black raiment (including neo-terrorist balaclava).

We were on the road one night to see a game when he told me all this and my jaw was so far south of my top lip there was drool all over the crotch of my trousers: I had never met anyone like this. Rich also, it became clear in about ten seconds, was one of life's naturally gifted raconteurs, and, you might say, liked to laugh at life if he possibly could, even though he openly relished the fact that he was enormously attracted to extremes.

'I once went a whole year without chocolate and I *loved* chocolate,' he said, pronouncing the 'lov' with the emphasis of an angry drunk crashing his fist down on a bar top demanding service.

As I got to know him better I realised he didn't eat proper food and he didn't drink tea or coffee.

'Why did you want to do that?'

'To prove to myself I could do it.'

'And did you?' says I, goggling in admiration.

'Of course!'

Of course. How could I have doubted him for a second. I was trying to process the man as I did everyone I met: their politics, their taste in music, their job, their social class, tuck them away in a filing cabinet in my head. Usually I could do this when I first met someone and they'd rarely, if ever surprise you. Where the hell did I put Rich? I had to square all he'd just told me with the fact that he now had short, neatly cut hair, wore immaculate designer casual clothes and worked for a snack food company as a rep. He was gloriously un-pidgeonholable. The more he talked, the more you could see there was something about him that was completely uncontainable.

'How did you get from punk with mohican to repping for this mob?' There were samples all over the car which we were in the process of eat-

ing.
     'Eve and I..'
     'Who's Eve?'
     'Well, her real name's Paula, but I call her Eve..'
     'What, is that her middle name, then?'
     'No. She's my wife. We got married on a beach in California. Anyway, we were living in a squat in Islington and one of our flatmates was on smack and Paula became pregnant again, so we thought, this is ridiculous, this is no place to bring up children, so I got a job.'
     He joined the Post Office working behind the counter, 'sonze mohican' as he might say, and he and Paula gradually moved across into the straight world, getting on a council housing list before they did almost exactly what Louise and I did: grab a better quality of life for our kids while it was still there. Like me he wanted out of the south.
     'Not me, Paula: I'd go back tomorrow if it was my choice.'
     The next fork in the road saw one point west off junction 28 of the M1, the other pointing east: there were two jobs to apply for: one in Mansfield, the other in Chesterfield. Two fields. Rich knew the local teams' colours: he preferred blue. He got the job, with a paint company as a sales representative, and they moved north.
     Rich had been poleaxed by the Town bug in pretty much exactly the same way as me. He had wondered along to a Tuesday night match because his next door neighbour was going, not because he was remotely interested per se, took one look at Saltergate and bang, that was it: hooked. This astounded me as much as I understood perfectly what he had gone through. What on earth was it about lower division football, its grounds, its clubs that reeled us in like gormless fish clapping their mouths onto that fat worm? It was, as I believe they say across the Atlantic, the darnest thing.
     Me, I've always had a thing for the romantic, but Rich is about as romantic as a ten foot length of tubular steel. Or so he says. Yet we would both drive ridiculous lengths to see a game: we drove one Christmas to Brighton for a night match, straight there, straight back. No ceremony, barely a stop for chips and chocolate. And we'd laugh all the way there, and laugh all the way back, as the engine purred on the company motor to the sound of a London accent as raw as a plunge in the Thames in November, and an irrepressible flow of language, peppered with fucks and other choice expletives and a love of making the best of life that was totally infectious. He was one of that very rare breed of people you instinctively want to like you. Third phone call, something like that, it was clear I'd somehow won his approval. I was telling him I'd been off work with a

virus.

'You fackin' teachers. Tell you what: education attracts layabouts.'

If I'd been talking to anyone else I'd be taking off my coat ready for a bit of verbal roughousing before he'd finished the sentence, but I was laughing.

'You can talk, you, you corporate lackey: free tickets for this, another bloody junket there: you call riding in a car all day work? You're just a sell-out, Rich,' and he was laughing now too as he put his foot down a little harder,

'Dead right,' he replied, ruefully. There was a very large part of him that belonged under a pink mohican still. For all his larger than life persona, there was a depth inside that made you want to spend more and more time with him, to see if you could uncover it. The neo-cockney, in-your-face Rich was enough for me though. He played Sunday football in Chesterfield, doubtless the only player in the whole district who sounded like a Saturday night import from Hackney Marshes. Sweeper, he reckoned. I saw him with a ball once and he was very talented indeed, one amongst thousands who could have played the game professionally if they'd been desperate and disciplined enough. I always wanted to hear him in action on a muddy pitch somewhere shouting the odds after getting clattered: 'You northern wanker,' he'd go, under his breath, and if pushed, right in the bloke's face.

Players from each side would pull them apart but Rich would still be going strong,

'Any time, mate: any fackin' time...'

And if his adversary was ever waiting for him afterwards, he'd just laugh the argument away, I bet. The other bloke would have been determined to plant at least one prime clout on this mouthy cockney bastard's face, but would change his mind without knowing exactly why later on that night when he stopped to think about the incident again.

So even if it slammed with rain on an ice cold night on a roofless terrace, as it did in Bath one year when Bristol Rovers were having to play there, it was still nothing less than total enjoyment to be there with him, even if your knackers were frozen half off.

These were the pieces of him that fascinated me most about him: the bits of him which weren't at all like me. Despite being a multi-layered being alright, there was something hard, implacable about him. I could have done with some of that attitude down through the years. This came out in his seemingly hopeless xenophobia: he had a chance of a better job in Scotland, but, he thought, 'I'm not going up to that dump of a country: full of pasty fackin' jocks.'

The statement was layered with such contempt you could have plastered the walls of an entire estate of Wimpey homes. Yet this was the man who came back from Barcelona glowing with pleasure at what a wonderful, sophisticated place it was and how superior the lifestyle was to England's. You were better off not trying to work him out; the best thing was just to enjoy him.

This ruthless side also came out in Rich when he applied for jobs. When I prised a potted life story out of him on our first trip it turned out that when he applied for a job he didn't just turn up for the interview and hope his gift of the gab would see him through as I would tend to do: when he left the post office it was because he had audio taped his presentation and listened to it over and over again until it was slick and ready. Then when he went from paint to snacks he videotaped his spiel: 'I looked at it and I was scratchin' my balls and pickin' my nose and all sorts of rubbish.'

But he honed the talk until he knew he would probably win. Then, on one of our journeys he told me he'd applied for a job with a massive multinational clothes firm. As he began his research, ringing up the company for information various, he was told something which would have had me putting down the receiver and throwing in the towel: 'Apparently, a thousand people 'ave put in for this job.'

'You'll get it,' I replied, not even having to think about the issue.

'I don't know about that,' said Rich, and he laughed mischievously. But he would already be putting the final touches to the master plan in his head and be throwing the switches that would spell ruin for all the other hopefuls, all nine hundred and ninety-nine of them.

Meanwhile, as The Chairman of the Bored he gladly, though miserably contributed to our campaign to either get rid of Chris McMenemy's successor, John Duncan, or get him to change his arse-clenchingly dull approach to winning football matches.

It was Duncan who'd managed the club when I came in, ten years before. He'd organised the successful promotion campaign of that season. But he was also the one presiding over the sleep inducing outfit I saw lose to Chester and Brentford when I decided that I had to find a way to the inside of my adopted football club. And here he was, back again, after a failed attempt to return Ipswich Town to the former glories of the Bobby Robson days.

While in East Anglia he had kept in contact with the club and was still the darling of the two chiefs of the mid and late-eighties, bluff Barrie Hubbard (or Scouse Barrie as we called him after we found out that his favourite club was actually Liverpool!) and J. Norton Lea, our ageing north-Midlands mogul and Chesterfield chairman. With the creeping caution of a night animal wary of being easy prey, in February 1993 Norton slipped Duncan back in to see if he might get Town up a division a second time.

From the off me and my happy band of back shed satirists were dead against this move. Having heard a plethora of horror stories from Ipswich fanzines about strikers playing full back, international Russian creative midfielders playing sweeper and the tactics soundly based on route one 'football' we quickly decided that we'd give him a few months to see whether he had the same in mind for us; then if it didn't work, we'd massacre him. He came in a February, won six games out of sixteen and we finished twelfth. The jury was out. However, we weren't playing passing football, and the situation looked ominous.

26

Nozzer and The Revolution

'The chairman of this boredom is a compliment collector;
I'd like to be his funeral director.'

Elvis Costello

i

Nozzer

Whether the dropped piece of toast fell butter side up or down that next season, 1993-4, seemed to depend for us upon Duncan's attitude to the fans' favourite: the somewhat afore-mentioned Steve Norris. He was beloved of me, and he was beloved of Rich too: we both loved a goalscorer and Nozzer was a natural. At the time he signed for us in March 1992, we needed a striker, but the fans thought the arrival of the greedily, lusciously successful Nozzer at Saltergate to be about as likely as Batman. Even at 31, the only way for one like him must surely be up. And yet, there it was on Ceefax one afternoon, signed on loan with a view to permanent move. A dream. This quick, tricky little forward would rescue us from oblivion.

He had come to league football quite late at 27, and was already thirty when McMenemy bagged him, a year before Duncan's arrival, and immediately started scoring at a rate of one every two games. As all aficionados of the game will tell you, when you can score at that rate, you're any team's ticket to success, or should be if the defensive side of things is right and if the manager isn't a total pillock.

Unbelievably, the season after Nozzer notched over forty times, *forty times* for Halifax Town, a new manager in the form of dour ex-centre half from the old days called John McGrath came in, and shipped our hero out. Steve, not exactly your archetypal big bustling hulk of an English centre-forward, didn't work hard enough, he said. Said to achieve success they would have to adopt a different style of play, which Steve, so the manager said, couldn't adapt to: the big lumping style we at Spireite Mansions unaf-fectionately called 'the Big Boot.' Nozzer was off-loaded to us for a mere thirty thousand quid. And did Halifart Town win promotion without him?

No, they finished bottom of the fourth division the following season and were duly relegated out of the league. Now there's a surprise.

Funnily enough, the morning after Duncan's arrival as the players got stripped for training, goalkeeper Chris Marples, who'd played under the new gaffer as a young rookie the first time, turned to Town's top scorer and predicted, emphatically,

'You won't last five minutes, Nozzer; you're not 'is type of player.'

Not that we were aware of this at the time. Nozzer played every week under the new man during the new season to start with and up to the new year, in nineteen league games, had scored thirteen goals, a fabulous ratio. Yet Duncan's lack of public support for our hero led us to the inescapable conclusion, incredible though it seemed, that he wanted to drop Nozzer and would do at the first available opportunity. The opportunity never arose, because there was no let up in the goal supply but Duncan outed him anyway, to the total dismay of almost all the Saltergate hardcore support. He'd actually got in an overweight reserve from Ipswich to try to upstage Nozzer. The lad actually scored in his first game but that couldn't disguise his inferiority in terms of sharpness and team play. This was classic Duncan stuff and we: Rich, Radders and me, were utterly outraged. After Christmas we went five games at home without a win, but none of this could possibly have been down to Nozzer. He scored in two of them and didn't play in the last one. We all understood that playing football successfully meant you had to score goals. And we had experts to back us. Steve Norris scored them, this was indisputable. Yet it wasn't good enough for Duncan. The part of his brain which he used to think about football was wired differently to ours ('wired to his arse,' as one wag put it at the time). Or, he was jealous of Nozzer's popularity and wanted to destroy it. He could easily have transferred him, but didn't dare. So he bided his time and waited for the moment.

Then we played Carlisle United at home and in the second half at 0-0 were struggling really badly. Nozzer was on the bench and with no sign of his entry into the proceedings, the crowd were on Duncan's back. Club physio Dave Rushbury kept on and on at the manager to put him on the pitch. With just under thirty minutes to go, the manager caved in and on he came. The rest of the afternoon was the most and least enjoyable of all the games I saw at Saltergate.

Steve scored the first with a header, laid on a second for seventeen year old prodigy Kevin Davies (his first ever league goal) and netted a beautifully crafted third. He had now scored twenty goals for the season*.

---

* Steve went on to score a total of twenty league goals that season, the first Town player to do so for thirteen seasons.

This was such a perfect half an hour of football, I was practically delerious. Duncan's stupidity football-wise had been publically exposed so explicitly it was almost embarrassing. However, it didn't alter the fact that the boss was a cussed son of a bitch who would still be determined to face down his critics and have his own way. Then an appalling thing occurred that made things far worse and probably decided my whole future: the final whistle had gone and while we were still clapping and celebrating on the Kop, we saw that Duncan had walked right on to the pitch and had gone up to Nozzer and put his arm around him. Or tried to.

'I tried to shake him off me and told him to 'fuck off," Nozzer told me a year later.

It was the middle of the end of Nozzer's road with Town: he was to play only ten or so times the following season, and we all looked on with resignation as Nozzer was periodically benched in what appeared to be a concerted effort to undermine his confidence and form, what a tribunal would call 'creative dismissal.' Nonetheless we Norris fans still walked around in a state of permanent disgust. The Carlisle game had done it for me. I had never seen such a display of gutless hypocrisy before and haven't seen one since and decided there and then that 1) I hated Duncan and 2) would do all I reasonably could to use the power of the fanzine to get him out.

ii
The Revolution

I didn't do something Rich did in protest at the methods of the manager around this time, although I'd always be honest and straight with friends, acquaintances and everyone who read The Crooked Spireite, I didn't have the guts to do myself: write directly to Duncan to tell him what I thought. What put me off this completely was that one night I got a phone call from the H-man to report the fact that Scotch John had called round his house personally to see him!

Rich - if I use the word 'disappointingly' I would be guilty of the most criminal use of understatement in the history of the English language, you'll understand that there isn't an adequate word to describe the situation - was not at home. A conversation between these two I would have paid ten pounds, twenty pounds to see, not least because, according to Paula, who answered the door, Scotch was in a mood for a scrap: a verbal one, anyway.

Rich loathed Duncan as much as I did, and we sat together in the family stand at home games with our eldest sons, and watched our team play a system of football over the first four months of the next season which tore us and most of the rest of the crowd to pieces. Boring was not the word. Crude, Neanderthal and antediluvian might just get us most of the way there. Goals were in shorter supply than giraffe meat at Tesco's. In fact Duncan managed the team as if he was intensely suspicious of scoring goals, which is a Titanic irony as he'd been a striker himself - most famously and successfully at Tottenham - and a very good one, but with the reputation as a lazy one. A good result was a win, a great result a one-nil win.

Whether Scotch came from one of these horrifically uptight, repressed Presbyterian families I know not, but his team played like a child from one: denied the right to enjoy itself, so punished if it ever did. In bed at nine o'clock, no television except on special occasions and definitely no sweets. Tactics and training methods were always based on perfecting the art of never conceding and the game plan always tight, highly organised defence - seemingly seen as an end in itself rather than a means to an end - and a long ball from the back a staple. Rich and I would often fantasize about making a spectacularly vast banner a hundred feet long at least, which we'd unfurl from the Compton roof facing the managerial dug-outs saying, 'Campaign For Real Football - In The Name Of God Go (and take your bloody awful brand of football with you).' I half-fancied that if we'd have been able to go out to a shop and buy one, and get someone to fix it to the roof at five to three for a reasonable price, say a hundred quid, the idea would have been a real go-er. Sadly, fantasy it would remain.

And yet. One skill Duncan undoubtedly had as a manager - and I hated to admit it with every strand of my DNA - was that of being able to buy good players. Nicky Law, centre back and captain. An excellent defender and stupendous leader*. Lawrie Madden: almost forty but on his day, still a great man to have. Mark Jules: flying winger with great attacking potential. David Moss: classy forward who could score. Phil Robinson: about to emerge as one of the most important midfield players in the club's history. Tony Lormor: neat, skilful forward who could score goals too. He brought in good people alright, but he didn't want to let them off the leash to play some attacking football. It simply was not the Duncan way.

In the autumn of 1994, events seemed to be moving towards a final showdown between the manager and the crowd. Nozzer, in one of Scotch's not very subtle attempts at image-management, had been made captain at the start of the season, He appeared in the first five games, scoring twice and playing well. He was moved out in early September though. This may

*Note: he took the club to promotion in his first season as manager in 2001

have been precipitated by his skipper's hand in ignoring the boss' tactics at Blackpool, the players deciding to attack instead and winning 2-1 against a side a division higher. Nozzer was bound to be dropped sooner or later, we all knew that, and it proved to be sooner.

Come October, the team playing like a sick dog, especially at home, Duncan's public stock hit the drop zone. We won 3-0 at Colchester on the 8th, the Big Boot working to good effect for a change, but at Saltergate the standard of play was abysmal, the route one stuff insulting and insufferable, and the 'Duncan Out' chants began in real earnest. 'We want football' the Kop intoned, almost zombie like in keeping with the performance of the players, who obviously hadn't become professional footballers to play the game like this. On the 1st of the month we beat Torquay 1-0 thanks to an own goal. On the 15th we drew 0-0 with Darlington. On the 22nd we drew 1-1 with Fulham.

The crowds for these games were all very poor indeed: under two and a half thousand locals turned up to watch the team, creating a sound economic case for a change of personnel in the manager's office. Beyond the absolutely committed and the permanently obsessed, there were another few thousand passive fans in the area ready to turn up to see a winning team heading for higher places and of those, a thousand or so who will pay their money to see their team involved in a decent game of football. But here we were, down to those prepared to be morbidly attracted to the match or folk who were so used to going their shoes walked over to them sat in a chair at two o'clock, clasped themselves around the sitter and marched him (or her) off to Saltergate whether they wanted to or not.

Was there any chance of me finding an alternative method of deploying my time on Saturday afternoons? Er, no. The day of the Fulham game, Louise's cousin's daughter was to be married in the church of the Crooked Spire no less, at two o'clock. The nuptials would be completed by ten-to-three I reckoned, so I could run up the road then in time for the kick off, but then there was the matter of a number of fanzines that needed selling, so I nipped out of church at about twenty-five to and legged it as fast as I could so I could shift at least forty copies of the latest issue. Much later, I arrived at the reception in time for the profiteroles.

A suitably historical day, the 5th of November, saw Nozzer's last hurrah, scoring the winner as we somehow overcame Hereford 1-0 with only nine men. No matter how much contempt he had for Scotch, Rich always had more for whoever we were playing, their players and their supporters, so threw himself into every game with the passion of an angry Italian. When United missed a penalty in the last minute, he was beside himself, screaming abuse at the taker and his eighty supporters behind the Cross

Street goal with wild, joyful abandon. Mine was confined by my hostility to all things Duncan: the three handy points had to be offset against his diminished chances of getting the sack.

Events swung my way as November passed. Two more games at home, two poor cup draws. Then two more reverses: a draw at Gillingham thanks to an horrendous blunder by keeper Marples, then a pitiful collapse in a cup replay against Scarborough, an outfit who were to finish one off the bottom of the division the following May thanks only to goal difference, to go crashing out of the FA Cup at the first round stage yet again: we had the worst record in the competition of all the professional clubs. The longingly awaited exit of the man responsible for this misery (as far as I was concerned) had to be imminent.

The next game, at home was gratifyingly odd. We beat Preston North End, but in such a forlorn, joyless way, the Kop received the winning goal with another chant of 'Duncan Out,' which was repeated with a certain amount of ghoulish enthusiasm at the final whistle. The match-winning goal - a brilliant one - was scored by a player just arrived on loan, Sean McCauley, who looked so classy on the left side of midfield that Rich and I turned to each other and pronounced judgement in unison as soon as we'd seen five minutes of him:

'This boy's way too good for us.'

However, rumour had it Scotch had the opportunity to sign him, but wasn't interested, which to us coloured in even more of the caricature we were painting.

The following Tuesday we were put out of the Mickey Mouse Trophy held for lower division clubs* then back on home base on the Saturday took on Rochdale. Leading twice we were levelled twice: points shared, more disgruntlement. Miraculously we were still eighth in the table, but it was as sure a bet as Britney Spears not winning a Barnsley Coal Digging Championship that we weren't going to win promotion with this man in charge.

Next up it was hated rivals the Shags, the Handbags, at their place.

At the half way stage we were two goals behind and there were some angry people on the terraces. One in front of me borrowed a mobile

---

* This has been variously been known officially as the Associate Members Cup, the Freight Rover Trophy, the Sherpa Van Trophy, the Leyland DAF Trophy,the Autoglass Trophy and the Auto Windscreens Shield, according to the sense of humour of the man with the power to ascribe it a title and is always derided by fans of the smaller clubs. Until Wembley appears over the horizon, at which point our attitude changes dramatically. A cup final is, after all, a cup final, and a trophy well, a trophy.

phone, rang Mansfield Town FC and asked to speak to Chesterfield chairman Norton Lea. No way would he get Norton out of the boardroom, especially as he'd once been a director here himself. However, a minute later it was clear that this bloke was actually haranguing someone down the other end of the line on the subject about Town being two-nil down at Mansfield: the CFC supremo *himself*, we learned as soon as the mobile was safely back in the hand of the owner. Amazing.

This sort of pressure had to be getting to old Norts, we thought: how long could he put up with the meagre, desultory home crowds, the doggedly hostile chanting at matches, ('Norton Out' could occasionally be heard when the attraction of 'Duncan Out' wore off for a spell) and the letters we knew he was getting insisting he make a change? At the end of the match - it ended 4-2 to the Shags - Rich, Radders and I sat in the car and after a thirty minute symposium decided that one more defeat, in the next game on Boxing Day against Doncaster Rovers, third in the table, would be enough to finish Duncan, enabling us to move into some sort of light.

The most crucial game in my Boxing Day Football career so far arrived with me in the best of moods: this was it. Ten to five, no more Duncan and I could start enjoying my football again. It was going to be wonderful. Then of course, life being what it is, I was banjanxed. From the kick off, we played the game as nature intended - 'if football was supposed to be played in the air, God would have put grass there', as Brian Clough famously put it - passing the ball from blue shirt to blue shirt, with three men up front, and new player Phil Robinson scored twice with two flying headers to give us a great win.

I didn't know quite where to put myself, but before I had too much time to dwell on the situation we went off to Northampton the next day and won there 3-2, again playing the new system. The run went on. Another home win (another Robinson goal) a draw away, then another two wins. Five wins out of six. Then a draw away at Preston then another three wins. This was crazy, this was ridiculous: we were sweeping all before us. Another new player, striker Tony Lormor was scoring goals and with his exuberant goal celebrations was fast becoming a new hero. Eight wins out of eleven had put us into the top three. Promotion, within two months of the team playing disastrously, seemed now to be a distinct possibility.

And there was no let up in the run of undefeated games. We won seven more out of the next eleven before champions elect Carlisle beat us 2-1 at Saltergate at the end of April only thanks to an offside opening goal (the great Dave Waller was pitch side to tell me so later that night) and

Tony Lormor missing a late penalty.* Twenty-one games unbeaten and though Walsall too had an amazing run of wins to prevent us barging our way into the second of only two automatic promotion spots, we were in the Play Offs and hot tips to blow away Mansfield in the semis and whoever turned up in the other dressing room at Wembley.

Much as I hated Duncan, I desperately wanted to get out of the basement. Every football fan follows a team to see them win and be successful; to turn up every year to see mediocre plodders finish in loser-land every season was nothing like enough. And there was this too: every club has a 'rightful' station, a position of equilibrium based on their history and fan base. Not long before I came on the scene, Town were banging on the door to the old Division Two (now One) hard enough for lumps of paint to come off it: a fourth division club we were not. So I went to all twenty-one of those games, and after the first two was desperate for us to keep winning. If Duncan had to stay manager, then so be it, I'd have to live with it. Stuck in Division Four was like living with a hundred foot wall between you and the rest of the world: I wanted to see what was over the other side. I could comfortably wear these feelings too because I did some digging that late winter of '95 and found out what had turned the whole scene around 180 degrees.

There was a fellow who bought every copy of The Crooked Spireite, a big Town fan, who used to go past me every home game on the street wearing a tie. He used to watch the match from the directors' box, or thereabouts, and hung out with the likes of Norton Lea and Scouse Barrie, who he said he'd known a long time. After an amount of time we got talking and discussing things surrounding the team and such, and little by little he would give me more snippets of info about likely transfers and so on. I always enjoyed meeting fans with info, and with this guy there was always a spot of good natured sparring as he was a bit of a Duncan fan. Three games or so into the record unbeaten run, he laid an absolute megaton bomb on me after I'd tried to coax out of him what had gone off behind the scenes to transform the team: told me the story.

'After the Preston match,' he said, hands in the pockets of a smart navy overcoat, 'Lea brought over an ex-Dutch international basically, to come in

---

* Hasland Harry would sheepishly confess much, much later, 'I let myself down badly that night, in front of my son.' He was referring to his standing up immediately David Reeves' superlative shot from twenty five yards crashed into the net, making a hand sign symbolising male onanism and shouting, 'Reeves, you fuckin' wanker' at the top of his voice in the direction of a grinning Carlisle centre forward now buried under delirious team-mates. Duncan tried to neutralise the memory by signing him in 1998.

and coach the team alongside Duncan.'

'Whaat!'

'Mmm,' he nodded eagerly, and moved on: 'He sat beside him at the Rochdale game, and after half an hour he turned to Duncan and told him, 'you'll never win promotion playing this way.'' Scotch was certain at this time that playing with one man up front, even at home, was the tactical masterstroke required to bring it all back home to Chesterfield.

'Blimey, Dave, we could all have told Scotch that! Then what happened?'

'That's it, that's all I know; work the rest out for yourself.'

'Who was this Dutch player then?'

'I don't know, I'll see if I can find out for you.'

There. That was all I needed to know. It was confirmed in my mind what anyone who followed every match closely and thought a little about human dynamics would easily work out: that the change in team formation and tactics had not been Duncan's work, but that the pressure of the sack had forced him into a corner. We'd also heard that after Mansfield, the players had told the gaffer they'd had enough of playing doomwatch football. It was so obvious. I'd seen almost every Duncan game in the previous two years: that was a hundred matches: there was his dour, sour, miserable method, or there was what all fans simply called 'playing football.' I called the first Spireite of the unbeaten run 'The Revolution Issue' and set out to let everyone know that this glory we were now moving inexorably towards had, essentially, bugger all to do with the manager and threw my whole footballing soul at the issue.

The Play Off home game against Mansfield was the night of my footballing life. The first leg had ended 1-1 at Field Mill, Phil Robinson scoring a goal of messianic proportions. There was so much tension at Saltergate two days later you could have loaded up your wheelbarrow with it and put it on your roses. Nightime football, even in front of a crowd as small as 8000, can have a powerful atmosphere. When each one of that 8000 is on their own an explosive container of nervous energy and adrenalin, their whole futures seemingly dependent upon ninety minutes' play, the air is charged with particles no machine known to humankind can measure.

The game went to two hours, scores level on 2-2 after a match that swayed from one side to the other like a small boat on a huge, rolling ocean. Admittedly, Mansfield, now down to ten men, had the chance to kill their opponents in injury time, but striker Wilkinson didn't have what it took to be a paid assassin. With a single failure to keep a cold head in a crucible of fire, their chance had gone. The Spireites ran out 5-2 winners just over thirty minutes later, the home fans in a pulsating explosion of completely unrestrained joy. Me included. I was with Lyall in the main stand and my head was throbbing with emotional exhaustion. I'd made a pact with myself at seven thirty to put my war against the manager aside for the night, to remember why I had become a Chesterfield supporter in the first place, and why I'd travelled from Torquay to Hartlepool, Gillingham to Carlisle these past seven years in pursuit of what it is and what it means to follow a football team.

I may have had a happier and more fulfilling night in my life to that step on the road, but I don't remember it. It was stupendous.

Rich had been there, on the terraces, and afterwards Radders told me he'd been in a practically demonic state for most of the night, at certain points howling like a deranged animal across a fence at Mansfield fans who tried to match this show of ardour; in the latter part of the evening as events swung the way of the Town, he was more positively possessed, shaking the gates of delirium in victory frenzy.

These events overshadowed Wembley almost completely. I can't say we were always going to win, but two first half goals from Robinson and Tony Lormor quickly put the game out of Bury's reach, as long as they couldn't get one goal back. It was not pretty stuff. By the end of the twenty-one game salute, Duncan had reigned in the natural attacking instincts of the players again. We ended the pre-play off season high on confidence but long again on direct football. Scotch could argue that it worked. The Dutch coach had long since returned home or on to another stop on the football planet, unrequired. The mere threat of him had been enough to allow JD to save himself.

There was a victory parade in Town and we were all there to see the players beaming radiantly like brides, making the most of their day in the sun. It doesn't come along to fourth division footballers very often and usually not at all. In the pleasant Chesterfield market square in front of a few hundred townsfolk basking happily on a hot May morning, Duncan made a speech which I booed, naturally. I was totally drowned by those who greeted a man now a hero: as far as they knew, this man had led the club to not one, but two promotions. This is how it would seem to the outside world too. They weren't interested in Crooked Spireites and revolution stories. To the victor the spoils.

The press and the TV only saw a team in blue winning at Wembley, and assumed, as they always do, that every part of this grand success was planned down to the finest detail by the manager. Andy King, who'd been only one competent swing of a striker's boot away from the decrepit old twin towers himself, could easily have been on the podium - a back of a covered lorry, actually - ten miles east that day. 'Is he lucky?' Sir Matt might have asked of him.

No. Andy King soon lost his job. John Duncan took Chesterfield Football Club off to division two of the football league, ten years exactly since he'd done it the last time.

27

Falling Out Of Love

*'Things are so bad I am reduced to scraping the
outside of the barrel.'*

Roger McGough

1995   Chesterfield Promoted To League Division Two.

I put a brave face on things, but I was torn in half. Part of me had a
spring in its step, was pleased to be going to Oxford and Swindon -
new grounds to chalk off the list, of course - and enjoyed the increased
self-respect of being a fan of a club which had at last tasted some success.
But the rest of me dragged its weary feet in a slough of depression and
defeat. I had lost. The Crooked Spireite had lost. The Nozzer issue had
been swepped away in the historical tide. Rich was full of the joys of being
upwardly mobile and I tried my best to follow his example but it was so
difficult. To make things better, or worse, we had a great first season in
Division 2.

Well, up to a point. By Christmas it was clear we weren't going to be
catapulted back in the direction we'd just come because we were in the top
six. The team played enough attacking football in the first half of the season to suggest that maybe, just maybe, Duncan was re-thinking his tactical approach to the game. We beat teams easily at Saltergate, 3-0, 4-2 and
managed to hold our own away from home. To add to our sense of self-
improvement, our own young genius, Kevin Davies was about to flower
after two seasons of exceptional promise. He was maturing now, was 18
years of age, and the higher grade of football seemed to very much agree
with him.

But I dreaded to think what I'd do with myself if we got promoted. I
still believed Duncan's success was fraudulent but I couldn't maintain this
if we went up. Would I resign as editor of the fanzine? Could I bear even
to keep going to matches? But what sort of a life beckoned me if I didn't
have football?

I made a pact with myself. If we got promoted, I'd have to accept that
Duncan was a good manager. Simple. The idea of getting promoted was

still profoundly attractive. God, can you imagine? Division One? Us? Playing Birmingham City, West Brom, Charlton? Cripes, that would be serious stuff. Yes, I could cope with that. But if we failed, then Duncan failed too and I would still be free, ethically and logically, to take Duncan to the cleaners.

Fortunately, Scotch John being Scotch John and me being right, he blew it. In the last weeks of the season we blew up badly. Davies got injured and with him went our footballing attempt to winning points. After that it was Howizer football all the way with the expected effect on our results which went in an Armitage Shanks kind of direction. There was some disappointment around the place, but hardly anyone was blaming the manager for lack of success. Chesterfield had just achieved their best position in the Football League for fifteen years so there was nothing approaching the revolutionary fervour in the air I'd have liked.

The following season, 1996-97, followed the same pattern as the previous one. Our defence was as mean as a convention of Swiss bankers so we nicked result after result - five 1-0s in the first seven games - and again spent the pre-Christmas period near the top of the table.

Looming over the Crooked Spireite writers now was another problem: the fact that Norton Lea wanted to move us away from Saltergate. This was the most drastic thought imaginable to me, short of the club folding completely, for this would destroy, at a stroke, over one hundred and twenty years of history. Queen Victoria was practically running around her palace garden with hair still in bunches when a town football team first played at Saltergate. Saltergate was as much a part of what made this club Chesterfield FC as the blue shirt, the players and the fans. Here lay the soul of the club, its essence and much of its substance. If you took the team from here and transplanted it somewhere else in however modern and plush a new stadium you might as well call it Willie Poo Knickers United or Scrumpscious Rumpscious Plaster Of Paris Athletic. It quite clearly wouldn't be Chesterfield FC.

And anyway. Here was another forceful point several of us made over and over again: a new ground would be a plastic and concrete disaster, done on the cheap. Like Chester, like Wycombe, we'd seen plenty of these shoddy, valueless disasters already. Even Millwall's New Den, which could hold over 20,000 fans was just a bloated concoction of the ugliest most tastelessly functional building materials ersatz modern Britain could offer. New ground, New Jerusalem? Nothing but an utterly and completely bankrupt idea.

On the pitch, the public were served shite on a platter alright but reasonable numbers of people turned up to watch because it was successful shite, and least in terms of points. It wasn't until our twelfth game that we managed to score two goals in a game, an appalling record, the ghost of D. Blanchflower would have convinced you if he sat beside you watching in this autumn of 1996.

The editor's diary in the CS reflected what seemed to be a growing number of critics of the implacably anti-Duncan stance, some of whom were making their feelings felt on a new Town fan web-site, home of the reactionary, Telegraph reading end of the fan-spectrum (as opposed to our Albanian Leninist-Marxist Death Or Glory approach):

Monday 28th October.

On the phone to an aquaintance this afternoon. Am informed that the Spireite and myself particularly are getting a pasting on a CFC fan website. Criticisms include the usual one about being 'too negative' and me not being born in Chesterfield. Plus, I'm supposed to have signed a pro-Dog Bin Park* petition at Blackpool and therefore am guilty of hypocrisy and furthermore I censor pro-club, pro-board, pro-Duncan, whatever, letters. Oh, I am sorry, but it's a bit late for me to do anything about my birthplace now. Is it my fault that I fell head over heels for a Tapland girl and head over heels for her football club as well?

All this was not quite what I had in mind when I signed on the dotted line for supporting Town now ten years after I sat in the wing stand at the Brentford home game in the sun. It was inevitable I suppose that when the team began to do well me as editor of the CS, the big mouth, would attract more stick. 'Negative' was what they hit us with, something akin to the 'unpatriotic' label that was hung around the necks of dissenters in war time. In the States they would have called us 'unamerican.'

I tried to hang tough: I knew I needed to grit my teeth and stick to my guns: Duncan couldn't possibly take this club forward in any meaningful way, but I'd never had thick skin and the team had been at least relatively successful for two years and the tension was tiring. It would have seemed to some, possibly many, that all I cared about was my war against Duncan. And they were right of course.

---

* Dog Bin Park refers to the Wheeldon Mill site for the new ground, 'The Norton Lea Stadium,' or whatever hideous name he'd cooked up for it. Lea was at this time trying to pressure the council into giving his company planning permission for the development by organising a petition. It was nice to see Mr Lea suddenly showing such enthusiasm for the democratic process.

The fact that I 'wasn't from round 'ere' nagged at me more and more, even though Radford told me where I was born made not a scrotum of difference to my value as a Chesterfield fan. I wasn't quite so sure. It always seemed wrong to me that the fanzine, a local flagship of the club's support, should be run by an outsider. Perhaps now a lot of folk now agreed and I felt all the time I could feel their hot breath on my coat collar.

'You have to be able to take this crap from people: they don't know anything about football anyway, compared to you.' My small heart said, 'what can I do to make these naughty people stop?' I felt exposed and miserable and wasted valuable time and energy the next few days getting on the Internet at lunchtimes and giving my detractors as good a punching as they were giving me.

The pressure to keep up a positive front in the magazine - I couldn't help myself from putting out issue after issue, the thing seemed to have a life of its own - saw me performing Baden Powell knot-tying feats to keep my real emotions connected to what I thought the punters wanted to hear.

Wednesday 4th December Town 2 (Fat Bloke, The Truth) Peterbro 1

We didn't really deserve it, but Duncan, now managing with the luck of the devil, made sure of the points. The fellers with me thought we'd never score but I kept reassuring them old golden bollocks would get his three points in the end, and so it proved. All in all it was a great night at the football. I froze my gonads off on Saltergate for three quarters of an hour selling this, the wind whistling down a semi-deserted road for much of the time, like a scene from a film that should have been entitled, 'The Desolation of Existence' or 'The Sad Bleeding Life Of The Eskimo Who Had No Trousers.' But under that old Compton roof in the second half we had a real good laugh about all manner of things on the pitch, stole a win and went home happy. Yer mates. Some good crack. Football on a Tuesday night. That'll do me.

Actually, the only word that describes the last part of that particular entry is 'lies.' 'Yer mates.' The false jollity of this excruciating expression is like a little man with hob nail boots dancing on the shredded nerves of my two front teeth when I read it now - it was a bald attempt to cover over the negative associations my psyche was now making with the words Chesterfield Football Club. In 1987 walking down Saltergate hearing fans chanting for the head of the manager, I'd failed to understand a) what the man who'd got the team promoted had done to deserve such unfair abuse and b) how fans could be so political about football when all I wanted to do was bask in the beauty of trolling along to the ground to support my new team come what may. Ten years later I would like to have walked around the streets of town with his bleeding head on a stick. And look where I'd arrived! There seemed to be a good few folk in Chesterfield (and outlying districts) who'd have been more than happy if it'd been mine.

I may well have had a ninety minutes full of laughs that night with my pal Radders, my now habitual Recreation Ground companion now that Rich had indeed carried off the championship trophy of his new job with his leisure clothes multi-national and been sent on to, as he would put it, 'the land of the pasty fackin' jock.' But underneath, my soul was sick, and getting worse. More and more now, a win for the team was a win for Duncan and a personal defeat for me. That was the trouble: I took everything so personally. When Nozzer was discarded I said over and over again to myself, 'how dare that man do this to Town fans', meaning 'how dare he do this to me'.

How miserable a person I was to live with at this time I dread to think. Louise gave me no indication, but I suspect that Ian Duncan Smith or a tax inspector from Guildford might have been more fun to have around than me. She did tell me though how much she dreaded weekends. Not least because she now worked hard all week teaching, this made me cringe, with guilt and regret. I was letting her down by being chained to matches and The Crooked Spireite, which by now had become the equivalent of a third son.

If I had had any decency or sense, for Louise I would have let go of the magazine and ditched some of the away trips, all of which, actually, were to the rest of the human race faintly ridiculous, but I couldn't. I would let my mind dwell on the idea for a few moments occasionally, but the thoughts went somewhere else within seconds: of course I couldn't stop doing the fanzine; that idea was as ridiculous as attacking a Chesterfield nightclub bouncer with a bouquet of daisies, or more pointedly, not going to away games. The thought of the Spireites running out on to a football pitch for a game without me there in person to witness it, made me literally shudder.

So football now took up practically all my time and more seemingly all of my available head space. Even in the summer I wrote articles, thought about new ideas for features and organised merchandise - we had enamel badges, t-shirts and aerial photographs of Saltergate on the go by now - and talked incessantly on phones still about transfer rumours, Duncan, the new ground, the fanzine, actual transfers, Duncan, staying at

Saltergate, the fanzine, the new ground, Duncan: round and round I went, day after day, like a little child on a fairground roundabout, slurping a comforting giant of a stick of candy floss. All of it I loved, all of it I was beginning to feel dismal and weary of. But the last thing I could possibly do was give it all up.

Then the cup run began.

28

The Cup Run

'It can come a bit hard sometimes to see one's own unique, heroic life pinned pitilessly to a wall.'

Stephen Fry

i

One to Four

There has only been one glorious cup run for my team,* any competition, during my time as a real football supporter**, but I would think those who have witnessed a lower division team cup run, one that sees round one as the starting gate, would agree that when you play your first game, there is not the slightest inkling of what lies ahead. People

---

* Why is a situation wherein a football team wins a small succession of games called a cup 'run'? Dunno. It's the only word you ever hear used to describe such a thing. I apologise for its apparent overuse in this chapter but plead the zero alternative.

**The only season since that opening season for me, 1984-5, where Town did anything at all in any of the cup competitions was in September 1992, under Chris McMenemy when we played a two-legged tie against Liverpool in the Coca Cola (League) Cup. I hobbled there on crutches (only the last hundred yards from where the coach dropped us off, to be fair) to see us, sensationally, draw 4-4. We took 9,000 fans, sang all night and nearly scored all night. Hardly being able to believe his luck, being 4-2 up well into the second half, McMenemy, like a man with vertigo finding himself three quarters the way up the north face of the Eiger, panicked. He took off strikers Nozzer and Dave Lancaster who'd both scored twice already, conceding all initiative to the home side, and instead of ending up winning 5 or 6-4, we allowed Liverpool to draw level. Sat in the stand with Stuart and other CS stalwart Billy Wheatcroft, we cracked jokes all night and had one hell of a hoot. It started off as gallows humour and soon became the sort of laugh you might conceivably have after you've died and know you're on the way up to eternal life in Heaven. Until that is, the last ten minutes when we were trying to hold on at 4-3; then we were perched on the edge of our seats with faces contorted with the tension of the desperate. When they equalised we'd come out of the clouds to become real football fans again: it felt like a defeat as it always does when you've led a game by two clear goals.

say afterwards they had hunches that 'this year was going to be our year' but there really is no internal conductor to signal to you the stone cold fact that you are going to end up on a field of play somewhere competing in the third round of the FA Cup, perhaps paired with Manchester United and facing ninety minutes at Old Trafford. In which case that hunch was the usual wishful thinking.

I learned not to bother having hunches about four years into my Chesterfield career. After Notts County, then Bolton Wanderers put us out in round one in the first two, the first full Paul Hart year gave us a magnificent tie at Shrewsbury Town, then a division higher, where we won 3-2 and were all singing 'Ooh, Waller, Wall-er!' in the open air toilets on the away end at half time. We all got an incredible buzz out of that and even managed not to piss all the way down the front of our trousers. This was only our third appearance in round two in eight years, and in all three we were put out. Huddersfield Town delivered the fatal blow to the back of the neck in the second round here too. We'd only been in round three three times since 1970, ten times since 1951 and had never, *never* got through to round four as a lower division side. For a number of years either side of the Second World War, the best Town side in the club's history had reached round five on three occasions. But Chesterfield FC had never been in a cup quarter final in their history, and worse for the Town fan of 1996-97, had not been even to round three since 1981, the last time they'd had a crash hot side (Town fans at the time said the team was so good, played such good football, they were 'too good' to win promotion. Danny Wilson was it's principal star among several).

In this 1996-97 FACup season, the only encouraging signs when the draw for round one was completed were two: firstly, we looked extremely likely to knock over any division three side - we'd made not so much mincemeat as clear soup of Scarborough the previous season, away, now looking miles ahead of such teams - and secondly, we were drawn at home.

Our round one opponents, Bury had been promoted to division two a year behind us but came to our place a top three side. However, their success was based on formidable home form, and it showed. Our centre back Mark Williams, a terrific purchase from Shrewsbury for next to nothing the previous season, scored with a solid header from a corner in the first half and we continued to look strong at the back for the rest of the half. One of the genuine strengths of the side was its spirit and determination. They were so mean in the footballing sense they wouldn't have given a drowning man a life belt. Whether they got this from Duncan or from themselves I couldn't say. Perhaps Scotch had some fearful punishment for them if they ever came off the pitch having conceded a goal. It was possible.

One existing certainty was Duncan's manic, pathological obsession for practicing the 'art' of defending during training. Over to Nozzer.

'One time we were rehearsing how to attack at corners and Duncan and Kevin Randall had spent most of the morning trying to work out how many men we could afford to have in the other team's box and, stupidly, we've only got two. So I turned to Duncan and said, 'shouldn't we only have one? What if we take the corner, the ball canons off the bar up the field: they could break away and we'd be struggling.' And Duncan actually took me seriously: he turned to Randall and said, 'what do you think?"

Anyhow. Back at the Bury game, we started playing for the final whistle after about ten minutes of the second half, 'shut up shop,' as the expression has it, and held on quite comfortably. It wasn't pretty: it never was any more. But that was round one out of the way.

The draw for round two was, on paper, perfect: Scarborough - at home. It was no thrashing though. They fought like stink but our players were too good for theirs, even performing here well below par, as happens many times when a team is a hot favourite. We conjured two goals from somewhere to no reply. Round three at last, the first time for fully sixteen years. It was ridiculous. Now we were there you could see it only took winning two games. You could either celebrate this and laugh your head off, or you could get really cheesed off thinking about how short changed Town fans had been for so, so bloody long. If you were me, you could start worrying.

Round three was another home draw: another division two opponent with a weak away record - Bristol City. By this stage of the competition, what was needed of the side was to be an occasion side. Not big occasion yet, because this tie was an anti-climax when one considered that we could very feasibly have been at Old Trafford in this round, or at Everton or Arsenal or Newcastle. But were we a side which really wanted to win a cup tie? We had a great defence, with tremendous steel at the back; that we knew from the Bury game. We also had an exceptionally competent goalkeeper, Billy Mercer and an emerging star in the centre back role in Sean Dyche. A supremely gifted right back, (for the lower divisions anyway) he had been moved to centre back after David Pleat, then of Luton Town, tried to buy him from us as one. He was now playing brilliantly there. If they could maintain form - they'd only conceded five goals in the previous ten games - we had to have a great chance of winning. It was only Bristol City after all. They were no great shakes.

The boys at the back, if you will, weren't truly put to the test. We were lucky, presented with a perfect opportunity to go onward: City had a man sent off in the first half. Again we produced not one goal but two, and were in the fourth round. The fourth round! This for me, a fan of only twelve year vintage was incredible. Those of longer service were to be seen in a daze, or in a state of advanced exuberance, at home, at the match, at work, wherever. For all of us this was big news.

But I oscillated between clouds of glory and black depression. There was no doubt that Duncan's stock was rising like a hot tip on Wall Street again, a crying shame, because although our league position was still high, - top eight-, those not definitively in the pro-Duncan camp were fed up with the inglorious style. Coming into the fourth round match, we'd managed only three goals in the previous six league games. You would normally get relegated if you couldn't do something to pep that up.

What also rankled desperately with me and the anti-Duncan camp, shrinking but still strong and fervent, was his attitude to certain players. Two of the key figures of the promotion season, Lormor and Robinson, were either gone (the latter) or in the process of being eased out (the former). It really did seem, as with Nozzer, that if you were a crowd favourite you were not looked favourably upon by Scotch. Unlikely as it may sound, and it may only be a coincidence, it was as if he was jealous of the popularity of the players who were the darlings of the Kop. Another who had been well liked as a hot winger whose pace had destroyed us three seasons earlier when playing for Scarborough, Mark Jules, had been converted to full back. Frustratingly, it looked in games that season as if he'd been told by Scotch that he'd be fined a tenner if he crossed the half way line. His cheetah-like speed across mud and grass meant that wingers never bested him, but to us he was a waste of a real, attacking asset. It seemed to be that man Scotch spoiling our fun again.

Why Robbo had been moved on, to (Notts County), we had no idea. It only appeared all too clear that he had fallen foul of the chief in some way or other, despite having been the heart of the team in midfield for the best part of two seasons. He scored goals with an eyebrow-raising alacrity for a midfield player too: 10 in his first half a season, 11 the other side of Christmas in the next.

Tony Lormor was one you couldn't help liking. Lacking in pace but a technically competent striker, he was a Geordie, a character, a smiler and a cheeky corner flag goal celebrator also. Every fan needs at least one Tony Lormor in the side to keep the spirits up on the dark days of winter, especially when you've come a long way from home to be there. Goals there were from Tony too: 11 in his first half a season, almost 20 in the next at a higher level. This season he'd managed 10 again, but now he was in and out of the side, and the word on Saltergate was that it was nothing to do with injury.

There were replacements for these men, and young Paul Holland, Robbo's replacement, was a fine player without a shadow of a doubt. However, he didn't seem to enjoy his football as much as he had when he came to Saltergate with Mansfield and scored goals against us. Typical of Duncan, we said, to waste another talent.

And if that wasn't having all your toys put away in a box in the loft, there was the Kevin Davies mystery. The mesmerically gifted tyro of the previous season was withering like a prize orchid in November frost. He had one or two injuries so missed games, but the fact was, his form had deserted him completely. Shadow. Self. Former. Deeply worrying. Again the rumours were strong around town. Fall outs with the boss. Disillusioned with the style of play. Training dull, dull, dull. He'd lost interest and wanted away. Wasn't disciplined enough. Went out too much. Wouldn't have been the first and wouldn't be the last. You listened to your story and took your choice. Horrible as it was to watch such a talent struggling so badly, the thought that his transfer value was imploding week by week, was the thing that had you thinking that finding some sort of refuge in heavy drinking wasn't such a bad idea as you'd once thought.

It was all like this then, when we went to table topping division one side Bolton Wanderers, 6-2 demolishers of Luton in a delayed round three game, on Tuesday February 4th for the biggest cup game for the club possibly since 1939. The omens were good. Bolton had rested players for this. They thought this was going to be a straightforward job for a fine side on their way to the Premiership. Scouts would have seen a Town side that offered their regular opponents little threat in front of goal - who were, well, rubbish really by comparison with us.

One big, defensive ricket* after six minutes and Kev Davies was offered a cow's arse with a banjo he couldn't but thwack, form or no form: underdogs one-up. Cue for a lot of game defending for the rest of the half and an equaliser just before the break. The clouds were looming for a traditional second half a la Chesterfield - Scarborough in round two: we'd surely lose by a couple of goals, at least.

Or sunshine. I was again in a state of inner torment. Half of me was pulled towards the kudos, the prestige, the plain pure joy that went with pulling off a major cup upset - that's what the 1-0 scoreline had promised only minutes before the break. If you can get back in the dressing room at one-none: I can hear Big Ron telling me this right now, you were in with a hell of a chance. With that tough Chesterfield defence? What then? Duncan's Heroes Storm Into Round 5. Duncan Makes History For Town. The thought made me ill. I wanted that Bolton equaliser.

---

* A Ricket is a footballing term for a blunder, especially in the south.

I went out for the second half hoping that this was the cup run over. We'd lose, the burst bubble and all that clichéd stuff, then be back to the big boot of league football. Then we'd see what Scotch was made of. I knew he wasn't good enough to take this team up, I felt it in my bones and had learned enough from watching lower division football twice a week for nine years to be certain that his sphincter clenching defensive tactics were doomed to failure. So it was Come On You Whites, put us out of our misery, we lovers of all that's noble and true in the great game of football, then we can go home and write it up as one great year in the cup (at last) and get back to real life.

But Kevin Davies ruined it. He knew he was in the shop window. If he could find a bit more of that which had left him, he'd be away from Chesterfield to a big club and a big world: he was still only nineteen. It was all ahead of him and all to play for as he came out for the second half........

........and took it by storm. Twice he was put through, one on one with the keeper and twice he rammed the ball into the net to make it two, then three-one. Even I had to admit they both made glorious sights, poetic, artistic sights. He was brilliant, I had to give him that. I loved him, and I hated him. Lucky, lucky Duncan again. Bolton were horrifically disappointing, they hadn't turned up and had given three bad goals away. They had totally underestimated us.

I was still pulled down to the pitchside from the seats that Rick had wheedled out of a new business acquaintance, to applaud the team off the pitch and would have walked on to the pitch to do it had there not been a ruddy great fence in the way. I had come this far, four hundred games with Town since 1984 and I wasn't going to let my loathing for a manager deprive me of displaying my affection and admiration for a performance that made the heart feel well and truly massaged and the eye misty with emotion.

Round five - this was getting serious - would be at home, against a Premiership side, Nottingham Forest. No more, no less.

ii
Forest

I knew we were going to win when we heard Stuart Pearce wasn't playing. Even with him in it they were the most wretched Forest side for twenty years - sorry: the only wretched Forest side of the past twenty years. We were as certain as a crowd turning up for a public execution to be up for the cup and they were as ready for dumping out of the competition as a big fat turkey ready for my oven on Christmas Day. If you had any knowledge of football you could see this coming from the hills and dales of, ooh, miles and flipping miles away.

Forest were so bad you could almost have felt sorry for their fans. I can't honestly say I gave a tuppenny stuff for them however, steeped and pickling as I was up the other end of the ground in my own misery. My meagre critical faculties as a football observer - and we who have not played the game to a high standard will always have limited skill in this area - and the fact that whatever I was feeling a thick part of me was blue where it used to be an ugly fleshy pink, told me that we had performed heroically despite the meagre threat from players who should have known and played far, far better. They played with zero spirit and less confidence. Psychologically, if it had been a heavyweight boxing contest, it would all have been over in fifteen seconds. Duncan. Lucky. Yet again. I was like old England being invaded by the Danes, if you'll excuse the peculiar analogy. The part of me taken up by the traitor who made me feel sickened at beating Forest was spreading rapidly, but there was still plenty of me, the Chesterfield fan left.

Forest finished with ten men and we won 1-0. A penalty.

I went round to the main entrance of the club with Stuart, Radders and Billy, another confirmed Duncan-outer, determined to grasp Paul Holland by the hand: I often felt sentimental like this after a major win, but he was nowhere to be seen ages after the final whistle. We did see a mob of disconsolate, angry adult Forest fans, not kids, who were only a few beers away from being a lynch mob. They barracked keeper Mark Crossley, brave or foolish enough to be standing in the car park with his father, and a couple of late middle aged men who looked nondescript but were recognised as Forest directors and were given a fearful coating before they moved hurriedly back inside the football club.

We walked behind the now empty Cross Street end where the gates were still open to let BBC blokes clear up their cables and so on. I wanted to go onto the terrace to see if I could track down a programme perhaps thrown away in disgust.* There was one there alright, a little torn but still worth having. On this event, I later indulged myself in full view of the readers of the fanzine thusly:

> So we go in and hunt on the floor for a prog, and wouldn't you
> know it, Stuart finds one. It's crushed, as if thrown away in anger,

---

*With characteristic sloppiness, the club hadn't printed enough programmes and had sold out by 2.20 pm.

bitterness or despair, or maybe a mixture of all three. That's the one I want. Not a pristine one which still looks unread, but a damaged one, one which has already got some history, which will always remind me of these moments. For these were great, memorable moments. We stood on the top steps of the Cross Street end. Looking over the pitch, still green at the end of winter, it lit up by brilliant floodlights, over the Kop the sky was pink and glorious away over towards Birdholme. The ground looked brilliant. Empty, warm, inviting. I wish I could have spread my arms around you and hugged you to my chest. Never let you go. That anyone could throw this away. I simply don't, don't understand. That we could leave this place, better and more special than any I have ever lived in, for a new 1990s pile of soulless concrete seems somehow impossible. But the beauty of the place wouldn't let negative thoughts get a hold of my brain, so for a minute or so we just stood there looking, thinking about Saltergate, thinking about the day. Precious, precious moments.

Later I stared at my television set in wonder as my team were featured on Match Of The Day for the first time, the full analysis bit, the whole Alan Hansen. I can't tell you how strange and disconcerting that felt when you've spent your adult football life at Peterborough, Wigan and Stockport.

iii
Wrexham

The morning of the game I was on the Radio 5. Sixth round day, nine something in the morning and the phone goes as expected. They'd rung me a few days earlier telling me they wanted to interview me, being the fanzine editor, at the same time as a Wrexham fan who'd be on another line somewhere. To be honest, the Welsh guy was struggling. He'd never been on the radio before, you could tell, and he was very nervous. At least I'd been humiliated by Danny Baker on 606 before, I'd be okay, even though my stomach was hot and pumping.

Then it was my turn and stone me to pieces if the presenter, a Brummie*, didn't put me right on the spot. Rick would have said he was

---

* Who I later found out was a johnnie called Adrian Chiles, who still does the same show at the same time on the same station, and, I have to say, is very very good. So good, in fact, that I've almost forgiven him.

'giving it the big one'. He stunned me with: 'You've got a reputation for being rather anti-John Duncan; don't you think you should be eating your words, now he's got you to the sixth round?'

And the question was absolutely hanging there in the air, and the fecker expected me to answer it. Now, I'd come on expecting a nice couple of questions like 'how does it feel to got this far in the cup?' I thought he'd buddy up a bit, but he really went for me, because when I said, 'Look, today's a day I want to celebrate; it's such a big day in the history of the club, blah, blah, bleh, bleh,' But he absolutely Paxman-ed me: he repeated the bloody question. So I came over all political and said, 'Look, I could bore you with statistics about how few games we've won in the league while all this has been going on,' and our league form had gone down the crapper in the previous few weeks, 'but this is a day when I want to forget about all that stuff and just enjoy another big day in the cup: ask me another.'

I forget what happened next: he may have gone back to Wrexham, though I seem to recall saying something later about how cup football being all about silencing fifteen hundred premier club fans on an away terrace which I thought might upset someone's cosy notions about small club fan attitudes somewhere, come to think of it. But I was livid. All the crappy, insufferably wanky bland interviews I'd heard on the Beeb down the years and when it was my turn, I get a baseball bat in the bollocks. Typical of the state I'm in, I thought.

As for the game, it was dour. We scored. They didn't. I found a part of me at the end which was still blue, as opposed to black, and thought 'bugger me sideways with a buttered parsnip: we're in the cup semi-final' like everyone else. The black part slumped on to the concrete steps next to the tea hut and beat the ground in despair. 'They're going to build a statue of John Duncan now, I know it'.

iv
Semi Final

The town of Chesterfield went completely mad for the next five weeks. I kid you not. Mad. People who had never heard of football, let alone knew there was a football ground in the town had 'Come On You Blues' car stickers in their windows that a Sheffield Radio station, a *Sheffield* radio station, if you please, dropped on Chesterfield and outlying districts from a couple of aeroplanes. Hospital consultants and solicitors who rode around in their huge 4x4 suburban assault vehicles stuck silly, curly blue and white paper party thingies on their radio aerials.

Tickets? Me a season ticket holder: I'd rushed to get one when the club released a shed load after round four or somewhere so as not to get caught out if this cup ride went the whole distance, I had an allocation of four in the bag. All along the way the club had screwed up the ticket allocation for the last three games. A trained monkey could have worked out a way for all the regular fans to have got a ticket for rounds 5, 6 and the semi, but Mr Chairman couldn't or wouldn't take the necessary steps and took a huge, huge amount of stick from fans, sometimes to his face, telling him what a shitbag they thought he was. Some were in tears, stuck with only £38 tickets to buy, with money they could barely afford, or were left with nothing. Nearly 30,000 tickets went from FA to CFC to 'fans' of the club and they all went in the time it took you to have a wash in the morning and therefore as easily as switching your central heating on. Lea seemed to panic though and encouraged people to book blocks of tickets for coach trips which were hurriedly being organised by every firm in the area that employed more than about ten people. Huge chunks of the last two CSs of the season were taken up with articles and letters about this farce, Mr Basson putting in typically superb work on it. He was never better than when writing about how thoughtless or just plain stupid the board, particularly the Chairman, were in their dealings with fans. That's my bid for this year's Understatement Of The Year award, by the way.

I was in demand as unofficial fan spokesperson. I let a rude man from the Daily Express violate my house asking me all sorts of questions the answers to which he showed not the slightest interest. He drank our tea, sat in my chair for a the best part of an hour with a sneer on his face, then didn't use a word of it, which served my ego right for letting him over the threshold in the first place. A bloke from the Sydney Morning Herald rang up and was as nice as could be and I was nothing short of thrilled to my fillings about it. Any chance to be the centre of attention for a bit was fine by me. Mike Ticher himself, now working for a national rag, rang me up which pleased me to pieces, him virtually starting the fanzine movement and everything. It was like working for a massive corporation and the chairman getting in touch with you and taking a personal interest in you. That nearly made me happy.

For the most part the whole scene was a complete nightmare covered with sugar. The fans now cheered Duncan at every home game when he walked from the pitch door to the dugout. The team would play badly and boringly for the most part - we hardly won a game in the league the rest of the season - and he would be applauded back from the dug out to the door. Since that night in Bolton we'd played twelve league games and won only once. And no-one apart from me and a handful of spiteful, jealous losers, that's how we were painted, gave a fuck. Draw, loss or occasional grim victory (I should record for accuracy that we did beat Wycombe 4-2 soon after the Wrexham game), supporters turned up, laughed and grinned for the better part of two hours, bought more and more souvenirs and went home again to wait for Middlesbrough, who we were soon to play at, where else? Old Trafford.

I got the last magazine to the printer and back well in time for the semi: writers had much to clear from their chests what with club history being made and fans being so enraged at ticket foul ups. It filled up in no time at all. For the first time, I didn't write an editorial. I had nothing left to say. The board were taking Saltergate away from us which would become nice new housing for young couples who needed somewhere to put their assault vehicles, Duncan was going to be presented with a massive key twenty feet long, and as we weren't a city he could be given the freedom of, it would be a key with which he could claim free stuff like beer for the rest of his life, and I was as good as utterly and completely defeated.

And still things got worse. I had fanzines left to sell on the day of the club's first FA Cup semi-final, so I determinedly stood on Sir Matt Busby Way and sold 'em, shouting my usual 'Croogie-Spirwight, eighty pee' to any one of the fifty thousand people who were floating past me with red, then blue banners and flags and silly hats and painted faces. Who else but David Waller was one of them, and he was a sight for sore eyes: for once I was selling Crooked Spireites and recognised nobody going past me. I must have looked extremely happy to see him, because he beamed at me.

'EIGHTIE PEE!!......' I was hollering when I saw him, 'but free to legends,' as I always remembered to say whenever this happened on Saltergate. Then it was time to go and meet Louise and panic set in: I couldn't find her under the Munich clock. I ran to the main office where they couldn't have cared less about the fact that as far as I could see my wife had mistakenly gone inside the ground with my ticket. I cast around desperately to see a face I knew who would go inside and find Louise for me, which was ridiculous. They too were excited beyond words, this was the day of their lives, what did they want to help me for? Me, not even born in Chesterfield, nor anywhere in Derbyshire, not even the north of England. My parents weren't born in Derbyshire, nor my grandparents. I was born in Edmonton, London, the son of a bus conductor's daughter and a no good sailor's son. I'd turned up to a place where I no longer belonged; had never belonged.

I was frantic, it was ten to three. I went back to the clock and saw her dark-haired head wearing one hell of a frown. We made it past the 'where the hell have you beens?' and the ticket tearer on the turnstile, and when the teams came out three minutes later into the sunshine there was a noise around our heads that nearly woke the local dead, amid an Argentina 1978 paper shower. Inside, my throat caught itself in a choke and tears welled up, exactly the experience I'd had the second I saw my daughter for the first time, spooned out of Louise in 1986 crying with the cord dangling down. I began to calm down; Duncan walked out and past us - we were twenty metres from the tunnel - and was cheered to the echo. I booed him as loudly as I could. The woman to my right gave me a mystified look indeed. But what did she know about me, I thought. How the hell would she know what it was like to be me, standing there in a daze, losing my religion.

Then my team kicked off and I wanted them to lose.

If we won this game, it was all over for me at Chesterfield. How would I be able to walk into Saltergate, into Wembley, if we reached the cup final; if *John Duncan* reached the cup final? How could there be a fanzine? What would people say to me? If we made it to Wembley, how could I prove that it wasn't Duncan that got us there? Who would listen? And who would care?

We scored first. It was nil-nil at half time and our amazing run of luck held. Kevin Davies was lively and got one of their defenders booked. Then before half time the player who'd decked Kevin kicked the ball away at a free kick. David Elleray, the bald schoolmaster from Harrow, sent him off. At ten v eleven, we had to have some sort of chance. We must have played with an incredible amount of spirit, heart, soul. We went out in the second half and Andy Morris, still there eight years after he'd joined the club as a raw gangling 19 year-old, scored. Pandemonium around us. Six minutes later, Bruno was tripped, went down in installments, but Elleray gave the penalty. Captain Dick Dyche: slammed the ball low and straight, 2-0. This was beyond fiction.

But. This was the Middlesborough of Ravanelli, temperamental they said, but a truly excellent player, what they used to call a freescoring centre forward, and Juninho, the most brilliant player I had ever seen apart from Best, maybe. They surely could not go on playing this poorly, even with ten. Even with Bryan Robson managing them. Juninho ran and ran, so hard they as good as had eleven still. They pulled a goal back only four minutes after our penalty. This so often happens: the better team will rally, if only for a while, and in that time have to score, or else lose the game. Then an incredible, incredible thing happened. If you were writing a screenplay and included this, you'd be laughed at: we scored again.

However, though the ball rebounded from the bar well over the line, the linesman said he hadn't seen the ball cross the line. Elleray wasn't at an angle to know one way or the other. No goal. Within minutes, a Middlesborough equaliser: a penalty, non-stop flying machine Juninho being tripped as he surged past Dyche into a scoring position. Then, with the Premiership side inevitably recovering self-belief, they scored a third; obviously, the winner.

We were out. I was relieved. We'd given a magnificent account of ourselves, scored two goals against a Premiership side, which defied belief. But now, the story was over. I could reassemble myself again somehow, and stumble on into some sort of future. Then a minute to go, a ball bouncing in the Middlesborough box. Jamie Hewitt, who I'd seen play literally hundreds of times for Town, who'd scored that day in 1987 when Shaggy Caldwell had been injured, but had missed in the dying minutes at Wembley in 1990 when he could have saved my day and who'd been on the receiving end of appalling stick fans many, many times in the years which followed, was running to meet the bounce: headed it.

It looped, it sailed, it floated, over a goalie who just watched it. He had time to take his jock strap off, throw it at the ball and divert it over the bar, but he didn't. It fell to earth into the back of the net of the Stretford End - there was a nano-second of silence in the ground: there and gone but perceptible nevertheless, because it looked at first as if the ball had dropped harmlessly over the bar. Then an eruption of incredulity from one half of the ground and the game was drawn.

The players spent a long time on a lap of honour, where Boro fans richly applauded them too. Near the tunnel once again, the players were distracted by two men who had climbed on to seats to make themselves seen, and better heard.

'Oy, Dick! Jamie!" they yelled, trying to make themselves heard above the general commotion and waved their arms about exuberantly. Suddenly they were spotted by one player, who grabbed an arm of a second, and both smiled big smiles back to the two men standing on the seats, who were wearing extravagantly happy faces. One belonged to Chris Marples. And the one trying hardest to get his congratulations across to his old team mates, was Nozzer.

A far, far better and bigger man than me.

So we all jumped on the roundabout and went round again. More ticket fiascos, more crying, more queuing up at seven o'clock the night before, more hairdressers and people who'd never seen the team play before, in their thousands, whacking wads of hard-earned onto counters to be there. A replay at Hillsborough. The television after Old Trafford, the papers, they all said what a fantastic job John Duncan was doing at Chesterfield. Brilliant. Superb. So what could I know. Sky TV asked me to meet them for an interview at the ground, but I wasn't interested. How was I, in any way, now representative of the fans of Chesterfield football club? I'd wanted them to lose at Old Trafford, just so I, me, Craig Thomas, wouldn't be proved wrong in terms of what I thought I knew about football. How was I even to fit to sit to watch these players any more: who had given everything unto the last drop in that first game and would again?

In the replay the result was right for me, wrong for everybody else. 3-0 to them (or was it us, now?), Juninho again brilliant. As Paul Hart had once told me in the office under the stand, a lesser side can raise themselves once for a big game, but it was impossible for them to keep on doing it. So it proved. I had a very unenjoyable time, though. A gruesome time. Fans all around me on another charabanc trip. It was to football, but it might have been ice skating, basketball, a trip to a pantomime starring local town people who made it to fame and fortune. It was all about municipal spirit and a big occasion.

A new phenomenon really bugged me. Every few minutes, a chant went up behind me which we got caught up in. 'Stand up, if you're Chesterfield, stand up...' and we all had to get to our feet, as if the Queen had walked in. We never did this at Wycombe or Millwall, or anywhere. It seemed to typify a situation that had slipped way, way beyond my control. This wasn't supporting Chesterfield any more: this was not an experience that connected itself to what I'd spent the last nine years of my life doing. Going to football was about the familiar, about going through established rituals that were all immaculately observed. This was strange. This wasn't football anymore.

The final whistle went. The charabanc engines would be coughing into life any minute, ready to cart twenty five thousand people in blue back to their home town, which all too plainly wasn't mine. I went across to a fence that separated Boro from Town like concentration camp inmate of different nationalities, and to Rick's complete and utter disgust, shook hands with Middlesborough fans and wished them well in the final. And that was the last time I saw Chesterfield play.

29

Losing My Religion

'I guess you'd say I'm on my way to Burma Shave..'
Tom Waits

No spotlight. To start with I decided I couldn't face another home game that season - away games? forget that: I'd had enough Route One to last me a full lifetime. There were no more fanzines to produce before we all went our separate ways for the Summer break, so there was no pressure there, for a while at least. I'd have to go back in August though; have to.

So the team played - and I wasn't there. The feeling of alienation produced by the townspeople's orgy of euphoria over the two semi-finals was my methadone. In a few weeks the end of season arrived. I survived. I coped. I watched the Final, between Boro and Chelsea and thought, along with everyone else: that could have been us playing Chelsea. Can you imagine that? But for David Elleray and a linesman, we would have been there. We'd have all been there. A statue for Duncan then, definitely; manager 'til he got fed up with it; then a seat on the board. He'd still be there when I died. But there was no question about the fact that I would carry on with the Spireite and that I would be there to see Duncan fail next season. Just you wait, I thought. I will be proved right in the end.

Until one Sunday night in late May. Up at the local sports centre playing some fairly serious badminton my friend Clarkie gave me an absolute pasting. Competitive, remember. I came home and threw myself down in the chair, furious. And as quickly as a fork of lightning comes out of nowhere and splits the sky, it came to me.

'That's it. I have to give up the Spireite.'

'What's that got to do with badminton?' said Louise.

'Nothing. I'm giving the thing up. That's it.'

'Well, I'll believe that when I see it. But you do exactly what you like.'

I didn't give up the magazine for Louise: I gave it up for me. I tried on the idea for a day or two and it suited me very well indeed. I told what you might call my closest associate, Radders, and he said, 'I can see why. It's been less fun for me too.'

'Do you want to take it over?'

'No, I haven't got the time.' Or the inclination, I thought. Very wise.

I asked Stuart. It had been his baby: it could be his adolescent. It was his still, in a way. I owed it to him to make him the offer. He wasn't remotely interested. I think I may have mentioned it to Bob Wort, as a nod of respect, but he laughed. There was Billy, another of the clan, but it wasn't for him either. That was it. Nine and a half years, sixty-five individual magazines. A million words and more. So many laughs. So much hostility, hatred even. So much love. But no longer fun.

It was like cutting my own arm off with rusty wire to let go. To let it go.

Stuart's last cover was great. Randall, Dr Luther's assistant these past four years, was hugging a (for once) gleeful John Duncan and looking like he was whispering in his ear. Mr Basson put a bubble next to his mouth which said: 'Five forwards...Everyone up when we get a corner...Rehearsing set pieces during training...Short passes...Keeping the ball on the deck...Phil Robinson...Steve Norris...'

Duncan replies,

'Oooh, I love it when you talk dirty!!' A fitting way to leave, I think.

I sent a letter of thanks to all the subscribers explaining, lying, I should say, about why I was giving up. It was true - get this - I wanted to spend more time with my family, and there were other things I wanted to do with my life. But deep inside, in the places you let no-one in your life go, I knew that if it hadn't been for the cup run, I would perhaps still be there doing the same thing, observing all the same old rituals.

The new season was about to start but it felt so good to have cut myself free. I thought, 'no, I won't go to games. Not yet'. Then I could see another miserable Thomasonian trait arriving over the hill. My friends all expect me to go. They think this is me, what I do. So I wont. I'll stop.

August became September. The leaves did their autumn thing, observing their usual rituals and still I didn't go. I began to like Saturdays again. I would get up when I felt like it, look through the bedroom window at fields and woods and think, 'all this time in front of me today: it's all mine'. Oh, but that was a good feeling. For the first time in nine years I went to the shops on a weekend, and bought books, CDs and drank coffee in a pretend Italian coffee bar in Derby. I stopped going to Chesterfield for things. It was a year before I went again. When I did, the music shop wasn't where it was supposed to be and there was now the ugliest pub near the Crooked Spire you have ever seen in your life. 'The town has moved on and it doesn't need you', it seemed to be saying.

The Town, the cup semi-finalists, were not doing well, but though I always looked at their result in the paper and looked at the team to see who was playing, I thought about them less and less. Soon it felt natural, was natural, not to think like a supporter, not to be a supporter. Lyall had always had a thing for Tottenham because that's where I used to live - I told him the family stories just as Mabel Jnr had once done - and because his cousin, who he idolised, had a thing for them. For some reason I began to look more kindly upon the team I used to watch to see lose, and like it if they did well. But when they played Manchester United, I found myself always behind the Red Devils (as I had first known them).

I found I liked United doing well. I was quite beside myself when they won that European Cup final (let's forget silly names just this once more, shall we?) in the last minute, which really surprised me. Through the Chesterfield years I'd hardly thought of them apart from them symbolising all that was wrong with the game from an economic point of view: their aspirations were dangerous too and still are. But I could watch them on the box and it would be, well, only a game. I found myself feeling comfortable when they won. Which was fine for me because that was mostly all the time.

I didn't speak to Stuart anymore, or any other football people, and I saw much less of Radders. But we did go to hear some poetry: Brian Patten, then Roger McGough. Radders and I had compared favourite writers, poets and books the very first time we contacted each other through the post. Football fanatics are not so one-dimensional you know. They just appear to be that way. And now we even had a telephone conversation for ten minutes where we talked about the things going on in our lives, the important things, and we didn't once mention football. With the team going nowhere and the club's administration sinking into chaos in the first couple of years after Old Trafford, it was just as well.

But. Some time after I stopped going to football, I realised that all that time I had not been a fanatic. It had been more than an obsession. I had been addicted to football. Really, properly addicted, as men and women are to drink, hard drugs and gambling. After a while back then football started controlling me and I'd reached a point where I was going to games, those Tuesday nights at Bristol and Carlisle, Saturdays in Torquay, not because I genuinely wanted to go; not because I expected to enjoy myself, but because I had to. I needed the Spireites far, far more than they had ever needed me, my money and my support. The knowledge shocked me when I saw it there wafting across my mind. I thought I'd loved football. Loved the fanzine. I did. But way before the end I'd lost a grasp of where love stopped and the pure blind need of the addict began.

And I felt soothed by that knowledge. It meant that I could forget about ever going again to see them. I'd made a promise to myself back at the start of the post-Crooked Spireite period that I would not go back to Saltergate until I proved to myself that I could be a success in some tangible way in another area of my life. Because I felt now that football, Chesterfield, had robbed me of the other parts of me that were worth developing; that this whole, crucial non-football part of me had been neglected and damaged and I had to fix it. I thought of Rich and the year 'sonze chocolate' and knew that I would be faithful to the pact I'd made with my better self even if it meant I had to stay away forever.

And I have.

The year of The Cup Run still comes back to haunt me sometimes. The statue of Scotch John was never built, of course, but it would have served me right if it had. I now know that the struggle between him and those fans who in their minds and hearts wanted him gone was one which should have been fought by the people of Chesterfield; that it had nothing to do with me all along. Like the stranger in the cliched western movie who arrives in a strange town, he stays only as a guest, and when one day he leaves, no matter how many years later that is, he leaves understanding that he has always been a guest, that essentially, he hadn't rightly belonged there all that time. I had never belonged at Chesterfield. I now realised I had gone along to Saltergate to steal something and steal it I did. It was time to put it back and let real Chesterfield people try to look after all the fan things, carrying all the responsibilities and burdens, and enjoying all the glories. It is their club after all.

Where you're born or where you are brought up, is where you always belong. Football has taught me that. Through my Chesterfield years I denied this, that I might be accepted in a new place. I spoke ill of my mother. If I could not have bitten my tongue, I should at least have paid my respects to where she came from. I was fast out of the blocks to claim my father's heritage from Scotland and the north, but I was a charlatan to try to pull this little stunt. I am no more a Scot than a Dutchman. I am no more a northerner than Jimmy Greaves or Barbara Windsor. In the end I am from Tottenham or I am from nowhere. I may not wish to go back - there are a hundred reasons for choosing a place to live - but if there is a place where my ashes should be scattered or my body buried, it is there.

Am I doomed to wonder, clubless for the rest of my days, after all this time with football? I think so. It looks that way. This is something for me to wrestle with. Rick is as fanatical about Town: more so, in fact, than ever. He has lived in Holland and come back to England again in recent years. Whilst in the land of the coffee shop he organised a birthday treat for himself: flying to Maine Road to see the Spireites, which came as a shock to

Paula who was expecting to spend the evening with her husband. Is he crazy? I'm the last one you should allow to pass an opinion. I'm sure you'll find a way of making one on your own. For Rick though, there is no end in sight to his personal journey with the Spireites.*

Me, perhaps I will have to come to some arrangement with the Spurs, but it's a hundred and forty miles for a home game and have you seen the season ticket prices? The future looks difficult, then. I thought I had the solution a little while ago and it was this.

When I began this journey here, it was to try, amongst other things, to convince you that football doesn't matter. Because I'd convinced myself that this was so: this was my excuse for leaving it all behind completely. Unfortunately I was wrong: of course it matters. You don't need me to tell you any more how much fun it can be, all the good it can do. And after all: you've got to do something with your time off. What else is there? Rugby? Please. Shopping? It palls, believe me. Writing down coach numbers? Well, there's travel in there and I bet you meet some nice people. The Internet? (excuse me while I yawn). Reading? A large way to spend the long afternoons, I grant you, but in the end, reading is not living. In the last analysis you have to get up and do something with the life that's given you; there's a world out there!

I'll find something: I have to. But it can't be football. Just as one drink is far too many for the alcoholic, one match is one too many for me. I am an addict. Remember that.

I can never ever afford to forget.

---

* His journey is, at long last, one to be made without Duncan. I swore after the semi-final that if I knew just one thing about football after all the years I spent with it, it was that he would never win another promotion with Town. He didn't even get close and was sacked nearly three years after the semi-final, the team certain to be relegated. I could now go around saying 'I told you so,' but I no longer knew anyone who would be remotely interested.